Dr. John Chung's

SAT II
Math Level 1

10 Tests

Good Luck!

NO MATERIAL ON THIS PAGE

Dear Beloved Students,

With these new editions, I would like to thank all the students who sent me emails to encourage me to revise my books. As I said, while creating this series of math tests has brought great pleasure to my career, my only wish is that these books will help the many students who are preparing for college entrance. I have had the honor and the pleasure of working with numerous students and realized the need for prep books that can clearly explain the fundamentals of mathematics. Most importantly, the questions in these books focus on building a solid understanding of basic mathematical concepts. Without these solid foundations, it will be difficult to score well on the exams. These books emphasize that any difficult math question can be completely solved with a solid understanding of basic concepts.

As the old proverb says, "Where there is a will, there is a way." I still remember vividly a fifth-grader who was last in his class who eventually ended up at Harvard University seven years later. I cannot stress enough how such perseverance in the endless quest to master mathematical concepts and problems will yield fruitful results.

You may sometimes find that the explanations in these books might not be sufficient. In such a case, you can email me at drjcmath@gmail.com and I will do my best to provide a more detailed explanation. Additionally, as you work with these books, please notify me if you encounter any grammatical or typographical errors so that I can provide an updated version.

It is my great wish that all students who work with these books can reach their ultimate goals and enter the college of their dreams.

Thank you.

Sincerely,

Dr. John Chung

NO MATERIAL ON THIS PAGE

Contents

10 Tests

NO MATERIAL ON THIS PAGE

Dr. John Chung's SAT II

Math Level 1

Test 1

MATHEMATICS LEVEL 1 TEST

TEST 1

REFERENCE INFORMATION

THE FOLLOWING INFORMATION IS FOR YOUR REFERENCE IN ANSWERING SOME OF THE QUESTIONS IN THIS TEST

Volume of a right circular cone with radius r and height h: $V = \frac{1}{3}\pi r^2 h$

Lateral Area of a right circular cone with circumference of the base c and slant height ℓ: $S = \frac{1}{2}c\ell$

Volume of a sphere with radius r: $V = \frac{4}{3}\pi r^3$

Surface Area of a sphere with radius r: $S = 4\pi r^2$

Volume of a pyramid with base area B and height h: $V = \frac{1}{3}Bh$

Dr. John Chung's SAT II Math Level 1

Answer Sheet

1	Ⓐ Ⓑ Ⓒ Ⓓ Ⓔ		26	Ⓐ Ⓑ Ⓒ Ⓓ Ⓔ
2	Ⓐ Ⓑ Ⓒ Ⓓ Ⓔ		27	Ⓐ Ⓑ Ⓒ Ⓓ Ⓔ
3	Ⓐ Ⓑ Ⓒ Ⓓ Ⓔ		28	Ⓐ Ⓑ Ⓒ Ⓓ Ⓔ
4	Ⓐ Ⓑ Ⓒ Ⓓ Ⓔ		29	Ⓐ Ⓑ Ⓒ Ⓓ Ⓔ
5	Ⓐ Ⓑ Ⓒ Ⓓ Ⓔ		30	Ⓐ Ⓑ Ⓒ Ⓓ Ⓔ
6	Ⓐ Ⓑ Ⓒ Ⓓ Ⓔ		31	Ⓐ Ⓑ Ⓒ Ⓓ Ⓔ
7	Ⓐ Ⓑ Ⓒ Ⓓ Ⓔ		32	Ⓐ Ⓑ Ⓒ Ⓓ Ⓔ
8	Ⓐ Ⓑ Ⓒ Ⓓ Ⓔ		33	Ⓐ Ⓑ Ⓒ Ⓓ Ⓔ
9	Ⓐ Ⓑ Ⓒ Ⓓ Ⓔ		34	Ⓐ Ⓑ Ⓒ Ⓓ Ⓔ
10	Ⓐ Ⓑ Ⓒ Ⓓ Ⓔ		35	Ⓐ Ⓑ Ⓒ Ⓓ Ⓔ
11	Ⓐ Ⓑ Ⓒ Ⓓ Ⓔ		36	Ⓐ Ⓑ Ⓒ Ⓓ Ⓔ
12	Ⓐ Ⓑ Ⓒ Ⓓ Ⓔ		37	Ⓐ Ⓑ Ⓒ Ⓓ Ⓔ
13	Ⓐ Ⓑ Ⓒ Ⓓ Ⓔ		38	Ⓐ Ⓑ Ⓒ Ⓓ Ⓔ
14	Ⓐ Ⓑ Ⓒ Ⓓ Ⓔ		39	Ⓐ Ⓑ Ⓒ Ⓓ Ⓔ
15	Ⓐ Ⓑ Ⓒ Ⓓ Ⓔ		40	Ⓐ Ⓑ Ⓒ Ⓓ Ⓔ
16	Ⓐ Ⓑ Ⓒ Ⓓ Ⓔ		41	Ⓐ Ⓑ Ⓒ Ⓓ Ⓔ
17	Ⓐ Ⓑ Ⓒ Ⓓ Ⓔ		42	Ⓐ Ⓑ Ⓒ Ⓓ Ⓔ
18	Ⓐ Ⓑ Ⓒ Ⓓ Ⓔ		43	Ⓐ Ⓑ Ⓒ Ⓓ Ⓔ
19	Ⓐ Ⓑ Ⓒ Ⓓ Ⓔ		44	Ⓐ Ⓑ Ⓒ Ⓓ Ⓔ
20	Ⓐ Ⓑ Ⓒ Ⓓ Ⓔ		45	Ⓐ Ⓑ Ⓒ Ⓓ Ⓔ
21	Ⓐ Ⓑ Ⓒ Ⓓ Ⓔ		46	Ⓐ Ⓑ Ⓒ Ⓓ Ⓔ
22	Ⓐ Ⓑ Ⓒ Ⓓ Ⓔ		47	Ⓐ Ⓑ Ⓒ Ⓓ Ⓔ
23	Ⓐ Ⓑ Ⓒ Ⓓ Ⓔ		48	Ⓐ Ⓑ Ⓒ Ⓓ Ⓔ
24	Ⓐ Ⓑ Ⓒ Ⓓ Ⓔ		49	Ⓐ Ⓑ Ⓒ Ⓓ Ⓔ
25	Ⓐ Ⓑ Ⓒ Ⓓ Ⓔ		50	Ⓐ Ⓑ Ⓒ Ⓓ Ⓔ

The number of right answers : [　　　　]

The number of wrong answers : [　　　　]

$$\frac{[\quad\quad]}{\text{\# of correct}} - \frac{1}{4} \times \frac{[\quad\quad]}{\text{\# of wrong}} = \frac{[\quad\quad]}{\text{Raw score}}$$

Score Conversion Table

Raw Score	Scaled Score	Raw Score	Scaled Score	Raw Score	Scaled Score
50	800	28	630	6	480
49	800	27	620	5	470
48	800	26	610	4	470
47	800	25	600	3	460
46	790	24	590	2	460
45	780	23	580	1	450
44	770	22	570	0	450
43	760	21	550		
42	750	20	540		
41	740	19	530		
40	740	18	520		
39	730	17	510		
38	720	16	500		
37	710	15	490		
36	710	14	480		
35	700	13	470		
34	690	12	460		
33	680	11	450		
32	670	10	440		
31	660	9	430		
30	650	8	420		
29	640	7	410		

MATHEMATICS LEVEL 1 TEST

For each of the following problems, decide which is the BEST of the choices given. If the exact numerical value is not one of the choices, select the choice that best approximates this value. Then fill in the corresponding circle on the answer sheet.

Notes: (1) A scientific or graphing calculator will be necessary for answering some (but not all) of the questions in this test. For each question you will have to decide whether or not you should use a calculator.

(2) The only angle measure used on this test is degree measure. Make sure your calculator is in the degree mode.

(3) Figures that accompany problems in this test are intended to provide information useful in solving the problems. They are drawn as accurately as possible EXCEPT when it is stated in a specific problem that its figure is not drawn to scale. All figures lie in a plane unless otherwise indicated.

(4) Unless otherwise specified, the domain of any function f is assumed to be the set of all real numbers x for which $f(x)$ is a real number. The range of f is assumed to be the set of all real numbers $f(x)$, where x is in the domain of f.

(5) Reference information that may be useful in answering the questions in this test can be found on the page preceding Question 1.

USE THIS SPACE FOR SCRATCHWORK

1. If $ab - 3b = 30$ and $2a + 8 = 12$, what is the value of b?

   (A) −30
   (B) −10
   (C) −6
   (D) 10
   (E) 30

2. If $a + 2b = 2$ and $a - 2b = 10$, then $a^2 - 4b^2 =$

   (A) 5   (B) 10   (C) 12   (D) 20   (E) 24

GO ON TO THE NEXT PAGE

MATHEMATICS LEVEL 1 TEST - *Continued*

USE THIS SPACE FOR SCRATCHWORK.

3. In Figure 1, the area of the circular shaded region is 2π and the radius of circle O is 3. What is the value of w ?

    (A) 100
    (B) 120
    (C) 130
    (D) 140
    (E) 150

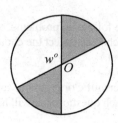

Figure 1

4. Which of the following is the graph of a linear function with a negative slope and a negative *y*-intercept?

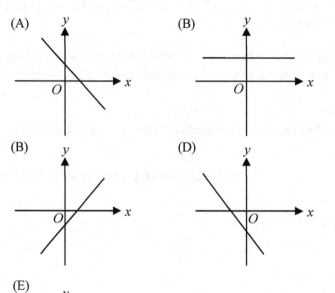

(E)

MATHEMATICS LEVEL 1 TEST - *Continued*

USE THIS SPACE FOR SCRATCHWORK.

5. If $x^3 = 16x$, what are all possible values of x?

(A) 0 only
(B) 0, 2, and -2
(C) 4 and -4 only
(D) 0 and 4 only
(E) 0, 4, and -4

6. If $3^{2x+1} = 9^{2x}$, what is the value of x?

(A) 3   (B) 2   (C) $\dfrac{1}{2}$ (D) $\dfrac{1}{4}$ (E) $-\dfrac{1}{2}$

7. If the equation is $x^2 - 2x + 3 = 0$, which of the following is true?

(A) The sum of the roots is -2.
(B) The product of the roots is -3.
(C) Both roots are greater than 0.
(D) Both roots are imaginary.
(E) Both roots are real.

8. Which of the following is the equation whose roots are -3 and 2?

(A) $x^2 + x - 4 = 0$
(B) $x^2 - x + 6 = 0$
(C) $x^2 - x - 6 = 0$
(D) $x^2 + x + 6 = 0$
(E) $x^2 + x - 6 = 0$

9. If $y = \sqrt{x^3 - 1.25}$, for what value of x is $y = 5$?

(A) 5.02
(B) 4.14
(C) 3.37
(D) 2.97
(E) 2.25

GO ON TO THE NEXT PAGE

MATHEMATICS LEVEL 1 TEST - *Continued*

USE THIS SPACE FOR SCRATCHWORK.

10. If the perimeter of a square is 18, which of the following is the length of a diagonal?

(A) 4.50
(B) 6.36
(C) 6.78
(D) 9.00
(E) 36.00

11. If $\dfrac{1}{1-\dfrac{1}{x}}$ is undefined, which of the following includes all possible value(s) of x ?

(A) $\{0\}$

(B) $\{1\}$

(C) $\{0,1\}$

(D) $\{0,-1\}$

(E) $\{0,-1,1\}$

12. If $\dfrac{2x-y}{x+3y}=\dfrac{2}{3}$, what is the ratio of x to y ?

(A) $\dfrac{2}{3}$

(B) $\dfrac{3}{2}$

(C) $\dfrac{9}{4}$

(D) $\dfrac{4}{9}$

(E) $\dfrac{3}{4}$

GO ON TO THE NEXT PAGE

MATHEMATICS LEVEL 1 TEST - *Continued*

USE THIS SPACE FOR SCRATCHWORK.

13. In isosceles triangle ABC in Figure 2, $\sin A = 0.5$.
    What is the length of $\overline{AC}$?

    (A) $15\sqrt{3}$
    (B) $10\sqrt{3}$
    (C) $10\sqrt{2}$
    (D) 10
    (E) 5

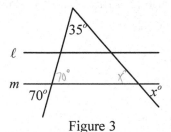

Figure 2
<u>Note</u>: Figure not drawn to scale.

14. Jennifer is 4 feet tall, and her shadow is 15 feet long. If
    the tree next to her casts a shadow that is 33 feet long,
    how tall is the tree?

    (A) 8.8 ft
    (B) 9.5 ft
    (C) 9.9 ft
    (D) 10.5ft
    (E) 11.2 ft

15. If $f(x) = \left| \dfrac{1-x}{x^2} \right|$, what is the value of $f(-0.1)$?

    (A) -110
    (B) -101
    (C) 101
    (D) 110
    (E) 120

16. In Figure 3, if $\ell \parallel m$, what is the value of x ?

    (A) 75
    (B) 80
    (C) 82
    (D) 83
    (E) 85

Figure 3

GO ON TO THE NEXT PAGE

MATHEMATICS LEVEL 1 TEST - *Continued*

USE THIS SPACE FOR SCRATCHWORK.

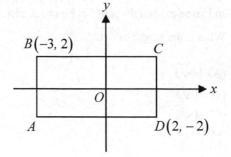

Figure 4

17. In Figure 4, $\overline{AB}$ of rectangle $ABCD$ is parallel to
    y-axis. What is the distance between point A and C?

    (A) 6
    (B) 6.4
    (C) 7.2
    (D) 8
    (E) 8.5

18. In how many different orders can the program for a music
    performance be arranged if 6 students are to perform?

    (A) 120
    (B) 240
    (C) 360
    (D) 480
    (E) 720

19. Corresponding altitudes of two similar triangles have
    lengths of 9 meters and 6 meters. If the perimeter of the
    larger triangle is 31.5 meters, what is the perimeter of the
    smaller triangle?

    (A) 21 m
    (B) 22.5 m
    (C) 23.2 m
    (D) 24 m
    (E) 27 m

20. Which of the following is an equation of a line which
    passes through $(5, 2)$ and is parallel to the line with
    equation $4x - 2y = -3$?

    (A) $y = 2x + 2$
    (B) $y = -2x - 2$
    (C) $y = 2x + 8$
    (D) $y = 2x - 8$
    (E) $y = -2x - 8$

GO ON TO THE NEXT PAGE

MATHEMATICS LEVEL 1 TEST - *Continued*

USE THIS SPACE FOR SCRATCHWORK.

21. In Figure 5, a tetrahedron is going to be cut from a corner of the cube with edge of 5. Which of the following is the volume of the tetrahedron?

    (A) 15
    (B) 20.8
    (C) 41.7
    (D) 62.6
    (E) 125

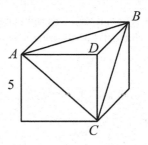

Figure 5

22. Which of the following statements is never true?

    (A) A square is a rhombus.
    (B) A rectangle is a rhombus.
    (C) A trapezoid is a parallelogram.
    (D) A square is a parallelogram.
    (E) A parallelogram is a square.

23. A power boat traveled 100 miles at an average speed of 25 miles per hour in still water. If the average speed had increased 16 percent, how much time, in percent, could have saved on this trip?

    (A) 10%
    (B) 13.8%
    (C) 14.5%
    (D) 25.2%
    (E) 40%

24. If b is a negative integer, for which of the following values of a is $\dfrac{|10-a|}{b}$ greatest ?

    (A) −20
    (B) −10
    (C) 10
    (D) 20
    (E) 30

GO ON TO THE NEXT PAGE

MATHEMATICS LEVEL 1 TEST - *Continued*

USE THIS SPACE FOR SCRATCHWORK.

25. In triangle ABC, if $\angle C$ is a right angle, $AC = 6$, and $BC = 8$, which of the following is equal to $\sin A$?

(A) 0.4
(B) 0.6
(C) 0.75
(D) 0.8
(E) 0.85

26. If Tiffany has 5 more dimes than quarters and the total value of the coins is $2.25, which of the following is the number of dimes?

(A) 3
(B) 5
(C) 7
(D) 9
(E) 10

27. In Figure 6, $ABCD$ is a parallelogram. Which of the following is the midpoint of $\overline{AC}$?

(A) $(2, 3)$
(B) $(4, 2)$
(C) $(3, 2)$
(D) $(3, 3)$
(E) $(4, 3)$

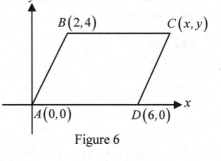

Figure 6

28. If 20 is 30% of $\dfrac{1}{3}$ of a certain number, what is that number?

(A) 200
(B) 180
(C) 150
(D) 120
(E) 90

GO ON TO THE NEXT PAGE

MATHEMATICS LEVEL 1 TEST - *Continued*

USE THIS SPACE FOR SCRATCHWORK.

29. In Figure 7, $\triangle ABC$ and $\triangle CDE$ are right triangles. If $AB = 12$, $AC = 16$, and $EC = 8$, which of the following is the length of $\overline{CD}$?

   (A) 14
   (B) 13
   (C) 12
   (D) 11
   (E) 10

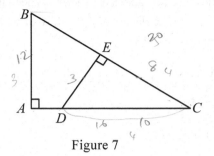

Figure 7

30. Which of the following numbers is contained in the domain of the function $f(x) = \dfrac{1}{x-5} - \dfrac{1}{\sqrt{x-5}}$?

   (A) 6
   (B) 5
   (C) 4
   (D) 3
   (E) 2

31. Which of the following is the graph for all values of x in $1 \le (x-1)^2 \le 9$?

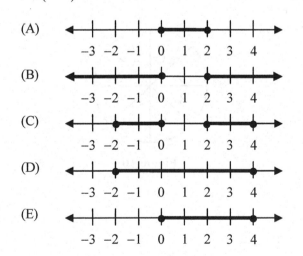

   (A)

   (B)

   (C)

   (D)

   (E)

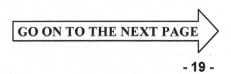

GO ON TO THE NEXT PAGE

MATHEMATICS LEVEL 1 TEST - *Continued*

USE THIS SPACE FOR SCRATCHWORK.

32. The circle in Figure 8 has center O and radius 10. If $\overline{BC}$ is perpendicular to $\overline{AD}$, which of the following is the length of $\overline{AC}$?

(A) 12
(B) 13
(C) 15
(D) 15.5
(E) 16

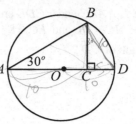

Figure 8

33. In Figure 9, if $\triangle ABC$ is a right triangle, $AD = BD$, $AC = \sqrt{3}$, and $CD = 1$, then $AB =$

(A) 2
(B) $2\sqrt{2}$
(C) $2\sqrt{3}$
(D) $3\sqrt{2}$
(E) $3\sqrt{3}$

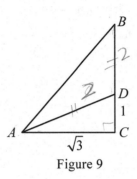

Figure 9

34. Figure 10 shows a disc with an arrow that can be spun so that it has an equal chance of landing on each of the 8 regions of the disc. If the spinner is spun 2 times, what is the probability that the spinner will land on a prime number at least once?

(A) $\dfrac{3}{8}$

(B) $\dfrac{9}{64}$

(C) $\dfrac{21}{64}$

(D) $\dfrac{30}{64}$

(E) $\dfrac{39}{64}$

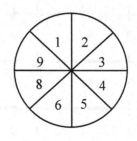

Figure 10

GO ON TO THE NEXT PAGE

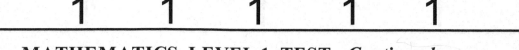

MATHEMATICS LEVEL 1 TEST - *Continued*

USE THIS SPACE FOR SCRATCHWORK.

35. Figure 11 shows the graph of function f. Which of the following is the value of $f(f(-4))$?

   (A) 2
   (B) 1
   (C) 0
   (D) −2
   (E) −4

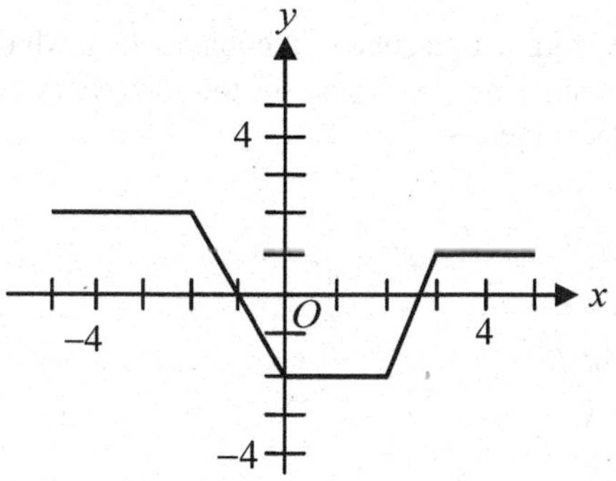

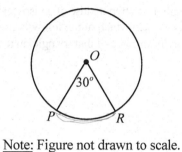

Figure 11

36. If circle O has an area of 16, what is the length of minor arc PR?

   (A) 0.95
   (B) 1.18
   (C) 2.56
   (D) 3.02
   (E) 3.98

37. If the graph of $y = x^2 - 2x + k$ intersects the line $y = 3$ exactly once, which of the following is the value of k?

   (A) 4
   (B) 3.5
   (C) 3
   (D) 2.5
   (E) 2

Note: Figure not drawn to scale.

Figure 12

38. In the xy-plane, which of the following is the equation of the line which passes through the points of intersection of the circles whose equations are $x^2 + y^2 = 4$ and $(x+2)^2 + (y-2)^2 = 4$?

   (A) $x + y - 2 = 0$
   (B) $x + y + 2 = 0$
   (C) $x - y - 2 = 0$
   (D) $x - y + 2 = 0$
   (E) $x - y + 4 = 0$

GO ON TO THE NEXT PAGE

MATHEMATICS LEVEL 1 TEST - *Continued*

USE THIS SPACE FOR SCRATCHWORK.

39. If the volume of a cube is k cubic meters, which of the following is an expression for the surface area of this cube, in square meters?

(A) $\sqrt{6k^3}$

(B) $6\sqrt[3]{k^2}$

(C) $6k\sqrt{k}$

(D) $6k^2$

(E) $6k^3$

40. If the length of the hypotenuse of an isosceles right triangle is x, then which of the following is the expression for the area of that triangle, in terms of x?

(A) $\dfrac{x}{2}$

(B) $\dfrac{x}{4}$

(C) x^2

(D) $\dfrac{x^2}{2}$

(E) $\dfrac{x^2}{4}$

41. If a and b are the roots of the equation $x^2 - 4x + 2 = 0$, which of the following is the value of $(a+1)(b+1)$?

(A) 5

(B) 6

(C) 7

(D) 10

(E) 15

GO ON TO THE NEXT PAGE

MATHEMATICS LEVEL 1 TEST - *Continued*

USE THIS SPACE FOR SCRATCHWORK.

42. The function f is defined by $f(x) = x^4 - x^3 + x - 1$. In which of the following intervals does the minimum value of f occur?

    (A) $-3 < x < -2$
    (B) $-2 < x < -1$
    (C) $-1 < x < 0$
    (D) $0 < x < 1$
    (E) $1 < x < 2$

43. If the ratio of an exterior angle to an interior angle of a regular polygon is 1:5, which of the following is the number of sides of that polygon?

    (A) 4
    (B) 8
    (C) 12
    (D) 16
    (E) 20

44. What is the greatest integer value of k such that $(k+1)x^2 - 2(k+1)x + 3 = 0$ has no real roots?

    (A) 1
    (B) 2
    (C) 3
    (D) 4
    (E) 5

USE THIS SPACE FOR SCRATCHWORK.

45. If $\csc x = -\dfrac{5}{3}$ and $\cot x = -\dfrac{4}{3}$, which of the following is

the value of $\cos x$?

(A) $-\dfrac{4}{5}$

(B) $-\dfrac{3}{5}$

(C) $-\dfrac{3}{4}$

(D) $\dfrac{3}{5}$

(E) $\dfrac{4}{5}$

46. A right circular cylinder has radius r and a height of $2r$. A right circular cone has a radius of r and a height of kr where k is a constant. Which of the following is the value of k if the cylinder and cone have equal lateral area?

(A) $\sqrt{10}$
(B) $\sqrt{12}$
(C) $\sqrt{14}$
(D) $\sqrt{15}$
(E) $\sqrt{18}$

47. If the function f is defined by $f(x-2) = x^2 + x - 2$,

which of the following gives the expression for $f(x)$?

(A) $x^2 - 3x$
(B) $x^2 - 3x + 4$
(C) $x^2 + 3x + 4$
(D) $x^2 - 3x + 5$
(E) $x^2 + 5x + 4$

MATHEMATICS LEVEL 1 TEST - *Continued*

USE THIS SPACE FOR SCRATCHWORK.

48. In Figure 13, if $ABCD$ is a rhombus with $BD = 24$ and $AB = 20$, which of the following is the area of the rhombus?

(A) 192
(B) 384
(C) 480
(D) 768
(E) 1024

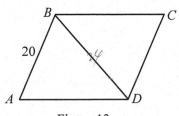

Figure 13
<u>Note</u>: Figure not drawn to scale.

49. If the function f is defined by $f(x) = -x^2 + 4x - 1$ for $0 \le x \le 3$, what is the range of f?

(A) $-1 \le f(x) \le 0$
(B) $-1 \le f(x) \le 2$
(C) $0 \le f(x) \le 2$
(D) $-1 \le f(x) \le 3$
(E) $2 \le f(x) \le 3$

50. If $f(x) = \sqrt{x^3 + 1}$ and f^{-1} is the inverse of f, which of the following is the value of $f^{-1}(5)$?

(A) 0.05
(B) 2.25
(C) 2.54
(D) 2.67
(E) 2.88

STOP
**IF YOU FINISH BEFORE TIME IS CALLED, YOU MAY CHECK YOUR WORK ON THIS TEST ONLY.
DO NOT TURN TO ANY OTHER TEST IN THIS BOOK.**

NO MATERIAL ON THIS PAGE

#	answer	#	answer	#	answer	#	answer	#	answer
1	A	11	C	21	B	31	C	41	C
2	D	12	C	22	C	32	C	42	C
3	D	13	B	23	B	33	C	43	C
4	D	14	A	24	C	34	E	44	A
5	E	15	D	25	D	35	D	45	E
6	C	16	A	26	E	36	B	46	D
7	D	17	B	27	B	37	A	47	E
8	E	18	E	28	A	38	D	48	B
9	D	19	A	29	E	39	B	49	D
10	B	20	D	30	A	40	E	50	E

Explanations: Test 1

1. (A) $\quad 2a+8=12 \ \Rightarrow\ a=2 \qquad (2)b-3b=30 \ \Rightarrow\ -b=30 \ \Rightarrow\ b=-30$

2. (D) $\quad$ Method 1: Solve system of equations. $\ a=6,\ b=-2$. Therefore $a^2-4b^2=20$.

Method 2: Since $(a-2b)(a+2b)=a^2-4b^2$, then $2\times 10=20$.

3. (D) $\quad$ The area of the circle is 9π. The area of a sector of a circle is proportion to its central angle. The area of the unshaded region is $9\pi-2\pi=7\pi$.

Therefore $\dfrac{7\pi}{9\pi}=\dfrac{2w}{360} \ \Rightarrow\ 2w=280 \ \Rightarrow\ w=140$.

4. (D) $\quad$ The graph in (D) has a negative slope and negative y-intercept.

5. (E) $\quad x^3=16x \ \Rightarrow\ x^3-16x=0 \ \Rightarrow\ x(x+4)(x-4)=0 \ \Rightarrow\ x=0,\ 4,\ \text{and}\ -4$

6. (C) $\quad 3^{2x+1}=9^{2x} \ \Rightarrow\ 3^{2x+1}=3^{4x} \ \Rightarrow\ 2x+1=4x \ \Rightarrow\ x=\dfrac{1}{2}$

7. (D)

> **Vieta's Formulas**
> If r and s are the roots of the equation $ax^2+bx+c=0$, then
> $$r+s=-\frac{b}{a} \quad \text{and} \quad rs=\frac{c}{a}.$$

> **Discriminant** b^2-4ac determines the nature of the roots of a quadratic equation when a, b, and c are rational numbers.
> If $b^2-4ac>0$, then there are two unequal real roots.
> If $b^2-4ac=0$, then there are two equal real roots.
> If $b^2-4ac<0$, then there are imaginary roots.

Sum of the roots $= 2$ and Product of the roots $= 3$.

Discriminant $b^2 - 4ac = -8 < 0 \Rightarrow$ Imaginary roots

Or use a graphic utility to find the nature of the roots of the graph.

8. (E) Method 1:

Since the roots are -3 and 2, the equation is $(x - {}^-3)(x - 2) = 0 \Rightarrow x^2 + x - 6 = 0$.

Method 2: Use Vieta's Formula.

$$ax^2 + bx + c = 0 \Rightarrow x^2 + \frac{b}{a}x + \frac{c}{a} = 0$$

Sum of the roots $-\dfrac{b}{a} = -3 + 2 = -1 \Rightarrow \dfrac{b}{a} = 1$ and

Product of the roots $\dfrac{c}{a} = (-3)(2) = -6$. Therefore $x^2 + \dfrac{b}{a}x + \dfrac{c}{a} = 0 \Rightarrow x^2 + x - 6 = 0.$

9. (D) $y^2 = x^3 - 1.25 \Rightarrow 5^2 = x^3 - 1.25 \Rightarrow x^3 = 26.25$

$x = 26.25^{\frac{1}{3}} \cong 2.97$

10. (B) The length of a side $= s \Rightarrow 4s = 18 \Rightarrow s = 4.5$

$s\sqrt{2} = 4.5\sqrt{2} \cong 6.36$

11. (C) If $x = 0$, then $\dfrac{1}{x}$ is undefined. $\dfrac{1}{1 - \dfrac{1}{x}} = \dfrac{x}{x - 1} \Rightarrow$ If $x = 1$, then $\dfrac{x}{x-1}$ is undefined.

12. (C) $\dfrac{2x - y}{x + 3y} = \dfrac{2}{3} \Rightarrow$ cross-mulitplication $6x - 3y = 2x + 6y \Rightarrow 4x = 9y \Rightarrow x = \dfrac{9}{4}y$

Therefore, $\dfrac{x}{y} = \dfrac{9}{4}$. (From the equation, you can use plug-in number. If $y = 4$, then $x = 9$.)

13. (B) $BD = 10\sin A = 10 \cdot 0.5 = 5 \Rightarrow AD = 5\sqrt{3} \Rightarrow AC = 10\sqrt{3}$

14. (A) Corresponding sides in similar figures are in proportion.

$\dfrac{4}{x} = \dfrac{15}{33} \Rightarrow x = \dfrac{4 \times 33}{15} = 8.8$

15. (D) $f(-0.1) = \left| \dfrac{1 - ^-0.1}{0.1^2} \right| = 110$

16. (A) Sum of the interior angles of a triangle is 180 and verticals angles are congruent.

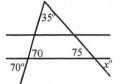

17. (B) The diagonals of a rectangle are congruent.

$AC = BD = \sqrt{\left(2 - ^-3\right)^2 + \left(-2 - 2\right)^2} = \sqrt{41} \cong 6.4$

18. (E) Order is important. Permutation

$_6P_6 = 6! = 720$

19. (A) The corresponding sides of the similar triangles are in proportion. The other perimeter $= x$.

$\dfrac{9}{6} = \dfrac{31.5}{x} \implies x = \dfrac{6 \times 31.5}{9} = 21$

20. (D) $4x - 2y = -3 \implies y = 2x + \dfrac{3}{2} \implies$ slope is 2.

Slope and a point form: $y - y_1 = m(x - x_1) \implies y - 2 = 2(x - 5) \implies y = 2x - 8$

21. (B) The tetrahedron is a triangular cone. $\triangle ADC$ is the base and $\overline{DB}$ is the height of the cone.

The area of $\triangle ADC = \dfrac{5 \times 5}{2} = 12.5$. The volume of the cone $= \dfrac{bh}{3} = \dfrac{12.5 \times 5}{3} \cong 20.8$.

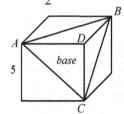

22. (C) A square is always a parallelogram. A trapezoid is never a parallelogram..

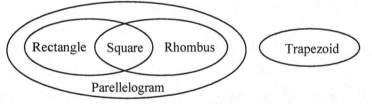

23. (B)

Distance	Speed	Time
100miles	25mph	100/25 = 4hr
	25(1.16) = 29mph	100/29 = 3.49hr

Therefore, % of the amount of time being saved is

$$\frac{4-3.49}{4}=\frac{x}{100} \quad\Rightarrow\quad x=\frac{100(4-3.49)}{4}\cong 13.8\%.$$

24. (C) Since b is a negative integer, $|10-a|$ must be the smallest number.

$$\frac{|10-a|}{b}=\begin{cases}(A)-20 \Rightarrow \dfrac{30}{b} & (B)-10 \Rightarrow \dfrac{20}{b} & (C)10 \Rightarrow \dfrac{0}{b}=0 \\[2mm] (D)20 \Rightarrow \dfrac{10}{b} & (E)30 \Rightarrow \dfrac{20}{b}\end{cases}$$

25. (D) Since $\triangle ABC$ is a right triangle, then $BC=8$, $AC=6$, and $AB=10$.

$$\sin A=\frac{\text{opp.}}{\text{hyp.}}=\frac{8}{10}=0.8$$

26. (E)

Coin	# of coins	Cents	Amount
Quarter	x	25	$25x$
Dime	$x+5$	10	$10(x+5)$

Total amount $=25x+10(x+5)=35x+50$

$35x+50=225 \quad\Rightarrow\quad x=5$ and $x+5=10$

27. (B) Diagonals of a parallelogram bisect each other. The midpoint of $\overline{BD}=$ The midpoint of $\overline{AC}$.

Midpoint of $\overline{BD}=\left(\dfrac{2+6}{2},\dfrac{4+0}{2}\right)=(4,2)$.

28. (A) Translate

The number $=x$: $\quad 20=0.3\times\dfrac{1}{3}\times x \quad\Rightarrow\quad 20=0.1x \quad\Rightarrow\quad x=200$

29. (E) In $\triangle ABC$, $AB=12$, $AC=16$, and $BC=20$. Use similarity.

$$\frac{AC}{EC}=\frac{BC}{CD} \quad\Rightarrow\quad \frac{16}{8}=\frac{20}{x} \quad\Rightarrow\quad x=10$$

30. (A) Domain: $\{x\,|\,x>5\}$

31. (C) $1\le(x-1)^2\le 9 \quad\Rightarrow\quad 1\le(x-1)^2$ and $(x-1)^2\ge 0$

(1) $1\le(x-1)^2 \quad\Rightarrow\quad x^2-2x\ge 0 \quad\Rightarrow\quad x(x-2)\ge 0 \quad\Rightarrow\quad x\ge 2$ or $x\le 0$

(2) $(x-1)^2\ge 9 \quad\Rightarrow\quad x^2-2x-8\le 0 \quad\Rightarrow\quad (x-4)(x+2)\le 0 \quad\Rightarrow\quad -2\le x\le 4$

From (1) and (2), the common intervals are $-2\le x\le 0$ or $2\le x\le 4$.

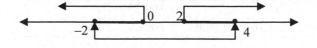

32. (C)   Since $\triangle AOB$ is isosceles, $BO = 10$ and $\angle BOC = 60^o$. Therefore $OC = 5$ and
$AC = 10 + 5 = 15$.

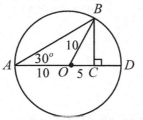

33. (C) $\triangle ACD$ is a special right triangle, $30^o - 60^o - 90^o$.
$AD = BD = 2$
$$AB = \sqrt{BC^2 + AC^2} = \sqrt{12} = 2\sqrt{3}$$
Or
Since $\angle B = \angle BAC = 60^o$, $AB = 2AC = 2\sqrt{3}$.

34. (E) $P(\text{prime at least once}) = 1 - P(\text{Both numbers are not prime})$
5 numbers out of 8 are not prime. Therefore, the number of pairs is $5 \times 5 = 25$.
$$P(\text{prime at least once}) = 1 - \frac{25}{64} = \frac{39}{64}$$

35. (D)   In the graph, $f(-4) = 2$ and $f(f(-4)) = f(2) = -2$.

36. (B)   Area $= \pi r^2 = 16 \;\Rightarrow\; r^2 = \dfrac{16}{\pi} \;\Rightarrow\; r = \dfrac{4}{\sqrt{\pi}}$

$$\overset{\frown}{PR} = 2\pi r \times \frac{30}{360} = \frac{\pi r}{6} \;\Rightarrow\; \frac{\pi \frac{4}{\sqrt{\pi}}}{6} = \frac{4\sqrt{\pi}}{6} \simeq 1.18$$

37. (A)   Since $y = 3$ is tangent to the parabola, axis of symmetry is
$$x = \frac{-b}{2a} = \frac{-(-2)}{2} = 1 . \text{ Therefore,}$$
$$f(1) = 1 - 2 + k = 3 \;\Rightarrow\; k = 4$$
Or
Perfect squared form is $y = (x-1)^2 + k - 1$.
The minimum value of $y = k - 1 = 3$. $k = 4$.

38. (D)   The graphs of circles are as follows. Two intersections are $(-2, 0)$ and $(0, 2)$.

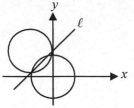

Slope $= \dfrac{2-0}{0-(-2)} = 1$ and y-intercept $= 2$.

The equation of line ℓ is $y = x + 2 \implies x - y + 2 = 0$

39. (B)   If the length of a side of the cube is s, the volume of the cube is s^3.

$$s^3 = k \implies \left(s^3\right)^{\frac{1}{3}} = k^{\frac{1}{3}} \implies s = k^{\frac{1}{3}}$$

Since the surface area of the cube is $6s^2$, therefore $6s^2 = 6\left(k^{\frac{1}{3}}\right)^2 = 6k^{\frac{2}{3}} = 6\sqrt[3]{k^2}$.

40. (E)   Since the length of the leg is $\dfrac{x}{\sqrt{2}}$, the area of the triangle is $\dfrac{x}{\sqrt{2}} \times \dfrac{x}{\sqrt{2}} \times \dfrac{1}{2} = \dfrac{x^2}{4}$.

41. (C)   From the equation, $a + b = 4$ and $ab = 2$.
Therefore, $(a+1)(b+1) = a + b + ab + 1 = 4 + 2 + 1 = 7$.

42. (C)   Use a graphic utility.

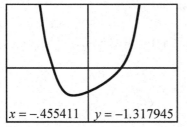

| $x = -.455411$ | $y = -1.317945$ |

43. (C)   Sum of the exterior angles of any polygon is 360°.

Interior angle $\leftarrow 5x \qquad x \rightarrow$ Exterior angle

An interior angle and an exterior angle form supplementary angles.
$5x + x = 6x = 180 \implies x = 30$

The number of sides is $\dfrac{360}{30} = 12$.

44. (A)   If discriminant $b^2 - 4ac < 0$, the equation has no real roots.

$4(k+1)^2 - 12(k+1) < 0 \implies (k+1)^2 - 3(k+1) < 0 \implies k^2 - k - 2 < 0$
$\implies (k-2)(k+1) < 0 \implies -1 < k < 2$

45. (E) $\csc x = -\dfrac{5}{3} \;\Rightarrow\; \sin x = -\dfrac{3}{5}, \quad \cot x = -\dfrac{4}{3} \;\Rightarrow\; \tan x = -\dfrac{3}{4}$

The terminal angle x lies in Quadrant IV.

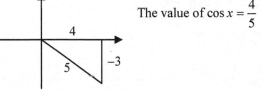

The value of $\cos x = \dfrac{4}{5}$

46. (D) The lateral area of the cylinder is $2\pi r h = 2\pi r (2r) = 4\pi r^2$ and

the lateral area of the cone is $\pi r \ell = \pi r \left(\sqrt{r^2 + k^2 r^2} \right) = \pi r^2 \left(\sqrt{1 + k^2} \right)$.

ℓ is slant height: $\ell = \sqrt{r^2 + (kr)^2}$

Therefore, $4\pi r^2 = \pi r^2 \left(\sqrt{1+k^2} \right) \;\Rightarrow\; 4 = \sqrt{1+k^2} \;\Rightarrow\; 16 = 1 + k^2 \;\Rightarrow\; k = \sqrt{15}$.

47. (E) $f(x-2) = x^2 + x - 2 \quad \underrightarrow{\text{change the variable to } k} \quad f(k-2) = k^2 + k - 2$

Let $k - 2 = x$, then $k = x + 2$. Replace k with $x + 2$.

$f(x) = (x+2)^2 + (x+2) - 2 \;\Rightarrow\; f(x) = x^2 + 5x + 4$

Or

If you substitute $(x+2)$ into x, you will get $f(x)$.

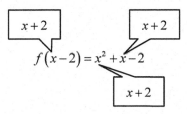

48. (B)

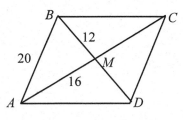

$\overline{AC} \perp \overline{BC}$ and $AM = 16$.
The area of the rhombus is
$\dfrac{12 \times 16}{2} \times 4 = 384$

49. (D) 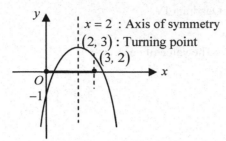 Since $f(0) = -1$, $f(2) = 3$, and $f(3) = 2$, the range of the graph is $-1 \le y \le 3$.

50. (E) $y = \sqrt{x^3 + 1} \xrightarrow{\text{Inverse}} x = \sqrt{\left(f^{-1}\right)^3 + 1}$

Therefore,

$$5 = \sqrt{\left(f^{-1}\right)^3 + 1} \Rightarrow 25 = \left(f^{-1}\right)^3 + 1 \Rightarrow \left(f^{-1}\right)^3 = 24 \Rightarrow f^{-1} = 24^{\frac{1}{3}} \cong 2.88$$

END

Dr. John Chung's SAT II

Math Level 1

Test 2

MATHEMATICS LEVEL 1 TEST

TEST 2

REFERENCE INFORMATION

THE FOLLOWING INFORMATION IS FOR YOUR REFERENCE IN ANSWERING SOME OF THE QUESTIONS IN THIS TEST

Volume of a right circular cone with radius r and height h: $V = \dfrac{1}{3}\pi r^2 h$

Lateral Area of a right circular cone with circumference of the base c and slant height ℓ: $S = \dfrac{1}{2}c\ell$

Volume of a sphere with radius r: $V = \dfrac{4}{3}\pi r^3$

Surface Area of a sphere with radius r: $S = 4\pi r^2$

Volume of a pyramid with base area B and height h: $V = \dfrac{1}{3}Bh$

Dr. John Chung's SAT II Math Level 1

Answer Sheet

1	Ⓐ Ⓑ Ⓒ Ⓓ Ⓔ	26	Ⓐ Ⓑ Ⓒ Ⓓ Ⓔ
2	Ⓐ Ⓑ Ⓒ Ⓓ Ⓔ	27	Ⓐ Ⓑ Ⓒ Ⓓ Ⓔ
3	Ⓐ Ⓑ Ⓒ Ⓓ Ⓔ	28	Ⓐ Ⓑ Ⓒ Ⓓ Ⓔ
4	Ⓐ Ⓑ Ⓒ Ⓓ Ⓔ	29	Ⓐ Ⓑ Ⓒ Ⓓ Ⓔ
5	Ⓐ Ⓑ Ⓒ Ⓓ Ⓔ	30	Ⓐ Ⓑ Ⓒ Ⓓ Ⓔ
6	Ⓐ Ⓑ Ⓒ Ⓓ Ⓔ	31	Ⓐ Ⓑ Ⓒ Ⓓ Ⓔ
7	Ⓐ Ⓑ Ⓒ Ⓓ Ⓔ	32	Ⓐ Ⓑ Ⓒ Ⓓ Ⓔ
8	Ⓐ Ⓑ Ⓒ Ⓓ Ⓔ	33	Ⓐ Ⓑ Ⓒ Ⓓ Ⓔ
9	Ⓐ Ⓑ Ⓒ Ⓓ Ⓔ	34	Ⓐ Ⓑ Ⓒ Ⓓ Ⓔ
10	Ⓐ Ⓑ Ⓒ Ⓓ Ⓔ	35	Ⓐ Ⓑ Ⓒ Ⓓ Ⓔ
11	Ⓐ Ⓑ Ⓒ Ⓓ Ⓔ	36	Ⓐ Ⓑ Ⓒ Ⓓ Ⓔ
12	Ⓐ Ⓑ Ⓒ Ⓓ Ⓔ	37	Ⓐ Ⓑ Ⓒ Ⓓ Ⓔ
13	Ⓐ Ⓑ Ⓒ Ⓓ Ⓔ	38	Ⓐ Ⓑ Ⓒ Ⓓ Ⓔ
14	Ⓐ Ⓑ Ⓒ Ⓓ Ⓔ	39	Ⓐ Ⓑ Ⓒ Ⓓ Ⓔ
15	Ⓐ Ⓑ Ⓒ Ⓓ Ⓔ	40	Ⓐ Ⓑ Ⓒ Ⓓ Ⓔ
16	Ⓐ Ⓑ Ⓒ Ⓓ Ⓔ	41	Ⓐ Ⓑ Ⓒ Ⓓ Ⓔ
17	Ⓐ Ⓑ Ⓒ Ⓓ Ⓔ	42	Ⓐ Ⓑ Ⓒ Ⓓ Ⓔ
18	Ⓐ Ⓑ Ⓒ Ⓓ Ⓔ	43	Ⓐ Ⓑ Ⓒ Ⓓ Ⓔ
19	Ⓐ Ⓑ Ⓒ Ⓓ Ⓔ	44	Ⓐ Ⓑ Ⓒ Ⓓ Ⓔ
20	Ⓐ Ⓑ Ⓒ Ⓓ Ⓔ	45	Ⓐ Ⓑ Ⓒ Ⓓ Ⓔ
21	Ⓐ Ⓑ Ⓒ Ⓓ Ⓔ	46	Ⓐ Ⓑ Ⓒ Ⓓ Ⓔ
22	Ⓐ Ⓑ Ⓒ Ⓓ Ⓔ	47	Ⓐ Ⓑ Ⓒ Ⓓ Ⓔ
23	Ⓐ Ⓑ Ⓒ Ⓓ Ⓔ	48	Ⓐ Ⓑ Ⓒ Ⓓ Ⓔ
24	Ⓐ Ⓑ Ⓒ Ⓓ Ⓔ	49	Ⓐ Ⓑ Ⓒ Ⓓ Ⓔ
25	Ⓐ Ⓑ Ⓒ Ⓓ Ⓔ	50	Ⓐ Ⓑ Ⓒ Ⓓ Ⓔ

The number of right answers : [   ]

The number of wrong answers : [   ]

$$\underbrace{[\qquad]}_{\text{\# of correct}} - \frac{1}{4} \times \underbrace{[\qquad]}_{\text{\# of wrong}} = \underbrace{[\qquad]}_{\text{Raw score}}$$

Score Conversion Table

Raw Score	Scaled Score	Raw Score	Scaled Score	Raw Score	Scaled Score
50	800	28	630	6	480
49	800	27	620	5	470
48	800	26	610	4	470
47	800	25	600	3	460
46	790	24	590	2	460
45	780	23	580	1	450
44	770	22	570	0	450
43	760	21	550		
42	750	20	540		
41	740	19	530		
40	740	18	520		
39	730	17	510		
38	720	16	500		
37	710	15	490		
36	710	14	480		
35	700	13	470		
34	690	12	460		
33	680	11	450		
32	670	10	440		
31	660	9	430		
30	650	8	420		
29	640	7	410		

MATHEMATICS LEVEL 1 TEST

For each of the following problems, decide which is the BEST of the choices given. If the exact numerical value is not one of the choices, select the choice that best approximates this value. Then fill in the corresponding circle on the answer sheet.

Notes: (1) A scientific or graphing calculator will be necessary for answering some (but not all) of the questions in this test. For each question you will have to decide whether or not you should use a calculator.

(2) For some questions in this test you may have to decide whether your calculator should be in the radian mode or the degree mode.

(3) Figures that accompany problems in this test are intended to provide information useful in solving the problems. They are drawn as accurately as possible EXCEPT when it is stated in a specific problem that its figure is not drawn to scale. All figures lie in a plane unless otherwise indicated.

(4) Unless otherwise specified, the domain of any function f is assumed to be the set of all real numbers x for which $f(x)$ is a real number. The range of f is assumed to be the set of all real numbers $f(x)$, where x is in the domain of f.

(5) Reference information that may be useful in answering the questions in this test can be found on the page preceding Question 1.

USE THIS SPACE FOR SCRATCHWORK

1.   If $\dfrac{1+2x}{3} - \dfrac{13}{4} = \dfrac{x}{4}$, then $x =$

(A) 7   (B) 10   (C) 12   (D) 15   (E) 17

2.   For all $a \neq 0$, $\dfrac{a-1}{a^{-1}-1} =$

(A) a (B) $-a$ (C) 1   (D) -1 (E) $\dfrac{1}{a}$

3.   If $x = 2$, then $\dfrac{2x^2 - 6x}{x-3} =$

(A) 2   (B) 4   (C) 6   (D) 8   (E) 10

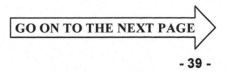

GO ON TO THE NEXT PAGE

USE THIS SPACE FOR SCRATCHWORK.

4. If $\dfrac{x-2y}{y} = 10$, then $\dfrac{x}{y} =$

(A) 4   (B) 8   (C) 10   (D) 12   (E) 14

5. If the length of a rectangle is twice its width, and the perimeter of the rectangle is 54, which of the following is the value of the area of the rectangle?

(A) 162
(B) 324
(C) 486
(D) 648
(E) 810

6. In parallelogram $ABCD$ in Figure 1, which of the following are the coordinates of vertex C ?

(A) $(1, 7)$

(B) $(2, 7)$

(C) $(6, 7)$

(D) $(7, 6)$

(E) $(8, 8)$

Figure 1

7. If $a^5 = 10$ and $a^7 = \dfrac{2}{x}$, which of the following is an expression for x in terms of a ?

(A) $2a^2$

(B) $\dfrac{5}{a^2}$

(C) $\dfrac{1}{5a^2}$

(D) $\dfrac{a^2}{100}$

(E) $\dfrac{100}{a^2}$

GO ON TO THE NEXT PAGE

MATHEMATICS LEVEL 1 TEST - *Continued*

USE THIS SPACE FOR SCRATCHWORK.

8. If the graph of $y = f(x)$ passes through point P, what is the value of a?

(A) 2
(B) 2.5
(C) 3
(D) 3.5
(E) 4.5

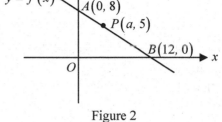

Figure 2

9. If $\sqrt{x^2 - 3} = 2$, then $(x-5)(x+5) =$

(A) 25
(B) 13
(C) 10
(D) −18
(E) −25

10. If $\left| \sqrt{a} - 3 \right| = 3 - \sqrt{a}$, which of the following could be the value of a?

(A) −5
(B) 7
(C) 10
(D) 16
(E) 25

11. If parallelogram $ABCD$ is intersected by line m in Figure 3, what is the sum of angle a and b?

(A) 90
(B) 135
(C) 180
(D) 235
(E) 270

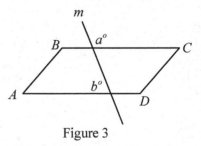

Figure 3

12. If $a^2 - b^2 = 6$ and $a + b = 3$, then $a =$

(A) 2.5 (B) 3 (C) 4.5 (D) 5 (E) 6.5

GO ON TO THE NEXT PAGE

MATHEMATICS LEVEL 1 TEST - *Continued*

USE THIS SPACE FOR SCRATCHWORK.

13. Which of the following is the solution of the inequality
$\dfrac{x+2}{x} > 3$?

(A) $x < 1$
(B) $x < 0$
(C) $0 < x < 1$
(D) $x > 1$
(E) $1 < x < 3$

14. If $a^2 - b^2 = 24$ and $a + b = 6$, then $2ab =$

(A) 5
(B) 8
(C) 10
(D) 12
(E) 18

15. If $x^3 = 10$, then $\sqrt{x} =$

(A) 1.47
(B) 1.72
(C) 2.45
(D) 2.76
(E) 3.33

16. If $20^m = 2^8 \cdot 5^4$, what is the value of m?

(A) 2
(B) 4
(C) 10
(D) 12
(E) 32

17. If the slope of line m is parallel to $-\dfrac{x}{3} + \dfrac{4y}{9} = 1$, what is
the slope of line m?

(A) $\dfrac{3}{4}$ (B) $\dfrac{1}{4}$ (C) $-\dfrac{1}{4}$ (D) $-\dfrac{3}{4}$ (E) $-\dfrac{4}{3}$

MATHEMATICS LEVEL 1 TEST - *Continued*

USE THIS SPACE FOR SCRATCHWORK.

18. What is the value of $5i^{-1} + 3i^{-3}$?

    (A) 2   (B) 5   (C) $2i$ (D) $-2i$ (E) $-5i$

19. If $f(x) = x^3 - 5$, then $f^{-1}(3) =$

    (A) 1   (B) 2   (C) 3   (D) 4   (E) 5

20. An equilateral triangle is inscribed in a circle in Figure 4. If the circle has a radius of 10, what is the length of $\overline{AB}$?

    (A) 10
    (B) 13.5
    (C) 15.6
    (D) 16.8
    (E) 17.3

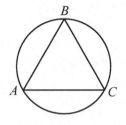

Figure 4

21. The histogram in Figure 5 shows the distribution of the number of children in the families of the employees in Company X. What percent of the employees have fewer than 4 children in the family?

    (A) 12.5
    (B) 25
    (C) 75
    (D) 87.5
    (E) 93.8

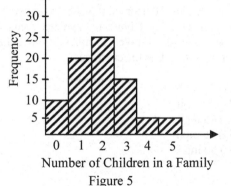

Number of Children in a Family
Figure 5

22. How many different four digit integers can be formed by rearranging the digits of 2525?

    (A) 24
    (B) 16
    (C) 12
    (D) 8
    (E) 6

GO ON TO THE NEXT PAGE

Dr. John Chung's SAT II Math Level 1 Test 2

USE THIS SPACE FOR SCRATCHWORK.

23. In Figure 6, *ABCD* is an isosceles trapezoid and $\overline{EF} \parallel \overline{AD}$. If $AE = BE = 4$, $AD = 8$, and $BC = 2$, what is the perimeter of quadrilateral *BCFE*?

    (A) 10
    (B) 15
    (C) 16
    (D) 18
    (E) 20

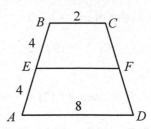

Note: Figure not drawn to scale.

Figure 6

24. If $i = \sqrt{-1}$ and if $i^{50} \cdot i^{20} \cdot i^{10k} = -1$, what is the smallest positive integer value of k?

    (A) 1
    (B) 2
    (C) 3
    (D) 4
    (E) 8

25. A truck takes 10 hours to travel between two cities, while a small car takes 8 hours to travel between the same cities. If the truck travels 15 miles per hour slower than the car, how fast does the car travel?

    (A) 75 mph
    (B) 70 mph
    (C) 68 mph
    (D) 65 mph
    (E) 60 mph

26. In Figure 7, if $AD = 10$, what is the length of $\overline{DC}$?

    (A) 10
    (B) 11.98
    (C) 13.57
    (D) 14.08
    (E) 15.16

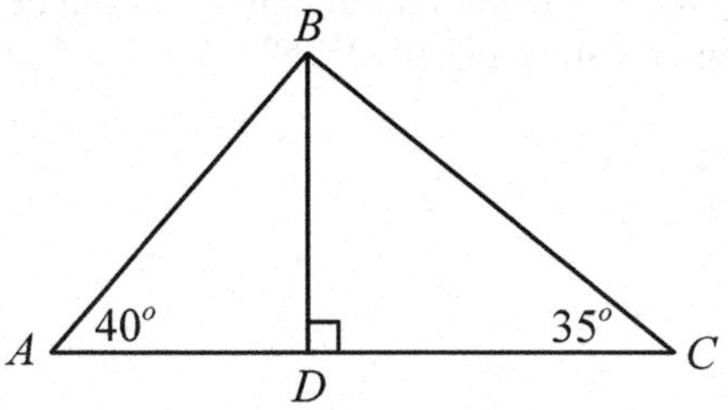

Note: Figure not drawn to scale.
Figure 7

27. Which of the following has the greatest value?

    (A) 20^{100} (B) 10^{150} (C) 5^{200} (D) 4^{250} (E) 2^{300}

GO ON TO THE NEXT PAGE

MATHEMATICS LEVEL 1 TEST - *Continued*

USE THIS SPACE FOR SCRATCHWORK.

28. The value of a laptop computer that depreciates for a number of days is modeled by the function

    $P(t) = P_o\left(1 - \dfrac{r}{100}\right)^t$, where P_o is the initial value of the laptop computer, r is the percent of depreciation per day, and t is the number of days. If you purchase the laptop computer for $800 and the value of the laptop computer decreases by 0.1% each day, what will be the value of the computer after 20 days from the date of purchase?

    (A) 600
    (B) 720
    (C) 745
    (D) 760
    (E) 784

29. In the xy-plane, the point P is equidistant from points $A(0, 0)$ and $B(4, 8)$. Which of the following could be the coordinates of the point P ?

    (A) $(2, 5)$

    (B) $(5, 3)$

    (C) $(6, 2)$

    (D) $(8, 4)$

    (E) $(9, 0)$

30. Tommy's average score on 10 quizzes is 85. When two of the lowest scores are dropped, the average increases to 90. What was the average score of the two lowest scores?

    (A) 50
    (B) 65
    (C) 70
    (D) 72
    (E) 75

31. If the circumference of the base of a right circular cylinder is 10π , and if the volume of the cylinder is 200π cubic units, what is the height of the cylinder?

    (A) 4   (B) 8   (C) 10   (D) 20   (E) 63

GO ON TO THE NEXT PAGE

MATHEMATICS LEVEL 1 TEST - *Continued*

USE THIS SPACE FOR SCRATCHWORK.

32. If α and β are the roots of the equation $x^2 - 3x + 1 = 0$, what is the value of $\dfrac{1}{\alpha} + \dfrac{1}{\beta}$?

    (A) 3 (B) $\dfrac{1}{3}$ (C) $-\dfrac{1}{3}$ (D) -3 (E) -6

33. In Figure 8, if $AD = 4$ and $CD = 15$, then what is the length of $\overline{AB}$?

    (A) 8.72
    (B) 7.75
    (C) 7.48
    (D) 7.15
    (E) 6.93

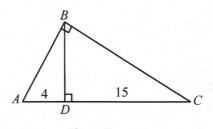

Figure 8

34. If $\sin\theta + \cos\theta = \dfrac{1}{2}$, which of the following is the value of $2\sin\theta\cos\theta$?

    (A) $-\dfrac{1}{2}$ (B) $-\dfrac{3}{4}$ (C) $\dfrac{1}{2}$ (D) $\dfrac{2}{3}$ (E) $\dfrac{3}{4}$

35. If point $P(-3, 5)$ is reflected in the line $y = -5$, what will be the coordinates of the reflection of point P ?

    (A) $(3, -10)$
    (B) $(-3, -10)$
    (C) $(-3, -15)$
    (D) $(2, 5)$
    (E) $(6, 5)$

GO ON TO THE NEXT PAGE

USE THIS SPACE FOR SCRATCHWORK.

36. If the function f is defined by $f(x) = (x-1)^2 - 3$, where $-1 \leq x \leq 3$, which of the following is the range of f?

(A) $-3 \leq f(x) \leq 1$

(B) $-3 \leq f(x) \leq -2$

(C) $-2 \leq f(x) \leq 1$

(D) $-2 \leq f(x) \leq 2$

(E) $-2 \leq f(x) \leq 3$

37. Figure 9 shows a right rectangular prism. If $BC = 5$, $CD = 6$, $DE = 8$, and M is the midpoint of $\overline{CD}$, what is the length of $\overline{AM}$?

(A) 8.4
(B) 8.8
(C) 9.3
(D) 9.5
(E) 9.9

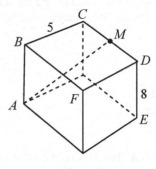

Figure 9

38. The triangle in Figure 10 is a right triangle. If $BC = 1$, what is the perimeter of $\triangle ABD$?

(A) 1.37
(B) 1.88
(C) 2
(D) 2.1
(E) 2.45

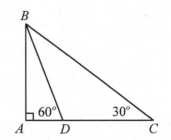

Note: Figure not drawn to scale.

Figure 10

39. What are the coordinates of the turning point of the parabola whose equation is $y = 2x^2 - 8x + 1$?

(A) $(2, 7)$

(B) $(2, -7)$

(C) $(-2, 7)$

(D) $(-2, -7)$

(E) $(-4, 7)$

GO ON TO THE NEXT PAGE

USE THIS SPACE FOR SCRATCHWORK.

40. Figure 11 shows the graphs of the equation $y = x$ and $(x-3)^2 + (y-2)^2 = 1$. What are the x-coordinates of the intersections of the graphs of the circle and the line?

    (A) 1 and 5
    (B) 1 and 4
    (C) 1 and 3
    (D) 2 and 3
    (E) 2 and 4

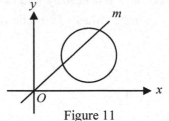

Figure 11

41. If a triangle is inscribed in a circle, and if the length of the radius of the circle is equal to one-half the length of a side of the triangle, then the triangle must be

    (A) acute
    (B) obtuse
    (C) right
    (D) isosceles
    (E) equilateral

42. In Figure 12, if *ABCDEF* is a regular hexagon inscribed in a circle, which of the following is the measure of $\angle ABD$?

    (A) 60°
    (B) 70°
    (C) 80°
    (D) 90°
    (E) 100°

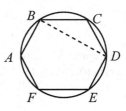

Figure 12

43. In Figure 13, a cone fits exactly in the cylinder. If the volume of the cone is 15 cubic units, then what is the volume of the cylinder?

    (A) 30 cubic units
    (B) 40 cubic units
    (C) 45 cubic units
    (D) 60 cubic units
    (E) 75 cubic units

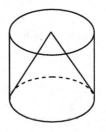

Figure 13

GO ON TO THE NEXT PAGE

MATHEMATICS LEVEL 1 TEST - *Continued*

USE THIS SPACE FOR SCRATCHWORK.

44. If Lee ate 123 pizzas in 6 days, each day eating 5more than on the previous day, how many pizzas did he eat on the third day?

(A) 8   (B) 13   (C) 18   (D) 23   (E) 28

45. In Figure 14, if $AB = 8$, what is the area of rhombus *ABCD*?

(A) 8
(B) 16
(C) 32
(D) 48
(E) 64

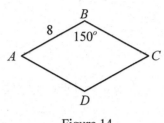

Figure 14

46. Triangles are formed according to a pattern as shown in Figure 15. Each arrangement after the first one is generated by adding a row of triangles to the bottom of the previous arrangement. If this pattern continues, which of the following is the number of triangles in the *n*th arrangement?

(A) $2n-1$

(B) $3n-2$

(C) $\dfrac{n(n+1)}{2}$

(D) n^2

(E) n^3

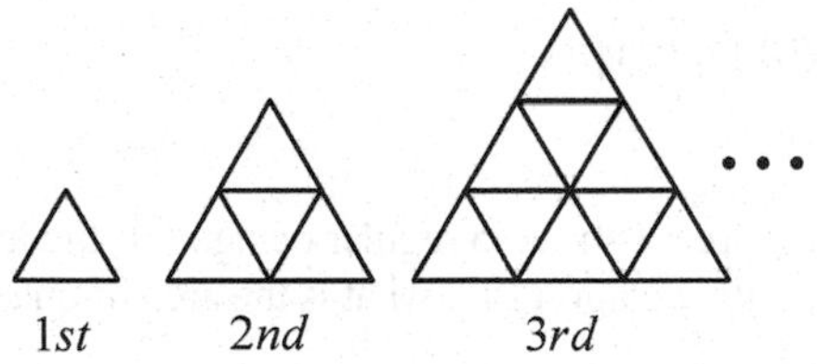

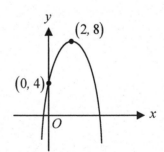

1*st*   2*nd*   3*rd*

Figure 15

47. Which of the following is the equation of the graph shown in Figure 16?

(A) $y = -x^2 + x + 4$
(B) $y = -x^2 - x + 4$
(C) $y = -x^2 + 4x + 4$
(D) $y = -x^2 - 4x + 4$
(E) $y = -2x^2 + x + 4$

Note: Figure not drawn to scale.

Figure 16

GO ON TO THE NEXT PAGE

USE THIS SPACE FOR SCRATCHWORK.

48.   How many gallons of a 8% salt solution must be mixed
with 15 gallons of a 30% salt solution to produce a 20%
solution?

(A) 12.5
(B) 10.8
(C) 9.6
(D) 8.2
(E) 6.7

49.   If $x^2 = y^2$, which of the following must be true?

(A) $x = y$
(B) $x = -y$
(C) $|x| = y$
(D) $x = |y|$
(E) $|x| = |y|$

50.   Figure 17 shows a regular octagon. If the length of a side
of the octagon is 2, what is the area of quadrilateral
ABCD ?

(A) 12
(B) $8 + 4\sqrt{2}$
(C) $4 + 4\sqrt{2}$
(D) $4 + 2\sqrt{2}$
(E) $2 + 2\sqrt{2}$

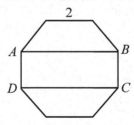

Figure 17

S T O P
IF YOU FINISH BEFORE TIME IS CALLED, YOU MAY CHECK YOUR WORK ON THIS TEST ONLY.
DO NOT TURN TO ANY OTHER TEST IN THIS BOOK.

NO MATERIAL ON THIS PAGE

NO MATERIAL ON THIS PAGE

#	answer	#	answer	#	answer	#	answer	#	answer
1	A	11	C	21	D	31	B	41	C
2	B	12	A	22	E	32	A	42	D
3	B	13	C	23	B	33	A	43	C
4	D	14	C	24	B	34	B	44	C
5	A	15	A	25	A	35	C	45	C
6	D	16	B	26	B	36	A	46	D
7	C	17	A	27	D	37	E	47	C
8	E	18	D	28	E	38	A	48	A
9	D	19	B	29	C	39	B	49	E
10	B	20	E	30	B	40	D	50	C

Explanations: Test 2

1. (A)   Multiply both sides by common denominator 12.

$$12\left(\frac{1+2x}{3}-\frac{13}{4}\right)=12\left(\frac{x}{4}\right) \;\Rightarrow\; 4(1+2x)-3(13)=3x \;\Rightarrow\; 5x=35$$

Therefore, $x=7$.

2. (B) $\dfrac{a-1}{\dfrac{1}{a}-1}=\dfrac{a(a-1)}{a\left(\dfrac{1}{a}-1\right)}=\dfrac{a(a-1)}{1-a}=-a$

> **Important:**
> $$\frac{a-b}{b-a}=-1$$

3. (B) $\dfrac{2x^2-6x}{x-3}=\dfrac{2x(x-3)}{x-3}=2x \;\Rightarrow\; 2(2)=4$

4. (D) $\dfrac{x-2y}{y}=10 \;\Rightarrow\; \dfrac{x}{y}-2=10 \;\Rightarrow\; \dfrac{x}{y}=12$

5. (A) $\ell=2w$ and $2(\ell+w)=54 \;\Rightarrow\; \ell+w=27$. Therefore, $2w+w=27 \;\Rightarrow\; w=9$ and $\ell=18$.

The area of the rectangle is $\ell w=9\times18=162$.

6. (D)   Diagonals bisect each other. The coordinates of the midpoint must be equal.

Midpoint of $\overline{BD}=\left(\dfrac{6+2}{2},\dfrac{m+6}{2}\right)$ and midpoint of $\overline{AC}=\left(\dfrac{x+1}{2},\dfrac{6+m}{2}\right)$.

Since $\overline{BC}\parallel\overline{AD}$, vertex C has coordinates $(x,6)$. Therefore,

$$6+2=x+1 \;\Rightarrow\; x=7.$$

The coordinates of the vertex C is $(7,6)$.

7. (C) $a^7 = \dfrac{2}{x}$ and $a^5 = 10$. $a^7 = a^5 a^2 = 10a^2$ $\Rightarrow$ $10a^2 = \dfrac{2}{x}$

Therefore, $x = \dfrac{2}{10a^2} = \dfrac{1}{5a^2}$.

8. (E) Since slope of the line is $-\dfrac{2}{3}$ and y-intercept is 8, the equation of the line is

$y = -\dfrac{2}{3}x + 8$. Point $(a, 5)$ lies on that line. Substitute into the equation.

$5 = -\dfrac{2}{3}a + 8$ $\Rightarrow$ $\dfrac{2}{3}a = 3$ $\Rightarrow$ $a = \dfrac{9}{2} = 4.5$

Or

Slopes between any two points on the line are constant.

Slope of $\overline{AB}$ = slope of $\overline{AP}$: $\dfrac{0-8}{12-0} = \dfrac{5-8}{a-0}$ $\Rightarrow$ $\dfrac{-2}{3} = \dfrac{-3}{a}$ $\Rightarrow$ $2a = 9$ $\Rightarrow$ $a = 4.5$

9. (D) $\sqrt{x^2 - 3} = 2$ $\Rightarrow$ $x^2 - 3 = 4$ $\Rightarrow$ $x^2 = 7$

$(x-5)(x+5) = x^2 - 25$ $\Rightarrow$ $\overset{\text{substitute}}{\left(x^2 = 7 \right)}$ $\Rightarrow$ $7 - 25 = -18$

10. (B) Since $\left| \sqrt{a} - 3 \right| = -\left(\sqrt{a} - 3 \right)$, then $\sqrt{a} - 3 \le 0$ and $a \ge 0$.

$\sqrt{a} \le 3$ $\Rightarrow$ $a \le 9$. Therefore, $0 \le a \le 9$.

Or

Check each choice.   (A) a cannot be negative.   (B) $\left| \sqrt{10} - 3 \right| = \sqrt{10} - 3$ because $\sqrt{10} > 3$.

11. (C) When two parallel lines are cut by a transversal, the sum of interior angles in the same side is 180°.

Therefore, $a + b = 180$.

12. (A) $a^2 - b^2 = 6$ $\Rightarrow$ $(a+b)(a-b) = 6$ $\Rightarrow$ If $a + b = 3$, then $a - b = 2$.

$$a + b = 3$$
System of equations : $\;\; +\underline{\left| a - b = 2 \right.}$
$$2a\;\; = 5 \;\Rightarrow\; a = 2.5$$

13. (C) 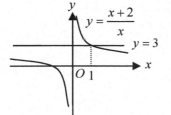 Method 1:

$\dfrac{x+2}{x} > 3 \quad \Rightarrow \quad$ If $x > 0$, $x+2 > 3x \quad \Rightarrow \quad 2x < 2 \quad \Rightarrow \quad x < 1$. Solution: $0 < x < 1$

If $x < 0$, $x+2 < 3x \quad \Rightarrow \quad 2x > 2 \quad \Rightarrow \quad x > 1$. No solution:

Method 2: Use a graphic utility. The graph of $y = \dfrac{x+2}{x}$ is over the graph of $y = 3$

in the interval of $0 < x < 1$.

14. (C) Since $a + b = 6$ and $a - b = 4$, then $a = 5$ and $b = 1$.
Therefore, $2ab = 2(5)(1) = 10$.

15. (A) $x^3 = 10 \quad \Rightarrow \quad \left(x^3\right)^{\frac{1}{6}} = 10^{\frac{1}{6}} \quad \Rightarrow \quad x^{\frac{1}{2}} \cong 1.47$

16. (B) $2^8 \cdot 5^4 = 4^4 \cdot 5^4 = \left(4 \cdot 5\right)^4 = 20^4 \quad \Rightarrow \quad 20^m = 20^4 \quad \Rightarrow \quad m = 4$

Or

Use a calculator.

$20^m = 2^8 \cdot 5^4 \quad \Rightarrow \quad m = \dfrac{\log \left(2^8 \cdot 5^4\right)}{\log 20} = 4$

17. (A) $9\left(-\dfrac{x}{3} + \dfrac{4y}{9} = 1\right) \quad \Rightarrow \quad -3x + 4y = 9 \quad \Rightarrow \quad 4y = 3x + 9 \quad \Rightarrow \quad y = \dfrac{3}{4}x + \dfrac{9}{4}$

Slope $= \dfrac{3}{4}$

18. (D) $\dfrac{5}{i} + \dfrac{3}{i^3} = \dfrac{5}{i} - \dfrac{3}{i} = \dfrac{2}{i}$ because $i^3 = -i$.

$\dfrac{2 \times i}{i \times i} = \dfrac{2i}{i^2} = -2i$

19. (B) $y = x^3 - 5 \quad \Rightarrow (\text{Inverse}) \quad x = y^3 - 5$, where $y = f^{-1}(x)$.
Since $x = 3$, $3 = y^3 - 5 \quad \Rightarrow \quad y^3 = 8 \quad \Rightarrow \quad y = f^{-1}(3) = 2$

20. (E)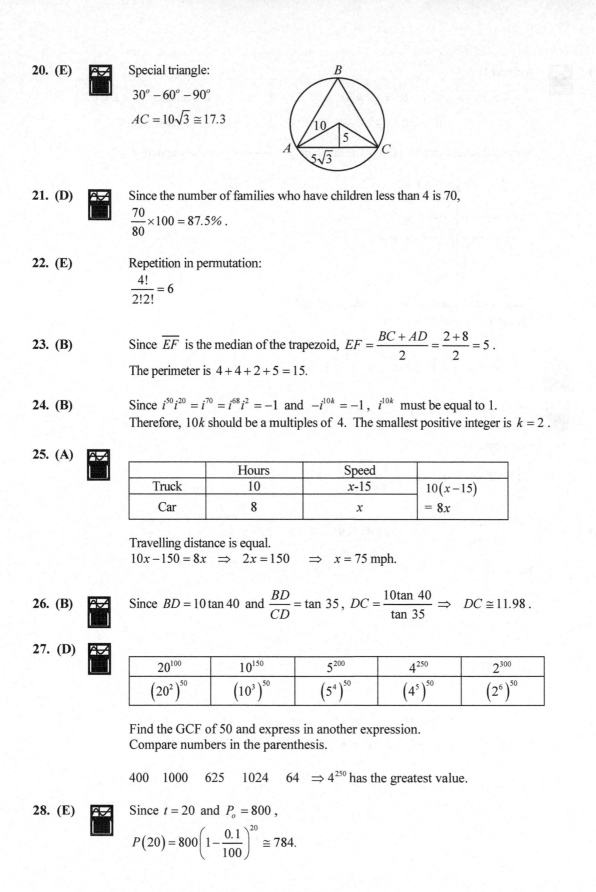

Special triangle:

$30^{\circ} - 60^{\circ} - 90^{\circ}$

$AC = 10\sqrt{3} \cong 17.3$

21. (D)

Since the number of families who have children less than 4 is 70,

$\dfrac{70}{80} \times 100 = 87.5\%$.

22. (E)

Repetition in permutation:

$\dfrac{4!}{2!2!} = 6$

23. (B)

Since $\overline{EF}$ is the median of the trapezoid, $EF = \dfrac{BC + AD}{2} = \dfrac{2+8}{2} = 5$.

The perimeter is $4 + 4 + 2 + 5 = 15$.

24. (B)

Since $i^{50} i^{20} = i^{70} = i^{68} i^{2} = -1$ and $-i^{10k} = -1$, i^{10k} must be equal to 1.

Therefore, $10k$ should be a multiples of 4. The smallest positive integer is $k = 2$.

25. (A)

	Hours	Speed	
Truck	10	x-15	$10(x-15)$
Car	8	x	$= 8x$

Travelling distance is equal.

$10x - 150 = 8x \implies 2x = 150 \implies x = 75$ mph.

26. (B)

Since $BD = 10 \tan 40$ and $\dfrac{BD}{CD} = \tan 35$, $DC = \dfrac{10 \tan 40}{\tan 35} \implies DC \cong 11.98$.

27. (D)

20^{100}	10^{150}	5^{200}	4^{250}	2^{300}
$\left(20^2\right)^{50}$	$\left(10^3\right)^{50}$	$\left(5^4\right)^{50}$	$\left(4^5\right)^{50}$	$\left(2^6\right)^{50}$

Find the GCF of 50 and express in another expression.
Compare numbers in the parenthesis.

400   1000   625   1024   64 $\implies 4^{250}$ has the greatest value.

28. (E)

Since $t = 20$ and $P_o = 800$,

$P(20) = 800\left(1 - \dfrac{0.1}{100}\right)^{20} \cong 784$.

29. (C)   Slope of the line is $\dfrac{8}{4} = 2$ and the midpoint is $\left(\dfrac{4+0}{2}, \dfrac{8+0}{2}\right) = (2, 4)$.

Slope of the equidistant line is $-\dfrac{1}{2}$.

Therefore, the equation of the line is $y = -\dfrac{1}{2}x + b$, where $(2, 4)$ on this line.

Since $b = 5$, the equation is $y = -\dfrac{1}{2}x + 5$

(C) $(6, 2)$: $2 = -\dfrac{1}{2}(6) + 5$ True.

30. (B)   Since the sum of 10 quizzes is $10 \times 85 = 850$ and the sum of 8 quizzes is $8 \times 90 = 720$, the sum of two quizzes is $850 - 720 = 130$.

The average of the two quizzes is $\dfrac{130}{2} = 65$.

31. (B)   Because $2\pi r = 10\pi \;\Rightarrow\; r = 5$.

Since $V = \pi r^2 h$, $200\pi = \pi 5^2 h \;\Rightarrow\; 200\pi = 25\pi h$, $h = 8$.

32. (A)   By Vieta's formula, $\alpha + \beta = 3$ and $\alpha\beta = 1$.

The value of $\dfrac{1}{\alpha} + \dfrac{1}{\beta} = \dfrac{\alpha + \beta}{\alpha\beta}$ is $\dfrac{3}{1} = 3$.

33. (A)

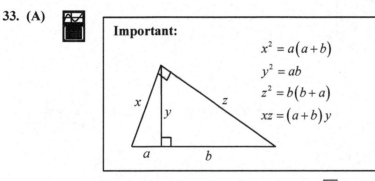

Important:

$$x^2 = a(a+b)$$
$$y^2 = ab$$
$$z^2 = b(b+a)$$
$$xz = (a+b)y$$

Therefore, $AB^2 = 4(4+15) \;\Rightarrow\; AB = \sqrt{76} \cong 8.72$.

34. (B)   Because $\sin\theta + \cos\theta = \dfrac{1}{2} \;\Rightarrow\; (\sin\theta + \cos\theta)^2 = \dfrac{1}{4}$,

$\sin^2\theta + \cos^2\theta + 2\sin\theta\cos\theta = \dfrac{1}{4}$.

Since $\sin^2\theta + \cos^2\theta = 1$, $2\sin\theta\cos\theta = -\dfrac{3}{4}$.

$\therefore\; \sin 2\theta = 2\sin\theta\cos\theta$.

35. (C)

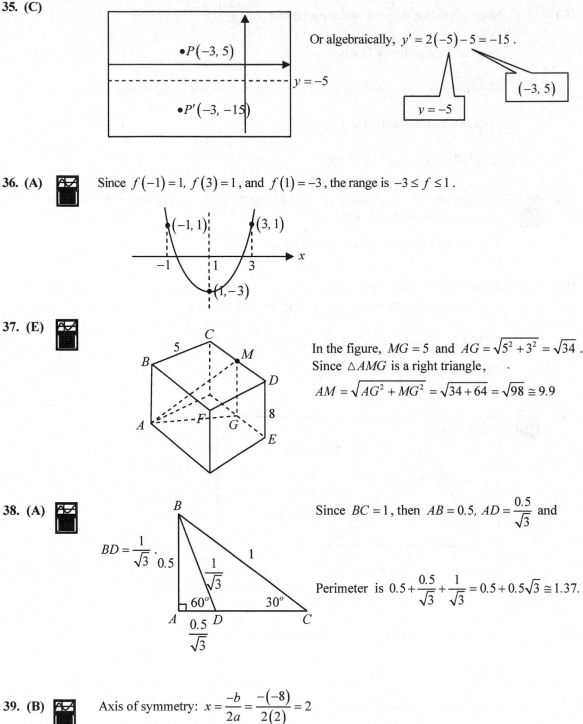

Or algebraically, $y' = 2(-5) - 5 = -15$.

$(-3, 5)$

$y = -5$

36. (A) Since $f(-1) = 1$, $f(3) = 1$, and $f(1) = -3$, the range is $-3 \le f \le 1$.

37. (E) In the figure, $MG = 5$ and $AG = \sqrt{5^2 + 3^2} = \sqrt{34}$.
Since $\triangle AMG$ is a right triangle,

$$AM = \sqrt{AG^2 + MG^2} = \sqrt{34 + 64} = \sqrt{98} \cong 9.9$$

38. (A) Since $BC = 1$, then $AB = 0.5$, $AD = \dfrac{0.5}{\sqrt{3}}$ and $BD = \dfrac{1}{\sqrt{3}}$.

Perimeter is $0.5 + \dfrac{0.5}{\sqrt{3}} + \dfrac{1}{\sqrt{3}} = 0.5 + 0.5\sqrt{3} \cong 1.37$.

39. (B) Axis of symmetry: $x = \dfrac{-b}{2a} = \dfrac{-(-8)}{2(2)} = 2$

Y-coordinate of the turning point: $y = f(2) = -7$

Therefore, the coordinates of the turning point is $(2, -7)$.

Or
Use graphic utility. Find minimum.

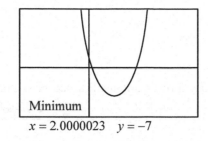

$$x = 2.0000023 \quad y = -7$$

40. (D)   System of equations:
Substitute $y = x$ into the equation of the circle.

$$(x-3)^2 + (x-2)^2 = 1 \quad \Rightarrow \quad 2x^2 - 10x + 12 = 0 \quad \Rightarrow \quad x^2 - 5x + 6 = 0$$

Factor : $(x-3)(x-2) = 0$

Therefore, $x = 3$ or $x - 2$.

41. (C)   Since the diameter must be a side of the triangle, any inscribed angle of a semicircle is a right angle.

42. (D) 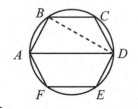   Total interior angle $= (6-2)180 = 720$

$$\angle ABC = \frac{720}{6} = 120$$

Since $\triangle BCD$ is isosceles,

$\angle CBD = 30$

$\therefore \angle ABD = 90$

Important

If n is the number of sides, the sum of interior angles is $(n-2) \times 180$.

The sum of all exterior angles of a polygon is 360°.

Or,

Since $\overline{AD}$ is the diameter of the circle, the inscribed angle for a semicircle is 90°.

43. (C) If r is the radius of the circular base and h is the height of the cone (or cylinder), the volume of the cone is $\dfrac{\pi r^2 h}{3}$ and the volume of the cylinder is $\pi r^2 h$.

$$\therefore \frac{\pi r^2 h}{3} = 15 \quad \Rightarrow \quad \pi r^2 h = 45$$

44. (C) The number a_n of pizzas each day form an arithmetic sequence with common difference 5.

If a is the first term, then $a_6 = a + (6-1)5 = a + 25$ and $S_6 = \dfrac{6(a + a + 25)}{2} = 6a + 25$.

Therefore, $6a + 25 = 123 \quad \Rightarrow \quad 6a = 48 \quad \Rightarrow \quad a = 8$.

$$\therefore a_3 = 8 + (3-1)5 = 18$$

> **Important**
> Arithmetic sequence: $a_1 =$ first term $\quad d =$ common difference
> $$a_n = a_1 + (n-1)d \quad \text{and} \quad S_n = \frac{n(a_1 + a_n)}{2}$$

45. (C) Since $\triangle ABE$ is a right triangle, $BE = 8\sin 15$ and $AE = 8\cos 15$.
Therefore, the area of the rhombus is
$$\left(\frac{AE \times BE}{2}\right)4 = \left(\frac{8\cos 15 \times 8\sin 15}{2}\right)4 = 128\cos 15 \sin 15 = 32$$

46. (D) The sequence has a pattern as follows.
$a_1 = 1$, $\quad a_2 = 1 + 3$, $\quad a_3 = 1 + 3 + 5, \ldots$
Therefore,
$a_n = 1 + 3 + 5 + \cdots + (2n - 1) \quad \because b_n = b_1 + (n-1)d$ where $b_1 = 1$ and $d = 2$
$$\therefore a_n = \frac{n(1 + 2n - 1)}{2} = n^2$$

47. (C) The equation of the graph is defined by $y = a(x - 2)^2 + 8$ (squared form).

Since point $(0, 4)$ lies on the graph, $4 = a(-2)^2 + 8 \quad \Rightarrow \quad a = -1$.

$$\therefore y = -(x - 2)^2 + 8 \quad \Rightarrow \quad y = -x^2 + 4x + 4$$

48. (A)

	% of Solute	Gallons of Solute
Solution A x gallons	8%	$0.08x$
Solution B 15 gallons	30%	4.5

When those two solutions are mixed, the % of solute is 20%.

$$\frac{0.08x+4.5}{x+15}=\frac{20}{100} \Rightarrow \frac{0.08x+4.5}{x+15}=\frac{1}{5}$$

$$0.4x+22.5=x+15 \Rightarrow 0.6x=7.5 \Rightarrow x=12.5 \text{ gallons}$$

49. (E)

$$x^2-y^2=0 \Rightarrow (x+y)(x-y)=0 \Rightarrow y=x \text{ or } y=-x$$

The equation represents two perpendicular lines.

It is equivalent to $|x|=|y|$.

50. (C)

Since $\angle AEF = 45^o$, $\triangle AEF$ is isosceles. Therefore, $AF=\sqrt{2}$.

The area of $\square ABCD$ is

$$2(2+2\sqrt{2})=4+4\sqrt{2}.$$

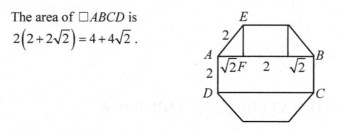

END

NO MATERIAL ON THIS PAGE

Dr. John Chung's SAT II

Math Level 1

Test 3

MATHEMATICS LEVEL 1 TEST

TEST 3

REFERENCE INFORMATION

THE FOLLOWING INFORMATION IS FOR YOUR REFERENCE IN ANSWERING SOME OF THE QUESTIONS IN THIS TEST

Volume of a right circular cone with radius r and height h: $V = \dfrac{1}{3}\pi r^2 h$

Lateral Area of a right circular cone with circumference of the base c and slant height ℓ: $S = \dfrac{1}{2}c\ell$

Volume of a sphere with radius r: $V = \dfrac{4}{3}\pi r^3$

Surface Area of a sphere with radius r: $S = 4\pi r^2$

Volume of a pyramid with base area B and height h: $V = \dfrac{1}{3}Bh$

Dr. John Chung's SAT II Math Level 1

Answer Sheet

1	Ⓐ Ⓑ Ⓒ Ⓓ Ⓔ	26	Ⓐ Ⓑ Ⓒ Ⓓ Ⓔ
2	Ⓐ Ⓑ Ⓒ Ⓓ Ⓔ	27	Ⓐ Ⓑ Ⓒ Ⓓ Ⓔ
3	Ⓐ Ⓑ Ⓒ Ⓓ Ⓔ	28	Ⓐ Ⓑ Ⓒ Ⓓ Ⓔ
4	Ⓐ Ⓑ Ⓒ Ⓓ Ⓔ	29	Ⓐ Ⓑ Ⓒ Ⓓ Ⓔ
5	Ⓐ Ⓑ Ⓒ Ⓓ Ⓔ	30	Ⓐ Ⓑ Ⓒ Ⓓ Ⓔ
6	Ⓐ Ⓑ Ⓒ Ⓓ Ⓔ	31	Ⓐ Ⓑ Ⓒ Ⓓ Ⓔ
7	Ⓐ Ⓑ Ⓒ Ⓓ Ⓔ	32	Ⓐ Ⓑ Ⓒ Ⓓ Ⓔ
8	Ⓐ Ⓑ Ⓒ Ⓓ Ⓔ	33	Ⓐ Ⓑ Ⓒ Ⓓ Ⓔ
9	Ⓐ Ⓑ Ⓒ Ⓓ Ⓔ	34	Ⓐ Ⓑ Ⓒ Ⓓ Ⓔ
10	Ⓐ Ⓑ Ⓒ Ⓓ Ⓔ	35	Ⓐ Ⓑ Ⓒ Ⓓ Ⓔ
11	Ⓐ Ⓑ Ⓒ Ⓓ Ⓔ	36	Ⓐ Ⓑ Ⓒ Ⓓ Ⓔ
12	Ⓐ Ⓑ Ⓒ Ⓓ Ⓔ	37	Ⓐ Ⓑ Ⓒ Ⓓ Ⓔ
13	Ⓐ Ⓑ Ⓒ Ⓓ Ⓔ	38	Ⓐ Ⓑ Ⓒ Ⓓ Ⓔ
14	Ⓐ Ⓑ Ⓒ Ⓓ Ⓔ	39	Ⓐ Ⓑ Ⓒ Ⓓ Ⓔ
15	Ⓐ Ⓑ Ⓒ Ⓓ Ⓔ	40	Ⓐ Ⓑ Ⓒ Ⓓ Ⓔ
16	Ⓐ Ⓑ Ⓒ Ⓓ Ⓔ	41	Ⓐ Ⓑ Ⓒ Ⓓ Ⓔ
17	Ⓐ Ⓑ Ⓒ Ⓓ Ⓔ	42	Ⓐ Ⓑ Ⓒ Ⓓ Ⓔ
18	Ⓐ Ⓑ Ⓒ Ⓓ Ⓔ	43	Ⓐ Ⓑ Ⓒ Ⓓ Ⓔ
19	Ⓐ Ⓑ Ⓒ Ⓓ Ⓔ	44	Ⓐ Ⓑ Ⓒ Ⓓ Ⓔ
20	Ⓐ Ⓑ Ⓒ Ⓓ Ⓔ	45	Ⓐ Ⓑ Ⓒ Ⓓ Ⓔ
21	Ⓐ Ⓑ Ⓒ Ⓓ Ⓔ	46	Ⓐ Ⓑ Ⓒ Ⓓ Ⓔ
22	Ⓐ Ⓑ Ⓒ Ⓓ Ⓔ	47	Ⓐ Ⓑ Ⓒ Ⓓ Ⓔ
23	Ⓐ Ⓑ Ⓒ Ⓓ Ⓔ	48	Ⓐ Ⓑ Ⓒ Ⓓ Ⓔ
24	Ⓐ Ⓑ Ⓒ Ⓓ Ⓔ	49	Ⓐ Ⓑ Ⓒ Ⓓ Ⓔ
25	Ⓐ Ⓑ Ⓒ Ⓓ Ⓔ	50	Ⓐ Ⓑ Ⓒ Ⓓ Ⓔ

The number of right answers : [   ]

The number of wrong answers : [   ]

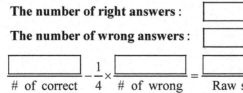

$$\boxed{} - \frac{1}{4} \times \boxed{} = \boxed{}$$

\# of correct   \# of wrong   Raw score

Score Conversion Table

Raw Score	Scaled Score	Raw Score	Scaled Score	Raw Score	Scaled Score
50	800	28	630	6	480
49	800	27	620	5	470
48	800	26	610	4	470
47	800	25	600	3	460
46	790	24	590	2	460
45	780	23	580	1	450
44	770	22	570	0	450
43	760	21	550		
42	750	20	540		
41	740	19	530		
40	740	18	520		
39	730	17	510		
38	720	16	500		
37	710	15	490		
36	710	14	480		
35	700	13	470		
34	690	12	460		
33	680	11	450		
32	670	10	440		
31	660	9	430		
30	650	8	420		
29	640	7	410		

MATHEMATICS LEVEL 1 TEST

For each of the following problems, decide which is the BEST of the choices given. If the exact numerical value is not one of the choices, select the choice that best approximates this value. Then fill in the corresponding circle on the answer sheet.

Notes: (1) A scientific or graphing calculator will be necessary for answering some (but not all) of the questions in this test. For each question you will have to decide whether or not you should use a calculator.

      (2) For some questions in this test you may have to decide whether your calculator should be in the radian mode or the degree mode.

      (3) Figures that accompany problems in this test are intended to provide information useful in solving the problems. They are drawn as accurately as possible EXCEPT when it is stated in a specific problem that its figure is not drawn to scale. All figures lie in a plane unless otherwise indicated.

      (4) Unless otherwise specified, the domain of any function f is assumed to be the set of all real numbers x for which $f(x)$ is a real number. The range of f is assumed to be the set of all real numbers $f(x)$, where x is in the domain of f.

      (5) Reference information that may be useful in answering the questions in this test can be found on the page preceding Question 1.

USE THIS SPACE FOR SCRATCHWORK

1.   If $\dfrac{1}{x^2-2}=\dfrac{1}{x}$, then $x=$

    (A) 2 only
    (B) $\sqrt{2}$ or $-\sqrt{2}$
    (C) 2 or -1
    (D) 2 or 3
    (E) -2 or 3

2.   The smallest positive integer that is divisible by 4, 9, and 12 is

    (A) 108   (B) 72   (C) 48   (D) 36   (E) 24

3.   If the edge of a cube is tripled, then the volume is multiplied by

    (A) 3   (B) 6   (C) 9   (D) 12   (E) 27

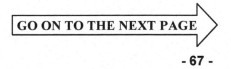

MATHEMATICS LEVEL 1 TEST - *Continued*

USE THIS SPACE FOR SCRATCHWORK.

4. The operation Ψ is defined by $x\,\Psi\,y = x - xy + y$, where x and y are real numbers. If $x\,\Psi\,5 = 0$, which of the following is the value of x?

(A) 0   (B) 1   (C) 1.25   (D) 2   (E) 2.5

5. If $y = -\sqrt{n^2}$ and $n = -4$, what is the value of y?

(A) 2
(B) 4
(C) -2
(D) -4
(E) -16

6. In Figure 2, if $\dfrac{AE}{DE} = \dfrac{1}{3}$, $\overline{AB} \parallel \overline{CD}$, and the area of $\triangle ABE = 6$, then what is the area of $\triangle CDE$?

(A) 12
(B) 18
(C) 24
(D) 42
(E) 54

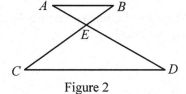

Figure 2

7. If $ab = 1$, then $\dfrac{3^{(a+b)^2}}{3^{(a-b)^2}} =$

(A) 9   (B) 27   (C) 36   (D) 81   (E) 243

8. If Figure 3 shows the graph of $y = f(x)$, which of the following could be the equation of the function?

(A) $f(x) = |x-2|$
(B) $f(x) = |x-2| + 3$
(C) $f(x) = -|x-2| + 3$
(D) $f(x) = -|x+2| + 3$
(E) $f(x) = -|x-4| - 3$

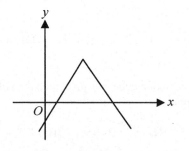

Note: Figure not drawn to scale.
Figure 3

GO ON TO THE NEXT PAGE

USE THIS SPACE FOR SCRATCHWORK.

9. $\left(\dfrac{1}{2}-\dfrac{1}{3}\right)+\left(\dfrac{1}{3}-\dfrac{1}{4}\right)+\left(\dfrac{1}{4}-\dfrac{1}{5}\right)+\cdots+\left(\dfrac{1}{19}-\dfrac{1}{20}\right)=$

(A) $\dfrac{1}{20}$ (B) $\dfrac{1}{5}$ (C) $\dfrac{9}{20}$ (D) $\dfrac{1}{2}$ (E) $\dfrac{2}{3}$

10. In Figure 4, triangle ABC is to be constructed using three points. Which of the following is the area of $\triangle ABC$?

(A) 10
(B) 12
(C) 14
(D) 18
(E) 24

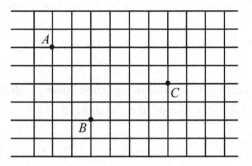

Figure 4

11. If $4^{a+b}=32$ and $3^{a-b}=81$, what is the value of a ?

(A) 2   (B) 2.75   (C) 3.25   (D) 4   (E) 5

12. If $a<b<c$, then $\Big|\,|a-b|+|b-c|\,\Big|=$

(A) $a+b$
(B) $b-a$
(C) $c-a$
(D) $c+a$
(E) $a+b+c$

13. If $(x+y)^2=10$ and $(x-y)^2=4$, then $xy=$

(A) 1   (B) 1.5   (C) 2   (D) 2.5   (E) 3

14. If $x+y=10$ and $x-y=5$, then $2x^2-2y^2=$

(A) 50
(B) 100
(C) 150
(D) 200
(E) 250

GO ON TO THE NEXT PAGE

MATHEMATICS LEVEL 1 TEST - *Continued*

USE THIS SPACE FOR SCRATCHWORK.

15. If the length of a rectangle is 3 more than twice the width, and if the perimeter is 24, what is the area of the rectangle?

(A) 18   (B) 24   (C) 27   (D) 30   (E) 72

16. If $f(x) = 1 - 2x$ and $g(x) = |1 - x|$, then $f(g(3)) =$

(A) 2   (B) 3   (C) –2   (D) –3   (E) –4

17. If the length of a side of equilateral triangle AOB is 10, which of the following is the slope of $\overline{AB}$?

(A) $-\sqrt{3}$

(B) $-\sqrt{2}$

(C) $-\dfrac{1}{2}$

(D) $-\dfrac{\sqrt{2}}{2}$

(E) $-\dfrac{\sqrt{3}}{3}$

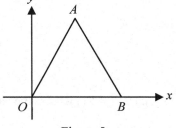

Figure 5

18. If $x = -1$ is a solution of the equation $3x^2 + 6kx = k$, then $k =$

(A) $\dfrac{1}{8}$ (B) $\dfrac{3}{7}$ (C) $\dfrac{7}{3}$ (D) 2   (E) 3

19. If one root of the equation $x^2 - 6x + k = 0$ is twice the value of the other root, what is the value of k ?

(A) 6
(B) 8
(C) 12
(D) 18
(E) 24

GO ON TO THE NEXT PAGE

MATHEMATICS LEVEL 1 TEST - *Continued*

USE THIS SPACE FOR SCRATCHWORK.

20. In rectangle $ABCD$ in Figure 6, $AB = 1$, M is the midpoint of $\overline{BC}$, and $\angle BAM = 45^\circ$. What is the perimeter of $\triangle ACM$?

    (A) 4.65
    (B) 5.32
    (C) 5.78
    (D) 6.02
    (E) 8.45

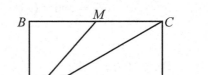

Figure 6

21. Each day, Jennifer ate 30% of the candy bars that were in her container at the beginning of the day. If 49 candy bars remained at the end of the second day, how many candy bars were in the container originally?

    (A) 80
    (B) 100
    (C) 120
    (D) 150
    (E) 200

22. If $x^3 + 3x^2 - x + 6 = (x + 2)P(x) + K$, where $P(x)$ is a polynomial and K is a constant, then $K =$

    (A) 10   (B) 12   (C) 15   (D) 20   (E) 24

23. Which of the following is a counterexample to the statement " All natural numbers are either prime or composite "?

    (A) 33   (B) 23   (C) 20   (D) 2   (E) 1

24. If $f(x) = -x^2 - (-x)^2$, then $f(-1) =$

    (A) −1
    (B) −2
    (C) 0
    (D) 1
    (E) 2

MATHEMATICS LEVEL 1 TEST - *Continued*

USE THIS SPACE FOR SCRATCHWORK.

25. If $f(x) = ax^5 + bx^3 + cx - 4$ and $f(-1) = 3$, then
$f(1) =$

(A) 10   (B) 7   (C) 3   (D) –3   (E) –11

26. If the sides of an obtuse triangle are lengths 3, 5, and x as shown in Figure 7, which of the following could be the value of x ?

(A) 3
(B) 4
(C) 5
(D) 5.5
(E) 7

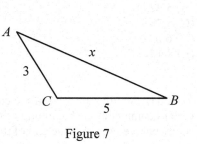

Figure 7

27. If $f\left(\dfrac{x}{3}\right) = x^2 - 2x + 3$, then $f(2) =$

(A) 3
(B) 15
(C) 27
(D) 30
(E) 48

28. If $\left(3^{x^2}\right)\left(3^{-4x}\right)\left(3^3\right) = 81^2$, which of the following could be the value of x ?

(A) 0   (B) 1   (C) 2   (D) 3   (E) 5

29. If $i^2 = -1$ and $S = i + i^2 + i^3 + i^4 + \cdots + i^{50}$, what is the value of S ?

(A) 1
(B) $1 - i$
(C) $1 + i$
(D) $i - 1$
(E) –1

GO ON TO THE NEXT PAGE

MATHEMATICS LEVEL 1 TEST - *Continued*

USE THIS SPACE FOR SCRATCHWORK.

30. Which of the following lines is perpendicular to the line $2x - 3y = 5$?

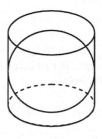

(A) $2x + 3y = 1$
(B) $2x - 3y = 4$
(C) $3x - 2y = -1$
(D) $3x + 2y = -3$
(E) $2x - 5y = -2$

31. In Figure 8, a sphere is inscribed in a cylinder. what is the ratio of the volume of the sphere to the volume of the cylinder?

(A) 1:2
(B) 1:3
(C) 2:3
(D) 2:5
(E) 3:4

Figure 8

32. The line with equation $x = 3$ is graphed on the same xy-plane as the circle with center $(7, 5)$ and radius 5. What are the coordinates of the points of intersection of the line and the circle?

(A) $(-3, 5)$ and $(3, 5)$

(B) $(3, 2)$ and $(3, 8)$

(C) $(3, 5)$ and $(3, -5)$

(D) $(3, 5)$ and $(3, 10)$

(E) $(5, 2)$ and $(5, 8)$

33. If the points of the parallelogram are given in Figure 9, what is the value of $a + b$?

(A) 4
(B) 5
(C) 6
(D) 7
(E) 8

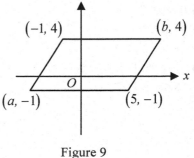

Figure 9

GO ON TO THE NEXT PAGE

MATHEMATICS LEVEL 1 TEST - *Continued*

USE THIS SPACE FOR SCRATCHWORK.

34. Which of the following is equivalent to
    $\{x: -4 < x < 10\}$?

    (A) $\{x: |x| < 7\}$
    (B) $\{x: |x+3| < 7\}$
    (C) $\{x: |x+3| > 7\}$
    (D) $\{x: |x-3| < 7\}$
    (E) $\{x: |x-3| > 7\}$

35. If two circles are externally tangent to each other, what is the greatest number of common tangents that can be drawn to both circles?

    (A) 0   (B) 1   (C) 2   (D) 3   (E) 4

36. The average age of a group of boys and girls is fourteen years. If the average of the boys' ages is sixteen and that of girls' ages is thirteen, what is the ratio of the numbers of boys to the number of girls?

    (A) 1:2
    (B) 1:3
    (C) 2:3
    (D) 2:1
    (E) 3:2

37. If $f(x) = -x^2 - 2x$ for $-2 \le x \le 2$, then which of the following is the range of f ?

    (A) $0 \le y \le 3$
    (B) $0 \le y \le 1$
    (C) $-8 \le y \le 0$
    (D) $-8 \le y \le 1$
    (E) $-8 \le y \le 3$

GO ON TO THE NEXT PAGE

MATHEMATICS LEVEL 1 TEST - *Continued*

USE THIS SPACE FOR SCRATCHWORK.

38. If $f(x) = \sqrt{x-2}$ and $g(x) = -x^2 + 1$, which of the following could be the graph of $g(f(x))$?

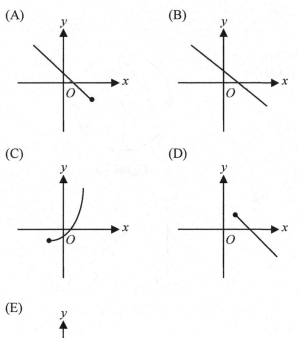

(A)

(B)

(C)

(D)

(E)

39. If $\dfrac{\sin 30^o}{5} = \dfrac{\sin \theta^o}{10}$, what is the value of θ?

(A) 0   (B) 30   (C) 45   (D) 60   (E) 90

40. Which of the following is the minimum value of $3^{x^2 - 2x - 1}$?

(A) $\dfrac{1}{9}$ (B) $\dfrac{1}{3}$ (C) 3   (D) 9   (E) 27

GO ON TO THE NEXT PAGE

MATHEMATICS LEVEL 1 TEST - *Continued*

USE THIS SPACE FOR SCRATCHWORK.

41. If the first four hexagonal numbers are 1, 7, 19, and 37, then which of the following is the fifteenth hexagonal number?

 (A) 427   (B) 538   (C) 613   (D) 631   (E) 721

42. In Figure 10, an equilateral triangle is inscribed in a circle. If the length of a side of the triangle is a and the radius of the circle is b, what is the ratio $\dfrac{b}{a}$?

 (A) $\dfrac{1}{2}$ (B) $\dfrac{2}{3}$ (C) $\dfrac{\sqrt{2}}{3}$ (D) $\dfrac{\sqrt{3}}{2}$ (E) $\dfrac{\sqrt{3}}{3}$

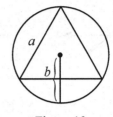

Figure 10

43. In triangle ABC shown in Figure 11, if $BC = a$, what is the area of the triangle?

 (A) $\dfrac{a^2}{4}$ (B) $\dfrac{a^2}{2}$ (C) $\dfrac{a^2}{\sqrt{2}}$ (D) $\dfrac{a^2}{\sqrt{3}}$ (E) $\dfrac{a^2}{3}$

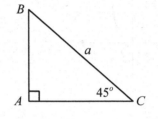

Figure 11

44. If $\sin\theta = k$, then $(\cos\theta)(\cot\theta)(\sin\theta) =$

 (A) k
 (B) $k-1$
 (C) k^2-1
 (D) $1-k^2$
 (E) $1+k^2$

45. In rectangle $ABCD$ in Figure 12 is rotated about side CD, what is the surface area of the resulting solid?

 (A) 50π
 (B) 100π
 (C) 125π
 (D) 150π
 (E) 200π

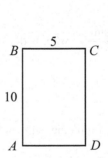

Figure 12

GO ON TO THE NEXT PAGE

MATHEMATICS LEVEL 1 TEST - *Continued*

USE THIS SPACE FOR SCRATCHWORK.

46. Which of the following is not a factor of the expression
$x^4 + 3x^3 - 4x^2 - 12x$?

(A) x
(B) $x - 2$
(C) $x + 2$
(D) $x + 4$
(E) $x + 3$

47. If $1 + 2 + 3 + 4 + \bullet\bullet\bullet + n > 125$, what is the least positive integer value of n ?

(A) 14
(B) 15
(C) 16
(D) 17
(E) 18

48. A box contains 5 red, 3 white, and 4 blue marbles. How many ways can 4 marbles be chosen if exactly 2 marbles are white?

(A) 108
(B) 216
(C) 324
(D) 432
(E) 540

49. In Figure 13, if $ABCD$ is a square and M is the midpoint of $\overline{AD}$. If $AB = 10$, what is the area of $\triangle BCE$?

(A) 27.8
(B) 30.3
(C) 31.3
(D) 33.3
(E) 66.7

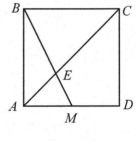

Figure 13

MATHEMATICS LEVEL 1 TEST - *Continued*

USE THIS SPACE FOR SCRATCHWORK.

50. If $f\big(g(x)\big) = x^2$ and $f(x) = 2x - 1$, which of the following is $g(x)$?

(A) $g(x) = \dfrac{x^2}{2}$

(B) $g(x) = \dfrac{x^2 + 1}{2}$

(C) $g(x) = \dfrac{x + 1}{2}$

(D) $g(x) = \dfrac{x^2 - 1}{2}$

(E) $g(x) = 2x^2 - 1$

STOP
IF YOU FINISH BEFORE TIME IS CALLED, YOU MAY CHECK YOUR WORK ON THIS TEST ONLY.
DO NOT TURN TO ANY OTHER TEST IN THIS BOOK.

NO MATERIAL ON THIS PAGE

NO MATERIAL ON THIS PAGE

#	answer	#	answer	#	answer	#	answer	#	answer
1	C	11	C	21	B	31	C	41	D
2	D	12	C	22	B	32	B	42	E
3	E	13	B	23	E	33	A	43	A
4	C	14	B	24	B	34	D	44	D
5	D	15	C	25	E	35	D	45	D
6	E	16	D	26	E	36	A	46	D
7	D	17	A	27	C	37	D	47	C
8	C	18	B	28	E	38	D	48	A
9	C	19	B	29	D	39	E	49	D
10	A	20	A	30	D	40	A	50	B

TEST 3   ANSWERS

Explanations: Test 3

1. (C)   Cross-multiplication:

$$x^2 - 2 = x \implies x^2 - x - 2 = 0 \implies (x-2)(x+1) = 0$$

$$\therefore x = 2 \text{ or } x = -1$$

2. (D)   LCM of the numbers is 36.

3. (E)

> **Important**
> In similar solids,
> Ratio of the corresponding sides $= a : b$
> Ratio of the areas $= a^2 : b^2$
> Ratio of the volumes $= a^3 : b^3$

Since ratio of the sides is 1:3, the ratio of the volumes is 1:27.

4. (C)   Since $x \Psi 5 = x - 5x + 5 = 0$, then $4x = 5 \implies x = 1.25$.

5. (D) $y = -\sqrt{(-4)^2} = -\sqrt{16} = -4$

6. (E)   Since $\triangle ABE \sim \triangle DCE$ and the ratio of the corresponding sides is 1:3, the ratio of the areas is 1:9.

Therefore, $\dfrac{1}{9} = \dfrac{6}{x} \implies x = 54$.

7. (D) $3^{(a+b)^2} \div 3^{(a-b)^2} = 3^{(a+b)^2 - (a-b)^2} = 3^{4ab} = 3^4$

$$\therefore 3^4 = 81$$

8. (C)   Since the coordinates of the vertex are both positive and the graph is open downward.

9. (C)
$$\left(\frac{1}{2}-\frac{1}{3}\right)+\left(\frac{1}{3}-\frac{1}{4}\right)+\left(\frac{1}{4}-\frac{1}{5}\right)+\cdots+\left(\frac{1}{19}-\frac{1}{20}\right)=\frac{1}{2}-\frac{1}{20}=\frac{9}{20}$$
The sum of all middle terms is 0.

10. (A)

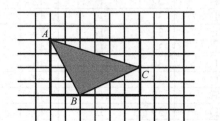

The area of the rectangle − the sum of the three triangles =
$$\left(4\times6\right)-\frac{1}{2}\left(4\cdot2+2\cdot6+2\cdot4\right)=10$$

11. (C)
$$4^{a+b}=\left(2^2\right)^{a+b}=2^{2a+2b}=2^5 \quad\Rightarrow\quad 2a+2b=5\cdots(1)$$
$$3^{a-b}=81=3^4 \quad\Rightarrow\quad a-b=4\cdots(2)$$
Add (1) and $2\times(2)$, then $4a=13 \quad\Rightarrow\quad a=3.25$.

12. (C) Since $a<b<c$, $|a-b|=b-a$ and $|b-c|=c-a$.

Therefore, $\||a-b|+|b-c\||=|b-a+c-b|=|c-a|=c-a$

13. (B)
$$(x+y)^2=10 \quad\Rightarrow\quad x^2+2xy+y^2=10 \quad (1)$$
$$(x-y)^2=4 \quad\Rightarrow\quad x^2-2xy+y^2=4 \quad (2)$$
$$(1)-(2)$$
$$4xy=6 \quad\Rightarrow\quad xy=\frac{6}{4}=1.5$$

14. (B) $2x^2-2y^2=2(x+y)(x-y)=2(10)(5)=100$.

15. (C) Since $L=2W+3$ and $L+W=12$, then $(2W+3)+W=12 \quad\Rightarrow\quad W=3$.
$L=2W+3=9$.
∴ The area of the rectangle $=3\times9=27$

16. (D) $g(3)=|1-3|=2 \quad\Rightarrow\quad f(g)=f(2)=1-2(2)=-3$

17. (A)

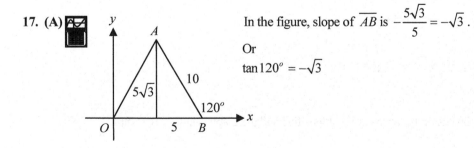

In the figure, slope of $\overline{AB}$ is $-\dfrac{5\sqrt{3}}{5}=-\sqrt{3}$.

Or
$$\tan 120^o=-\sqrt{3}$$

18. (B)   Since $x = -1$ is a solution, then $3(-1)^2 + 6k(-1) = k$.

$7k = 3 \implies k = \dfrac{3}{7}$

19. (B)   If s and $2s$ are the roots of the equation, then $s + 2s = 6$ and $2s(s) = k$.

$3s = 6 \implies s = 2$ and $k = 2s(s) = 2 \times 2(2) = 8$.

20. (A) 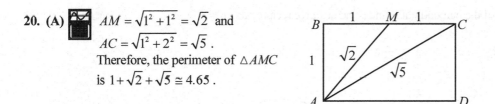 $AM = \sqrt{1^2 + 1^2} = \sqrt{2}$ and
$AC = \sqrt{1^2 + 2^2} = \sqrt{5}$.
Therefore, the perimeter of $\triangle AMC$
is $1 + \sqrt{2} + \sqrt{5} \cong 4.65$.

21. (B) $P = P_o(1 - 0.3)^t$, where P_o is the original number of candy bars.

Therefore, $49 = P_o(1 - 0.3)^2 \implies 49 = P_o(0.49) \implies P_o = 100$.

22. (B)   The equation is always equal for all real values of x, especially for $x = -2$.
Therefore,

$(-2)^3 + 3(-2)^2 - (-2) + 6 = k \implies 12 = k$.

23. (E)   1 is not prime or composite.

24. (B) $f(-1) = -(-1)^2 - (-1)^2 = -1 - 1 = -2$

25. (E)   Since $f(-1) = -a - b - c - 4 = 3 \implies -7 = a + b + c$,

$f(1) = a + b + c - 4 = -7 - 4 = -11$.

26. (E)   By triangular inequality: $5 - 3 < x < 5 + 3 \implies 2 < x < 8$

Pythagorean theorem: If the triangle is a right triangle, $c = \sqrt{3^2 + 5^2} = \sqrt{34}$.
If the triangle is an obtuse triangle, c must be greater than $\sqrt{34}$.
Therefore, $\sqrt{34} < x < 8 \implies 5.83 < x < 8$.

27. (C)   Method 1:

If $\dfrac{x}{3} = 2 \implies x = 6$, $f\left(\dfrac{6}{3}\right) = 6^2 - 2(6) + 3 = 27$.

28. (E) $3^{x^2 - 4x + 3} = (3^4)^2 \implies x^2 - 4x + 3 = 8 \implies x^2 - 4x - 5 = 0$

Since $(x - 5)(x + 1) = 0$, $x = 5$ or $x = -1$.

29. (D)   Because $i + i^2 + i^3 + i^4 = i - 1 - i + 1 = 0$, the sum of every four terms is 0.

$\underbrace{(i + i^2 + i^3 + i^4)}_{0} + \cdots + (i^{45} + i^{46} + i^{47} + i^{48}) + i^{49} + i^{50} = i - 1$

Or

Sum of geometric sequence:

$$S_{50} = \frac{a_1\left(1-r^{50}\right)}{1-r} = \frac{i\left(1-i^{50}\right)}{1-i} = \frac{i\left(1+1\right)}{1-i} = \frac{2i\left(1+i\right)}{\left(1-i\right)\left(1+i\right)} = i\left(1+i\right) = i+i^2 = i-1$$

30. (D) $2x-3y=5 \Rightarrow y = \frac{2}{3}x - \frac{5}{3}$ slope: $\frac{2}{3}$

The slope of the perpendicular line is the negative reciprocal: $m = -\frac{3}{2}$

(D) $3x+2y=-3 \Rightarrow y = -\frac{3}{2}x - \frac{3}{2}$

31. (C)   The ratio $= \dfrac{\frac{4}{3}\pi r^3}{\pi r^2\left(2r\right)} = \dfrac{\frac{4}{3}}{2} = \dfrac{2}{3}$

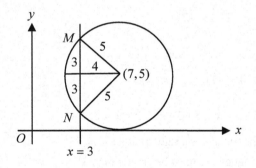

Volume of a cylinder $= \pi r^2 h$

Volume of a sphere $= \dfrac{4\pi r^3}{3}$

$h = 2r$

32. (B)   The graphs of the two equations are as follows. Using Pythagorean Theorem, we can find the coordinates of the points of intersection, $M(3,8)$ and $N(3,2)$.

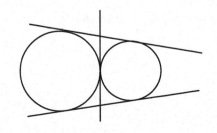

33. (A)   The midpoints of the diagonals are the same.

the x-coordinate of the midpoint : $\dfrac{-1+5}{2} = \dfrac{a+b}{2}$

$\therefore a+b=4$

34. (D)   Midpoint : $\dfrac{-4+10}{2} = 3$ Distance from midpoint to the numbers: $10-3=7$

$\therefore \left|x-3\right| < 7$

35. (D)

36. (A)

x: number of boys $\Rightarrow$ Total ages $= 16x$

y: number of girls $\Rightarrow$ Total ages $= 13y$

The average of the group: $= \dfrac{16x+13y}{x+y} = 14 \Rightarrow 16x+13y = 14x+14y \Rightarrow y = 2x$

Since $2x = y$, $\dfrac{x}{y} = \dfrac{x}{2x} = \dfrac{1}{2}$.

37. (D)

Axis of symmetry: $x = \dfrac{-b}{2a} = \dfrac{-(-2)}{2(-1)} = -1$

Since the graph opens downward, find y as follows.

$f(-1) = 1$, $f(-2) = 0$, and $f(2) = -8$

Therefore, $-8 \le y \le 1$.

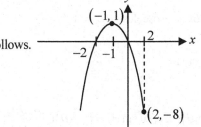

38. (D) $g(f) = -\left(\sqrt{x-2}\right)^2 + 1 \Rightarrow y = -x+3$, where $x \ge 2$.

39. (E) $\sin\theta = \dfrac{10\sin 30}{5} = 2\sin 30 = 2\left(\dfrac{1}{2}\right) = 1$

40. (A) The value of $x^2 - 2x - 1$ is minimum must be minimum.

Axis of symmetry: $x = \dfrac{-(-2)}{2(1)} = 1$ and the minimum: $f(1) = 1-2-1 = -2$

Therefore, the minimum is $3^{-2} = \dfrac{1}{9}$.

Or

Perfect squared form: $y = (x-1)^2 - 2 \Rightarrow$ minimum of $y = -2$

41. (D) Hexagonal numbers: Increased by multiples of 6.

a_n 1   7   19   37 $\cdots$

b_n 6   12   18

Since $a_n = a_1 + (b_1 + b_2 + \cdots b_{n-1})$,

$a_{15} = 1 + (6+12+18+\cdots) = 1 + 6(1+2+3+\cdots 14) = 1 + 6\left(\dfrac{14(1+14)}{2}\right) = 631$.

42. (E)   The length of the equilateral triangle in terms of b is

$$2\left(\frac{b\sqrt{3}}{2}\right) = b\sqrt{3}.$$

Therefore, $a = b\sqrt{3}$.

$$\therefore \frac{b}{a} = \frac{b}{b\sqrt{3}} = \frac{1}{\sqrt{3}} = \frac{\sqrt{3}}{3}.$$

43. (A) $\triangle ABC$ is isosceles. $AB = AC = \dfrac{a}{\sqrt{2}}$

The area $= \dfrac{1}{2}\left(\dfrac{a}{\sqrt{2}}\right)^2 = \dfrac{a^2}{4}.$

44. (D) $(\cos\theta)(\cot\theta)(\sin\theta) = (\cos\theta)\left(\dfrac{\cos\theta}{\sin\theta}\right)(\sin\theta) = \cos^2\theta$

Since $\cos^2\theta = 1 - \sin^2\theta$, the value is $1 - k^2$.

45. (D)   Surface area of a cylinder : $S = 2\pi r^2 + 2\pi rh$

Since $r = 5$ and $h = 10$, the area is $2\pi(5)^2 + 2\pi(5)(10) = 150\pi$.

46. (D)   Since $x^4 + 3x^3 - 4x^2 - 12x = x(x+3)(x+2)(x-2)$, $(x+4)$ is not a factor.

47. (C)   The sum of the arithmetic sequence $= \dfrac{n(1+n)}{2}$

(B) $n = 15 \implies \dfrac{15(1+15)}{2} = 120 < 125$

(C) $n = 16 \implies \dfrac{16(1+16)}{2} = 136 > 125$

Or

Use a graphic utility: $n(n+1) > 250 \implies y = n^2 + n - 250 > 0$

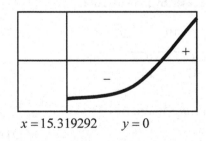

$x = 15.319292 \qquad y = 0$

48. (A)   Choose two white marbles out of 3 white marbles another two from 9 marbles (red or blue). Therefore, $_3C_2 \times {}_9C_2 = 108$.

49. (D)   For the given $AB = 10$ and $AM = 5$, we know that $\triangle BCE$ and $\triangle AEM$ are similar.

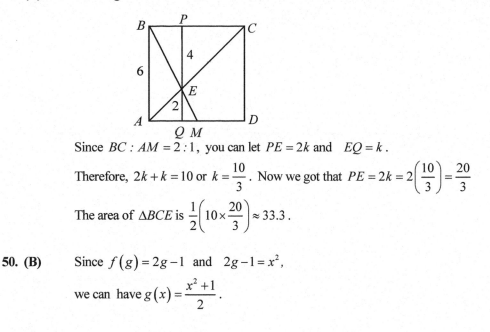

Since $BC : AM = 2 : 1$, you can let $PE = 2k$ and $EQ = k$.

Therefore, $2k + k = 10$ or $k = \dfrac{10}{3}$. Now we got that $PE = 2k = 2\left(\dfrac{10}{3}\right) = \dfrac{20}{3}$

The area of $\triangle BCE$ is $\dfrac{1}{2}\left(10 \times \dfrac{20}{3}\right) \approx 33.3$.

50. (B)   Since $f(g) = 2g - 1$ and $2g - 1 = x^2$,

we can have $g(x) = \dfrac{x^2 + 1}{2}$.

END

NO MATERIAL ON THIS PAGE

Dr. John Chung's SAT II

Math Level 1

Test 4

MATHEMATICS LEVEL 1 TEST

TEST 4

REFERENCE INFORMATION

THE FOLLOWING INFORMATION IS FOR YOUR REFERENCE IN ANSWERING SOME OF THE QUESTIONS IN THIS TEST

Volume of a right circular cone with radius r and height h: $V = \frac{1}{3}\pi r^2 h$

Lateral Area of a right circular cone with circumference of the base c and slant height ℓ: $S = \frac{1}{2}c\ell$

Volume of a sphere with radius r: $V = \frac{4}{3}\pi r^3$

Surface Area of a sphere with radius r: $S = 4\pi r^2$

Volume of a pyramid with base area B and height h: $V = \frac{1}{3}Bh$

Dr. John Chung's SAT II Math Level 1

Answer Sheet

1	Ⓐ Ⓑ Ⓒ Ⓓ Ⓔ	26	Ⓐ Ⓑ Ⓒ Ⓓ Ⓔ
2	Ⓐ Ⓑ Ⓒ Ⓓ Ⓔ	27	Ⓐ Ⓑ Ⓒ Ⓓ Ⓔ
3	Ⓐ Ⓑ Ⓒ Ⓓ Ⓔ	28	Ⓐ Ⓑ Ⓒ Ⓓ Ⓔ
4	Ⓐ Ⓑ Ⓒ Ⓓ Ⓔ	29	Ⓐ Ⓑ Ⓒ Ⓓ Ⓔ
5	Ⓐ Ⓑ Ⓒ Ⓓ Ⓔ	30	Ⓐ Ⓑ Ⓒ Ⓓ Ⓔ
6	Ⓐ Ⓑ Ⓒ Ⓓ Ⓔ	31	Ⓐ Ⓑ Ⓒ Ⓓ Ⓔ
7	Ⓐ Ⓑ Ⓒ Ⓓ Ⓔ	32	Ⓐ Ⓑ Ⓒ Ⓓ Ⓔ
8	Ⓐ Ⓑ Ⓒ Ⓓ Ⓔ	33	Ⓐ Ⓑ Ⓒ Ⓓ Ⓔ
9	Ⓐ Ⓑ Ⓒ Ⓓ Ⓔ	34	Ⓐ Ⓑ Ⓒ Ⓓ Ⓔ
10	Ⓐ Ⓑ Ⓒ Ⓓ Ⓔ	35	Ⓐ Ⓑ Ⓒ Ⓓ Ⓔ
11	Ⓐ Ⓑ Ⓒ Ⓓ Ⓔ	36	Ⓐ Ⓑ Ⓒ Ⓓ Ⓔ
12	Ⓐ Ⓑ Ⓒ Ⓓ Ⓔ	37	Ⓐ Ⓑ Ⓒ Ⓓ Ⓔ
13	Ⓐ Ⓑ Ⓒ Ⓓ Ⓔ	38	Ⓐ Ⓑ Ⓒ Ⓓ Ⓔ
14	Ⓐ Ⓑ Ⓒ Ⓓ Ⓔ	39	Ⓐ Ⓑ Ⓒ Ⓓ Ⓔ
15	Ⓐ Ⓑ Ⓒ Ⓓ Ⓔ	40	Ⓐ Ⓑ Ⓒ Ⓓ Ⓔ
16	Ⓐ Ⓑ Ⓒ Ⓓ Ⓔ	41	Ⓐ Ⓑ Ⓒ Ⓓ Ⓔ
17	Ⓐ Ⓑ Ⓒ Ⓓ Ⓔ	42	Ⓐ Ⓑ Ⓒ Ⓓ Ⓔ
18	Ⓐ Ⓑ Ⓒ Ⓓ Ⓔ	43	Ⓐ Ⓑ Ⓒ Ⓓ Ⓔ
19	Ⓐ Ⓑ Ⓒ Ⓓ Ⓔ	44	Ⓐ Ⓑ Ⓒ Ⓓ Ⓔ
20	Ⓐ Ⓑ Ⓒ Ⓓ Ⓔ	45	Ⓐ Ⓑ Ⓒ Ⓓ Ⓔ
21	Ⓐ Ⓑ Ⓒ Ⓓ Ⓔ	46	Ⓐ Ⓑ Ⓒ Ⓓ Ⓔ
22	Ⓐ Ⓑ Ⓒ Ⓓ Ⓔ	47	Ⓐ Ⓑ Ⓒ Ⓓ Ⓔ
23	Ⓐ Ⓑ Ⓒ Ⓓ Ⓔ	48	Ⓐ Ⓑ Ⓒ Ⓓ Ⓔ
24	Ⓐ Ⓑ Ⓒ Ⓓ Ⓔ	49	Ⓐ Ⓑ Ⓒ Ⓓ Ⓔ
25	Ⓐ Ⓑ Ⓒ Ⓓ Ⓔ	50	Ⓐ Ⓑ Ⓒ Ⓓ Ⓔ

The number of right answers : _____

The number of wrong answers : _____

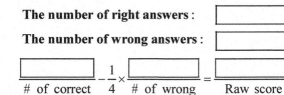

$$\underset{\text{\# of correct}}{\boxed{}} - \frac{1}{4} \times \underset{\text{\# of wrong}}{\boxed{}} = \underset{\text{Raw score}}{\boxed{}}$$

Score Conversion Table

Raw Score	Scaled Score	Raw Score	Scaled Score	Raw Score	Scaled Score
50	800	28	630	6	480
49	800	27	620	5	470
48	800	26	610	4	470
47	800	25	600	3	460
46	790	24	590	2	460
45	780	23	580	1	450
44	770	22	570	0	450
43	760	21	550		
42	750	20	540		
41	740	19	530		
40	740	18	520		
39	730	17	510		
38	720	16	500		
37	710	15	490		
36	710	14	480		
35	700	13	470		
34	690	12	460		
33	680	11	450		
32	670	10	440		
31	660	9	430		
30	650	8	420		
29	640	7	410		

MATHEMATICS LEVEL 1 TEST

For each of the following problems, decide which is the BEST of the choices given. If the exact numerical value is not one of the choices, select the choice that best approximates this value. Then fill in the corresponding circle on the answer sheet.

Notes: (1) A scientific or graphing calculator will be necessary for answering some (but not all) of the questions in this test. For each question you will have to decide whether or not you should use a calculator.

(2) For some questions in this test you may have to decide whether your calculator should be in the radian mode or the degree mode.

(3) Figures that accompany problems in this test are intended to provide information useful in solving the problems. They are drawn as accurately as possible EXCEPT when it is stated in a specific problem that its figure is not drawn to scale. All figures lie in a plane unless otherwise indicated.

(4) Unless otherwise specified, the domain of any function f is assumed to be the set of all real numbers x for which $f(x)$ is a real number. The range of f is assumed to be the set of all real numbers $f(x)$, where x is in the domain of f.

(5) Reference information that may be useful in answering the questions in this test can be found on the page preceding Question 1.

USE THIS SPACE FOR SCRATCHWORK

1. If $a + 3 = -4$, then $\dfrac{a^2 - 9}{3 - a} =$

    (A) -8 (B) -4 (C) 1 (D) 4 (E) 8

2. If x is greater than y, x is how much, in percent, greater than y?

    (A) $\dfrac{x}{y}$

    (B) $\dfrac{x - y}{y}$

    (C) $\dfrac{100(x - y)}{y}$

    (D) $\dfrac{100(x - y)}{x}$

    (E) $100(x - y)$

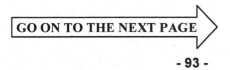
GO ON TO THE NEXT PAGE

MATHEMATICS LEVEL 1 TEST - *Continued*

USE THIS SPACE FOR SCRATCHWORK.

3.   If $\dfrac{25^4}{5^x} = 125$, then $x =$

(A) 5   (B) 4   (C) 3   (D) –4   (E) –5

4.   For what value of a is the expression $\dfrac{1}{1+\dfrac{1}{a}}$ undefined?

(A) 0 only
(B) 1 only
(C) –1 only
(D) 0 and –1
(E) 1 and –1

5.   If $\dfrac{5x-2y}{x+y} = \dfrac{1}{2}$, then what is the ratio of x to y ?

(A) $\dfrac{5}{9}$ (B) $\dfrac{4}{5}$ (C) $\dfrac{2}{3}$ (D) $\dfrac{5}{4}$ (E) $\dfrac{9}{5}$

6.   If a is 25% of b , then what percent of $5a$ is $2b$?

(A) 40%   (B) 80%   (C) 120%   (D) 160%   (E) 200%

7.   In Figure 1, line $\ell \parallel m \parallel n$, $AB = 5$, $BC = 8$, $DE = a$, and $EF = a+6$, then $a =$

(A) 10
(B) 5
(C) 4
(D) 3
(E) 2

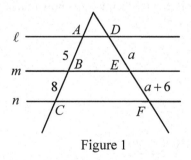

Figure 1

<u>Note</u>: Figure not drawn to scale.

GO ON TO THE NEXT PAGE

MATHEMATICS LEVEL 1 TEST - *Continued*

USE THIS SPACE FOR SCRATCHWORK.

8. In Figure 2, if O is the center of the circle and $\angle OCA = 40^o$, what is the measure of $\angle ACB$?

    (A) 20°
    (B) 22.5^o
    (C) 25°
    (D) 30°
    (E) 37.5^o

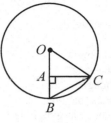

Figure 2

9. If the area of parallelogram $ABCD$ shown in Figure 3 is 120 and $AD = 20$, what is the perimeter of the parallelogram?

    (A) 60
    (B) 64
    (C) 80
    (D) 96
    (E) 100

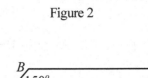

Figure 3

Note: Figure not drawn to scale.

10. If $\log_4 x = \dfrac{1}{2}$, then $\log_x 8 =$

    (A) 1   (B) 2   (C) 3   (D) 4   (E) 5

11. In triangle ABC shown in Figure 4, $AD = 5$ and $CD = 10$. If the area of $\triangle ABC$ is 40, what is the area of $\triangle ABD$?

    (A) 8
    (B) 10
    (C) 13.3
    (D) 15
    (E) 20

Figure 4

Note: Figure not drawn to scale.

12. A baseball is thrown into the air so that its height $h(t)$ at time t is defined by $h(t) = -12t^2 + 48t$. Which of the following is the maximum height that the ball can reach?

    (A) 12   (B) 24   (C) 48   (D) 60   (E) 96

GO ON TO THE NEXT PAGE

USE THIS SPACE FOR SCRATCHWORK.

13. If the measures of the angles of $\triangle ABC$ are a, b, and $a + b$, then the triangle is

(A) an acute triangle
(B) an obtuse triangle
(C) a right triangle
(D) an isosceles triangle
(E) an isosceles obtuse triangle

14. If $f(x+1) = 2x - 5$, then $f(x-1) =$

(A) $2x + 3$
(B) $2x + 1$
(C) $2x - 3$
(D) $2x - 5$
(E) $2x - 9$

15. In Figure 5, if $\dfrac{BD}{DE} = \dfrac{3}{2}$ and the area of $\triangle ABC$ is 30, which of the following is the area of $\triangle ADC$?

(A) 10
(B) 12
(C) 14
(D) 16
(E) 18

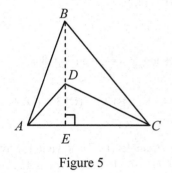

Figure 5

16. If $\left| x^2 - 3 \right| = 1$, which of the following is the solution set for the equation?

(A) $\{2\}$

(B) $\{2, -2\}$

(C) $\left\{2, -2, \sqrt{2}\right\}$

(D) $\left\{2, -2, \sqrt{2}, -\sqrt{2}\right\}$

(E) $\{2, -2, 4, -4\}$

GO ON TO THE NEXT PAGE

MATHEMATICS LEVEL 1 TEST - *Continued*

USE THIS SPACE FOR SCRATCHWORK.

17. The weight of a set of identical cubes varies directly with the number of cubes. If 20 of the identical cubes weigh 42 grams, how many of these cubes weigh 105 grams?

(A) 25   (B) 30   (C) 40   (D) 45   (E) 50

18. In triangle *ABC,* if $AB = 8$, $\angle A = 30^\circ$, and $\angle C = 45^\circ$, then $BC =$

(A) 4.25   (B) 5.12   (C) 5.66   (D) 6.31   (E) 8.58

19. In the triangle shown in Figure 6, $AD = 4$, $\angle A = 45^\circ$, and $\angle C = 30^\circ$. Which of the following is the area of $\triangle ABC$?

(A) 8
(B) $4 + 4\sqrt{3}$
(C) $8 + 4\sqrt{3}$
(D) $8 + 8\sqrt{3}$
(E) $14 + 8\sqrt{3}$

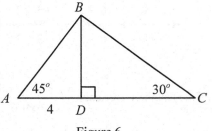

Figure 6

20. $\boxed{a, b, c} = ac + bc$ for all positive numbers a, b, and c.
If $\boxed{p, q, r} = 5r$, what is the average number of p and q ?

(A) 1
(B) 1.5
(C) 2
(D) 2.5
(E) 3

21. If $\dfrac{n!}{(n-2)!} = 72$, then $n =$

(A) 25
(B) 20
(C) 10
(D) 9
(E) 8

GO ON TO THE NEXT PAGE

MATHEMATICS LEVEL 1 TEST - *Continued*

USE THIS SPACE FOR SCRATCHWORK.

22. Which of the following is the graph of the solution set of $x^2 + x - 2 < 12x - 32$?

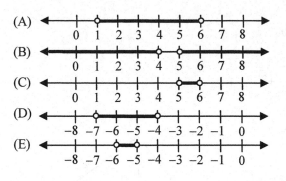

23. If the length of a rectangle is $\dfrac{x^2 + 4x + 3}{6x + 6}$ and the width of

the rectangle is $\dfrac{6x}{x^2 + 3x}$, what is the area of the rectangle?

(A) 1   (B) 2   (C) x (D) $3x$ (E) $6x$

24. Which of the following is the solution set of $\dfrac{2}{x} < 5$?

(A) $\{x \mid x > 0\}$

(B) $\{x \mid x < 0\}$

(C) $\{x \mid x > 0.4 \text{ or } x < -2\}$

(D) $\{x \mid x > 0.4 \text{ or } x < 0\}$

(E) $\{x \mid 0 < x < 4\}$

25. For what value(s) of x is the rational expression
$\dfrac{x\left(x^2 - 9\right)}{x^2 - 3x}$ undefined?

(A) $x = 0$
(B) $x = 3$
(C) $x = 0, x = 3$
(D) $x = -3$
(E) $x = 0, x = 3, x = -3$

MATHEMATICS LEVEL 1 TEST - *Continued*

USE THIS SPACE FOR SCRATCHWORK.

26. If quadrilateral $ABCD$ in Figure 7 is a parallelogram, which of the following statements must be true?

(A) $AB = BC$

(B) $AC = BD$

(C) $BM = CM$

(D) $\overline{AC}$ bisects $\angle BAD$.

(E) $\overline{BD}$ bisects $\overline{AC}$

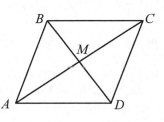

Figure 7

27. In a rectangular prism in Figure 8, what is the number of skewed lines to line BE ?

(A) 1
(B) 2
(C) 4
(D) 6
(E) 8

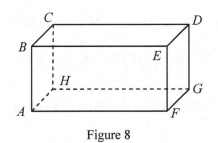

Figure 8

28. If $f(x) = \sqrt{x-1}$ and $g(x) = x$, which of the following is the domain of $g(f(x))$?

(A) $x > 1$
(B) $0 < x < 1$
(C) $x \geq 0$
(D) $x \geq 1$
(E) all real numbers

29. Using the function whose graph are shown in Figure 9, what is the value of the composition $f(f(-1.5))$?

(A) -2
(B) 0
(C) 2
(D) 4
(E) 5

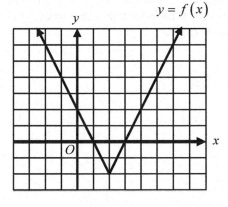

Figure 9

GO ON TO THE NEXT PAGE

USE THIS SPACE FOR SCRATCHWORK.

30. If $f(x) = \sqrt{\frac{2}{3}x - 1}$, then $f^{-1}(3) =$

(A) 1   (B) 10   (C) 15   (D) 24   (E) 32

31. If x varies directly with $y + 3$ and $x = 10$ when $y = 2$, what is x when $y = 10$?

(A) 26   (B) 30   (C) 52   (D) 80   (E) 100

32. If $(a + bi) - (2 - 4i) = 3 - 8i$, then $|a + bi| =$

(A) 10   (B) 13   (C) 15   (D) 20   (E) 27

33. How many ways can 3 students be seated in a row of 6 chairs?

(A) 6^3 (B) 3^6 (C) $_6P_3$ (D) $_3P_6$ (E) $_6C_3$

34. If $i^2 = -1$, then $\sum_{k=1}^{20}(i^k - 1) =$

(A) $-i$ (B) $-20i$ (C) -1 (D) -20 (E) $i - 20$

35. In Figure 10, quadrilateral $ABCD$ is a rectangle and $AB = 4$. What is the ratio of the area of $\triangle ABE$ to the area of $\triangle CED$?

(A) 1:3
(B) $\sqrt{3}:1$
(C) 3:1
(D) $2\sqrt{3}:1$
(E) $\sqrt{3}:2$

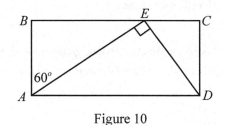

Figure 10

GO ON TO THE NEXT PAGE

MATHEMATICS LEVEL 1 TEST - *Continued*

USE THIS SPACE FOR SCRATCHWORK.

36. If $\dfrac{a-b}{c-b} = 3$, then $\dfrac{a-c}{b-c} =$

(A) –2　(B) –1　(C) 1　(D) 2　(E) 3

37. In circle O shown in Figure 11, if $AB > CD$, which of the following must be true?

I. $MO < NO$
II. $AM = BM$
III. $\overarc{AB} < \overarc{CD}$

(A) I only
(B) II only
(C) I and II only
(D) II and III only
(E) I, II, and III

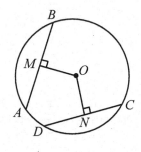

Figure 11

38. In a geometric sequence $\{a_n\}$, if $a_2 = 162$ and $a_5 = 6$, what is the value of a_6?

(A) –0.008
(B) –48
(C) 2
(D) 48
(E) 486

39. In Figure 12, if $AD = 12$, $AB = 5$, and $DE = 10$, what is the area of $\triangle ABC$?

(A) 5
(B) 10
(C) 15
(D) 20
(E) 25

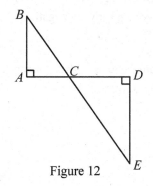

Figure 12

40. If $w = 3 - 4i$ and $z = 2 - 10i$, then $|w + 2z| =$

(A) 31　(B) 27　(C) 25　(D) 20　(E) 16

GO ON TO THE NEXT PAGE

MATHEMATICS LEVEL 1 TEST - *Continued*

USE THIS SPACE FOR SCRATCHWORK.

41. If $2\log_3 x - \log_3(x+4) = 2$, which of the following is the solution set of the equation?

(A) $\{-3\}$
(B) $\{3, 12\}$
(C) $\{-3, 12\}$
(D) $\{12\}$
(E) $\{-3, -12\}$

42. If $\sin\theta = -\dfrac{1}{2}$ and $\cos\theta = -\dfrac{\sqrt{3}}{2}$, what is the value of θ?

(A) 30°
(B) 150°
(C) 210°
(D) 240°
(E) 330°

43. If $\tan\theta > 0$, which of the following must be true?

(A) $\sin\theta$ must be positive.
(B) θ must be Quadrant III.
(C) $\cos\theta$ must be positive.
(D) $\sin\theta$ must be negative.
(E) $\cos\theta$ may be positive or negative.

44. If α and β are the roots of the equation $x^2 - 3x + 1 = 0$, what is the value of $|\alpha - \beta|$?

(A) 2
(B) $\sqrt{5}$
(C) $\sqrt{7}$
(D) 5
(E) 7

MATHEMATICS LEVEL 1 TEST - *Continued*

USE THIS SPACE FOR SCRATCHWORK.

45. In Figure 13, the equation of the graph of the circle is
$x^2 + y^2 = 4$ and the equation of line m is $y = \sqrt{3}\, x$.
Which of the following are the coordinates of point P ?

(A) $(1, 2)$

(B) $(1, \sqrt{3})$

(C) $(\sqrt{3}, 1)$

(D) $(2, 2\sqrt{3})$

(E) $(3, 3\sqrt{3})$

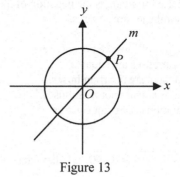

Figure 13

46. What is the range of the function g whose equation is
$g(x) = |x - 2| - 5$ and $0 \le x \le 10$?

(A) $-3 \le g(x) \le 0$

(B) $-3 \le g(x) \le 2$

(C) $-3 \le g(x) \le 3$

(D) $-5 \le g(x) \le 3$

(E) $-5 \le g(x) \le 2$

47. If $\log_a 5 \cdot \log_5 7 \cdot \log_7 b = \dfrac{1}{6}$, then $\log_b a =$

(A) 4   (B) 5   (C) 6   (D) 7   (E) 14

48. If line m with a slope of 1 and line ℓ with a slope of 2
intersect at point P, as shown in Figure 14, which of the
following is the area of $\triangle PQR$?

(A) 6
(B) 9
(C) 12
(D) 15
(E) 18

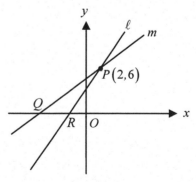

Figure 14

Note: Figure not drawn to scale.

GO ON TO THE NEXT PAGE

MATHEMATICS LEVEL 1 TEST - *Continued*

USE THIS SPACE FOR SCRATCHWORK.

49. Which of the following is the negation of the statement "Some rhombuses are squares."?

(A) Some rhombuses are not squares.
(B) All rhombuses are squares.
(C) All squares are not rhombuses.
(D) Some square are not rhombuses.
(E) All rhombuses are not squares.

50. In Figure 15, $\overline{AC}$ and $\overline{BD}$ are diameters of a circle with radius 5. If $\overline{AC}$ and $\overline{BD}$ are perpendicular, what is the area of the shaded region?

(A) 53.54
(B) 64.25
(C) 66.93
(D) 107.08
(E) 160.02

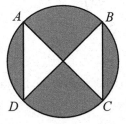

Figure 15

STOP
IF YOU FINISH BEFORE TIME IS CALLED, YOU MAY CHECK YOUR WORK ON THIS TEST ONLY.
DO NOT TURN TO ANY OTHER TEST IN THIS BOOK.

NO MATERIAL ON THIS PAGE

NO MATERIAL ON THIS PAGE

#	answer	#	answer	#	answer	#	answer	#	answer
1	D	11	C	21	D	31	A	41	D
2	C	12	C	22	C	32	B	42	C
3	A	13	C	23	A	33	C	43	E
4	D	14	E	24	D	34	D	44	B
5	A	15	B	25	C	35	C	45	B
6	D	16	D	26	E	36	A	46	D
7	A	17	E	27	C	37	C	47	C
8	C	18	C	28	D	38	C	48	B
9	B	19	D	29	D	39	B	49	E
10	C	20	D	30	C	40	C	50	A

Explanations: Test 4

1. (D) $a = -7 \implies \dfrac{a^2 - 9}{3 - a} = \dfrac{(-7)^2 - 9}{3 - (-7)} = \dfrac{40}{10} = 4$

$$\text{Or}$$

$$\dfrac{a^2 - 9}{3 - a} = \dfrac{(a+3)(a-3)}{(3-a)} = -(a+3) = -(-7+3) = 4$$

2. (C) $\left(\dfrac{x - y}{y} \times 100 \right)\%$

3. (A) $\dfrac{25^4}{5^x} = \dfrac{\left(5^2\right)^4}{5^x} = \dfrac{5^8}{5^x} = 5^{8-x}$

Since $5^{8-x} = 5^3$, $8 - x = 3 \implies x = 5$.

4. (D) If the denominator of a fraction, the value is undefined.

$\dfrac{1}{a} \implies$ undefined at $a = 0$

$1 + \dfrac{1}{a} \implies$ undefined at $a = -1$

5. (A) $\dfrac{5x + 2y}{x + y} = \dfrac{1}{2} \implies 10x - 4y = x + y \implies 9x = 5y$

Because $x = \dfrac{5y}{9}$, $\dfrac{x}{y} = \dfrac{5y/9}{y} = \dfrac{5}{9}$

6. (D) $a = \dfrac{b}{4} \Rightarrow b = 4a$ and $\dfrac{2b}{5a} = \dfrac{x}{100}(= x\%)$

$\dfrac{8a}{5a} = \dfrac{x}{100} \Rightarrow x = 160$

7. (A) $\dfrac{5}{a} = \dfrac{8}{a+6} \Rightarrow 8a = 5a + 30 \Rightarrow a = 10$

8. (C) Since $\triangle COB$ is isosceles, $\angle COB = 50^o$ and $\angle OBC = \angle OCB = 65$.

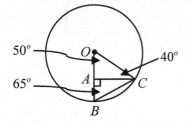

9. (B) Because the area of the parallelogram is 120,
$120 = 20h \Rightarrow h = 6$ and $AB = 12$.

Therefore, the perimeter is $2(12 + 20) = 64$.

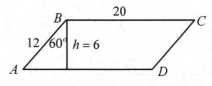

10. (C) $\log_4 x = \dfrac{1}{2} \Rightarrow x = 4^{\frac{1}{2}} = 2$

Therefore, $\log_x 8 = \log_2 8 = 3\log_2 2 = 3$.

11. (C) The ratio of the lengths of the bases is equal to the ratio of the areas. If the area of $\triangle ABD$ is k, the area of $\triangle BDC$ is $2k$.

$k + 2k = 3k = 40 \Rightarrow k = \dfrac{40}{3} \cong 13.3$

12. (C) Axis of symmetry: $x = \dfrac{-48}{2(-12)} = 2$

The maximum height: $h(2) = -12(2)^2 + 48(2) = 48$

13. (C) The sum of the interior angles of a triangle is 180 in degree,
then $a + b + (a + b) = 180 \Rightarrow 2(a + b) = 180 \Rightarrow a + b = 90$.
The triangle is a right triangle.

14. (E) When you replace x with $x - 2$, $f(x+1) \rightarrow f(x-2+1) = f(x-1)$ and
$f(x-1) = 2(x-2) - 5 \Rightarrow f(x-1) = 2x - 9$.

15. (B) 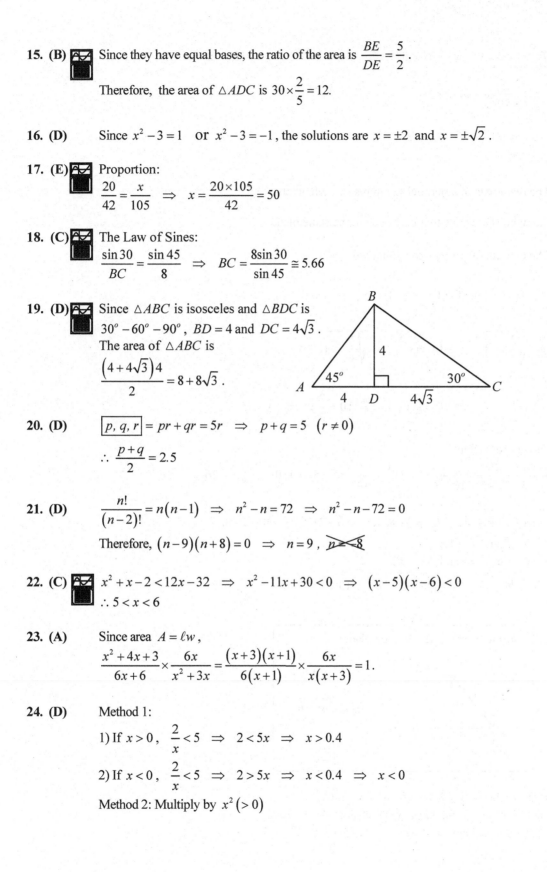 Since they have equal bases, the ratio of the area is $\dfrac{BE}{DE} = \dfrac{5}{2}$.

Therefore, the area of $\triangle ADC$ is $30 \times \dfrac{2}{5} = 12$.

16. (D) Since $x^2 - 3 = 1$ or $x^2 - 3 = -1$, the solutions are $x = \pm 2$ and $x = \pm\sqrt{2}$.

17. (E) Proportion:

$$\frac{20}{42} = \frac{x}{105} \implies x = \frac{20 \times 105}{42} = 50$$

18. (C) The Law of Sines:

$$\frac{\sin 30}{BC} = \frac{\sin 45}{8} \implies BC = \frac{8\sin 30}{\sin 45} \cong 5.66$$

19. (D) Since $\triangle ABC$ is isosceles and $\triangle BDC$ is $30^o - 60^o - 90^o$, $BD = 4$ and $DC = 4\sqrt{3}$.
The area of $\triangle ABC$ is

$$\frac{\left(4 + 4\sqrt{3}\right)4}{2} = 8 + 8\sqrt{3}.$$

20. (D) $\boxed{p, q, r} = pr + qr = 5r \implies p + q = 5 \quad (r \neq 0)$

$$\therefore \frac{p+q}{2} = 2.5$$

21. (D) $\dfrac{n!}{(n-2)!} = n(n-1) \implies n^2 - n = 72 \implies n^2 - n - 72 = 0$

Therefore, $(n-9)(n+8) = 0 \implies n = 9$, ~~$n = -8$~~

22. (C) $x^2 + x - 2 < 12x - 32 \implies x^2 - 11x + 30 < 0 \implies (x-5)(x-6) < 0$
$\therefore 5 < x < 6$

23. (A) Since area $A = \ell w$,

$$\frac{x^2 + 4x + 3}{6x + 6} \times \frac{6x}{x^2 + 3x} = \frac{(x+3)(x+1)}{6(x+1)} \times \frac{6x}{x(x+3)} = 1.$$

24. (D) Method 1:

1) If $x > 0$, $\dfrac{2}{x} < 5 \implies 2 < 5x \implies x > 0.4$

2) If $x < 0$, $\dfrac{2}{x} < 5 \implies 2 > 5x \implies x < 0.4 \implies x < 0$

Method 2: Multiply by $x^2 \, (> 0)$

$$\frac{2}{x} \times x^2 < 5 \times x^2 \implies 2x < 5x^2 \implies 5x^2 - 2x > 0 \implies x(5x-2) > 0$$

$$\therefore x > \frac{2}{5} = 0.4 \text{ or } x < 0$$

25. (C)   Denominator : $x^2 - 3x = x(x-3) = 0$

$$\therefore x = 0 \text{ or } x = 3$$

26. (E)   The diagonals of a parallelogram bisect each other.

27. (C)   Skew lines are lines that do not lie in the same plane.

28. (D)   The domain of $f(g)$ = the domain of g.

29. (D) $f(-0.5) = 5$ and $f(f(-0.5)) = f(5) = 4$

30. (C) $y = \sqrt{\frac{2}{3}x - 1} \implies$ Inverse : $x = \sqrt{\frac{2}{3}y - 1}$

If $x = 3$,

$$3 = \sqrt{\frac{2}{3}y - 1} \implies 9 = \frac{2}{3}y - 1 \implies 10 = \frac{2}{3}y \implies y = 15$$

31. (A)   Direct proportion:

$$\frac{x}{y+3} = \frac{10}{2+3} = \frac{x}{10+3} \implies \frac{10}{5} = \frac{x}{13} \implies 5x = 130 \implies x = 26$$

32. (B)   Since $(a + bi) - (2 - 4i) = 3 - 8i \implies (a-2) + (b+4)i = 3 - 8i$,

$a - 2 = 3$ and $b + 4 = -8$.

Therefore, $a = 5$ and $b = -12$.

$$\therefore |a + bi| = |5 - 12i| = \sqrt{5^2 + (-12)^2} = 13$$

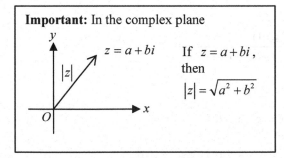

Important: In the complex plane

$z = a + bi$

If $z = a + bi$, then $|z| = \sqrt{a^2 + b^2}$

33. (C)   Step 1) Choose 3 chars out of 6. $\implies {_6}C_3$

Step 2) Assign 3 students to those chairs. $3 \times 2 \times 1 = 3!$

Therefore, the number of ways $= {_6}C_3 \times 3! = {_6}P_3$

34. (D) $\displaystyle\sum_{k=1}^{20}\left(i^k-1\right)=\left(i-1\right)+\left(i^2-1\right)+\left(i^3-1\right)+\cdots+\left(i^{20}-1\right)$

$$=\underbrace{\left(i+i^2+i^3+\cdots i^{20}\right)}_{0}-20=-20$$

35. (C) If $AB=4$, then $BE=4\sqrt{3}$ and $EC=\dfrac{4}{\sqrt{3}}$.

The heights of those two triangles are equal.

The ratio of the areas is $\dfrac{4\sqrt{3}}{\dfrac{4}{\sqrt{3}}}=\dfrac{12}{4}=\dfrac{3}{1}$.

36. (A) Since $\dfrac{a-b}{c-b}=\dfrac{3}{1}$, $3c=a+2b$.

$$\frac{a-c}{b-c}=\frac{3a-3c}{3b-3c}=\frac{3a-\left(a+2b\right)}{3b-\left(a+2b\right)}=\frac{2a-2b}{b-a}=\frac{2\left(a-b\right)}{\left(b-a\right)}=-2$$

37. (C) If two chords are unequal in length, then the shorter chord is farther from the center. A diameter perpendicular to a chord bisects the chord and its arc.

38. (C) $a_2=a_1 r=162$ and $a_5=a_1 r^4=6$

$$\frac{a_5}{a_2}=\frac{a_1 r^4}{a_1 r}=\frac{6}{162}\ \Rightarrow\ r^3=\frac{6}{162}=\frac{1}{27}\ \Rightarrow\ r=\frac{1}{3}$$

Therefore,

$$a_6=a_5\times r=6\times\frac{1}{3}=2.$$

39. (B) $\triangle ABC\sim\triangle DEC:\ \dfrac{AC}{CD}=\dfrac{5}{10}=\dfrac{1}{2}$

If $AD=12$, then $AC=12\times\dfrac{1}{3}=4$.

Therefore, the area of $\triangle ABC=\dfrac{4\times5}{2}=10.$

40. (C) $w+2z=3-4i+2\left(2-10i\right)=7-24i$

$$\left|w+2z\right|=\left|7-24i\right|=\sqrt{7^2+\left(-24\right)^2}=\sqrt{625}=25$$

41. (D) $2\log_3 x-\log_3\left(x+4\right)=2\ \Rightarrow\ \log_3 x^2-\log_3\left(x+4\right)=2$

$$\log_3\frac{x^2}{x+4}=2\ \Rightarrow\ \frac{x^2}{x+4}=9\ \Rightarrow\ x^2-9x-36=0$$

$(x-12)(x+3)=0 \implies x=12$ or $x=-3$

But $x>0$, the answer is $x=12$.

42. (C) Since $\sin\theta<0$ and $\cos\theta<0$, the angle lies in third quadrant.

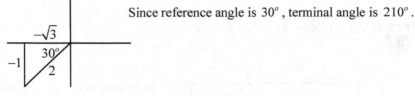

Since reference angle is 30°, terminal angle is 210°.

43. (E) Because $\tan\theta>0$ only in quadrant I and quadrant II, choice (E) is correct.

44. (B) From the quadratic equation, (α and β are the roots of the equation)

$\alpha+\beta=3$ and $\alpha\beta=1$.

Since $(\alpha-\beta)^2=(\alpha+\beta)^2-4\alpha\beta \implies (\alpha-\beta)^2=3^2-4(1)=5$,

$|\alpha-\beta|=\sqrt{5}$.

> **Important:**
> $(a-b)^2=(a+b)^2-4ab$
> $(a+b)^2=(a-b)^2+4ab$

45. (B) Since $y=\sqrt{3}x$ and the **x**-coordinate of point P is positive,

$x^2+y^2=4 \implies x^2+3x^2=4 \implies 4x^2=4 \implies x=1$ and $y=\sqrt{3}$

46. (D) The graph is as follows.
The range: $-5\le y\le 3$

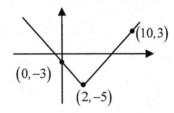

47. (C) $\log_a 5 \cdot \log_5 7 \cdot \log_7 b = \dfrac{1}{6}$

$\implies \dfrac{\log 5}{\log a}\cdot\dfrac{\log 7}{\log 5}\cdot\dfrac{\log b}{\log 7}=\dfrac{\log b}{\log a}=\log_a b$

Therefore, $\log_b a = \dfrac{1}{\log_a b}=6$

48. (B) Line m: $y=x+b_1$ passes through point $(2,6)$. $\therefore y=x+4$

Line ℓ: $y=2x+b_2$ passes through point $(2,6)$. $\therefore y=2x+2$

Points Q and R are the x-intercepts of the lines.

Therefore, $Q(-4, 0)$ and $R(-1, 0)$.
Since the height of $\triangle PQR$ is 6 and $QR = 3$,
the area of the triangle is
$$\frac{3 \times 6}{2} = 9$$

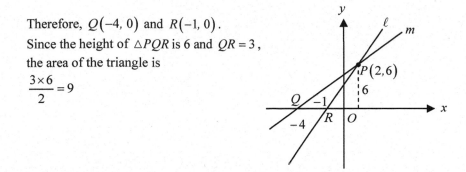

49. (E)   In the negation: some $\rightarrow$ all   or   all $\rightarrow$ some
            and $\rightarrow$ or   or   or $\rightarrow$ and

50. (A) The area of the circle: $\pi \cdot 5^2 = 25\pi$

The area of the two triangles: $\left(\dfrac{5 \times 5}{2}\right) \times 2 = 25$

$\therefore 25\pi - 25 \cong 53.54$

END

NO MATERIAL ON THIS PAGE

Dr. John Chung's SAT II

Math Level 1

Test 5

MATHEMATICS LEVEL 1 TEST

TEST 5

REFERENCE INFORMATION

THE FOLLOWING INFORMATION IS FOR YOUR REFERENCE IN ANSWERING SOME OF THE QUESTIONS IN THIS TEST

Volume of a right circular cone with radius r and height h: $V = \dfrac{1}{3}\pi r^2 h$

Lateral Area of a right circular cone with circumference of the base c and slant height ℓ: $S = \dfrac{1}{2}c\ell$

Volume of a sphere with radius r: $V = \dfrac{4}{3}\pi r^3$

Surface Area of a sphere with radius r: $S = 4\pi r^2$

Volume of a pyramid with base area B and height h: $V = \dfrac{1}{3}Bh$

Dr. John Chung's SAT II Math Level 1

Answer Sheet

#	Choices	#	Choices
1	Ⓐ Ⓑ Ⓒ Ⓓ Ⓔ	26	Ⓐ Ⓑ Ⓒ Ⓓ Ⓔ
2	Ⓐ Ⓑ Ⓒ Ⓓ Ⓔ	27	Ⓐ Ⓑ Ⓒ Ⓓ Ⓔ
3	Ⓐ Ⓑ Ⓒ Ⓓ Ⓔ	28	Ⓐ Ⓑ Ⓒ Ⓓ Ⓔ
4	Ⓐ Ⓑ Ⓒ Ⓓ Ⓔ	29	Ⓐ Ⓑ Ⓒ Ⓓ Ⓔ
5	Ⓐ Ⓑ Ⓒ Ⓓ Ⓔ	30	Ⓐ Ⓑ Ⓒ Ⓓ Ⓔ
6	Ⓐ Ⓑ Ⓒ Ⓓ Ⓔ	31	Ⓐ Ⓑ Ⓒ Ⓓ Ⓔ
7	Ⓐ Ⓑ Ⓒ Ⓓ Ⓔ	32	Ⓐ Ⓑ Ⓒ Ⓓ Ⓔ
8	Ⓐ Ⓑ Ⓒ Ⓓ Ⓔ	33	Ⓐ Ⓑ Ⓒ Ⓓ Ⓔ
9	Ⓐ Ⓑ Ⓒ Ⓓ Ⓔ	34	Ⓐ Ⓑ Ⓒ Ⓓ Ⓔ
10	Ⓐ Ⓑ Ⓒ Ⓓ Ⓔ	35	Ⓐ Ⓑ Ⓒ Ⓓ Ⓔ
11	Ⓐ Ⓑ Ⓒ Ⓓ Ⓔ	36	Ⓐ Ⓑ Ⓒ Ⓓ Ⓔ
12	Ⓐ Ⓑ Ⓒ Ⓓ Ⓔ	37	Ⓐ Ⓑ Ⓒ Ⓓ Ⓔ
13	Ⓐ Ⓑ Ⓒ Ⓓ Ⓔ	38	Ⓐ Ⓑ Ⓒ Ⓓ Ⓔ
14	Ⓐ Ⓑ Ⓒ Ⓓ Ⓔ	39	Ⓐ Ⓑ Ⓒ Ⓓ Ⓔ
15	Ⓐ Ⓑ Ⓒ Ⓓ Ⓔ	40	Ⓐ Ⓑ Ⓒ Ⓓ Ⓔ
16	Ⓐ Ⓑ Ⓒ Ⓓ Ⓔ	41	Ⓐ Ⓑ Ⓒ Ⓓ Ⓔ
17	Ⓐ Ⓑ Ⓒ Ⓓ Ⓔ	42	Ⓐ Ⓑ Ⓒ Ⓓ Ⓔ
18	Ⓐ Ⓑ Ⓒ Ⓓ Ⓔ	43	Ⓐ Ⓑ Ⓒ Ⓓ Ⓔ
19	Ⓐ Ⓑ Ⓒ Ⓓ Ⓔ	44	Ⓐ Ⓑ Ⓒ Ⓓ Ⓔ
20	Ⓐ Ⓑ Ⓒ Ⓓ Ⓔ	45	Ⓐ Ⓑ Ⓒ Ⓓ Ⓔ
21	Ⓐ Ⓑ Ⓒ Ⓓ Ⓔ	46	Ⓐ Ⓑ Ⓒ Ⓓ Ⓔ
22	Ⓐ Ⓑ Ⓒ Ⓓ Ⓔ	47	Ⓐ Ⓑ Ⓒ Ⓓ Ⓔ
23	Ⓐ Ⓑ Ⓒ Ⓓ Ⓔ	48	Ⓐ Ⓑ Ⓒ Ⓓ Ⓔ
24	Ⓐ Ⓑ Ⓒ Ⓓ Ⓔ	49	Ⓐ Ⓑ Ⓒ Ⓓ Ⓔ
25	Ⓐ Ⓑ Ⓒ Ⓓ Ⓔ	50	Ⓐ Ⓑ Ⓒ Ⓓ Ⓔ

The number of right answers : ☐

The number of wrong answers : ☐

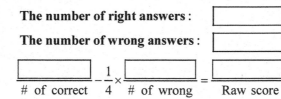

$$\boxed{} - \frac{1}{4} \times \boxed{} = \boxed{}$$

# of correct   # of wrong   Raw score

Score Conversion Table

Raw Score	Scaled Score	Raw Score	Scaled Score	Raw Score	Scaled Score
50	800	28	630	6	480
49	800	27	620	5	470
48	800	26	610	4	470
47	800	25	600	3	460
46	790	24	590	2	460
45	780	23	580	1	450
44	770	22	570	0	450
43	760	21	550		
42	750	20	540		
41	740	19	530		
40	740	18	520		
39	730	17	510		
38	720	16	500		
37	710	15	490		
36	710	14	480		
35	700	13	470		
34	690	12	460		
33	680	11	450		
32	670	10	440		
31	660	9	430		
30	650	8	420		
29	640	7	410		

MATHEMATICS LEVEL 1 TEST

For each of the following problems, decide which is the BEST of the choices given. If the exact numerical value is not one of the choices, select the choice that best approximates this value. Then fill in the corresponding circle on the answer sheet.

Notes: (1) A scientific or graphing calculator will be necessary for answering some (but not all) of the questions in this test. For each question you will have to decide whether or not you should use a calculator.

(2) For some questions in this test you may have to decide whether your calculator should be in the radian mode or the degree mode.

(3) Figures that accompany problems in this test are intended to provide information useful in solving the problems. They are drawn as accurately as possible EXCEPT when it is stated in a specific problem that its figure is not drawn to scale. All figures lie in a plane unless otherwise indicated.

(4) Unless otherwise specified, the domain of any function f is assumed to be the set of all real numbers x for which $f(x)$ is a real number. The range of f is assumed to be the set of all real numbers $f(x)$, where x is in the domain of f.

(5) Reference information that may be useful in answering the questions in this test can be found on the page preceding Question 1.

USE THIS SPACE FOR SCRATCHWORK.

1.   If $y = 5$, then $\dfrac{y^3 - y}{y^2 - 1} =$

(A) 5   (B) 10   (C) 15   (D) 20   (E) 25

2.   In Figure 1, $\overline{AC}$ is horizontal and $AB = 3\sqrt{2}$. If $BC = AC$ and the coordinates of point A are $(1, 2)$, what are the coordinates of point B?

(A) $(3, 3)$
(B) $(4, 4)$
(C) $(4, 5)$
(D) $(5, 5)$
(E) $(5, 6)$

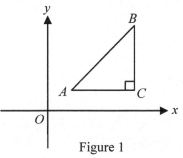

Figure 1

Note: Figure not drawn to scale.

MATHEMATICS LEVEL 1 TEST - *Continued*

USE THIS SPACE FOR SCRATCHWORK.

3. If $2^x = a$, then $2^{x+3} =$

    (A) 8   (B) a^3 (C) $8a$ (D) $a+8$ (E) $2a+3$

4. Which of the following statement is logically equivalent to the statement "If it is warm, then we go swimming"?

    (A) If we go swimming, then it is cold.
    (B) If it is not warm, then we don't go swimming.
    (C) If we go swimming, then it is warm.
    (D) If we don't go swimming, then it is not warm.
    (E) If we don't go swimming, then we go skiing.

5. If $\dfrac{6}{\sqrt{x}} = 3$, then $x^2 =$

    (A) 36   (B) 16   (C) 9   (D) 4   (E) 1

6. If $\dfrac{1}{a} = 2$ and $\dfrac{2}{a} + \dfrac{1}{b} = 5$, then $a+b =$

    (A) 1.5   (B) 2   (C) 2.5   (D) 3   (E) 3.5

7. In Figure 2, $\overline{AE}$ intersects $\overline{BD}$ at point C, $AB = BC$, and $CD = DE$. If $\angle B = 64°$, what is the measure of $\angle CDE$?

    (A) $60°$
    (B) $61°$
    (C) $62°$
    (D) $63°$
    (E) $64°$

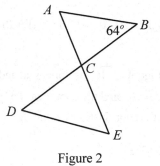

Figure 2

8. Which of the following is the distance between the points $(-2, 5)$ and $(3, -5)$?

    (A) 8.5   (B) 11.2   (C) 13   (D) 14.7   (E) 15.8

GO ON TO THE NEXT PAGE

MATHEMATICS LEVEL 1 TEST - *Continued*

USE THIS SPACE FOR SCRATCHWORK.

9. In Figure 3, what are the coordinates of point M ?

(A) $(2, 0)$

(B) $(3, 0)$

(C) $(4, 0)$

(D) $(6, 0)$

(E) $(8, 0)$

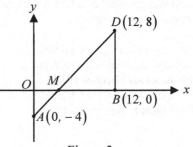

Figure 3

10. In $\triangle ABC$ shown in Figure 4, if $BD = 8$ and $CD = 4$, what is the area of $\triangle ABC$?

(A) $10\sqrt{3}$
(B) $20\sqrt{2}$
(C) $30\sqrt{3}$
(D) $40\sqrt{2}$
(E) $40\sqrt{3}$

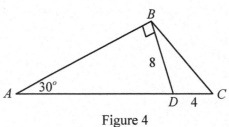

Figure 4

11. If $\cos A^{\circ} = \sin\left(2A^{\circ} + 30^{\circ}\right)$, which of the following could be the measure of A ?

(A) 10   (B) 20   (C) 30   (D) 40   (E) 90

12. What is the sum of the measures of the exterior angles of an octagon?

(A) 45° (B) 60° (C) 180° (D) 360° (E) 1080°

13. In the cube given in Figure 5, if P and Q are midpoints of the edges of the cube, and the cube has the edge of length 10, what is the length of $\overline{PQ}$?

(A) 10
(B) $5\sqrt{6}$
(C) $10\sqrt{2}$
(D) $10\sqrt{5}$
(E) $10\sqrt{6}$

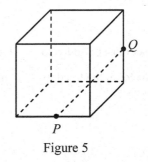

Figure 5

GO ON TO THE NEXT PAGE

MATHEMATICS LEVEL 1 TEST - *Continued*

USE THIS SPACE FOR SCRATCHWORK.

14.   If a parallelogram must be a rectangle, which of the
following could not be true?

(A) The diagonals are perpendicular.
(B) The opposite sides are congruent.
(C) The diagonals bisect each other.
(D) The opposite sides are parallel.
(E) The diagonals are congruent.

15.   In Figure 6, if $\ell \parallel m$ and $c = \dfrac{1}{3}b$, what is the measure of
a?

(A) 30°
(B) 35°
(C) 45°
(D) 60°
(E) 75°

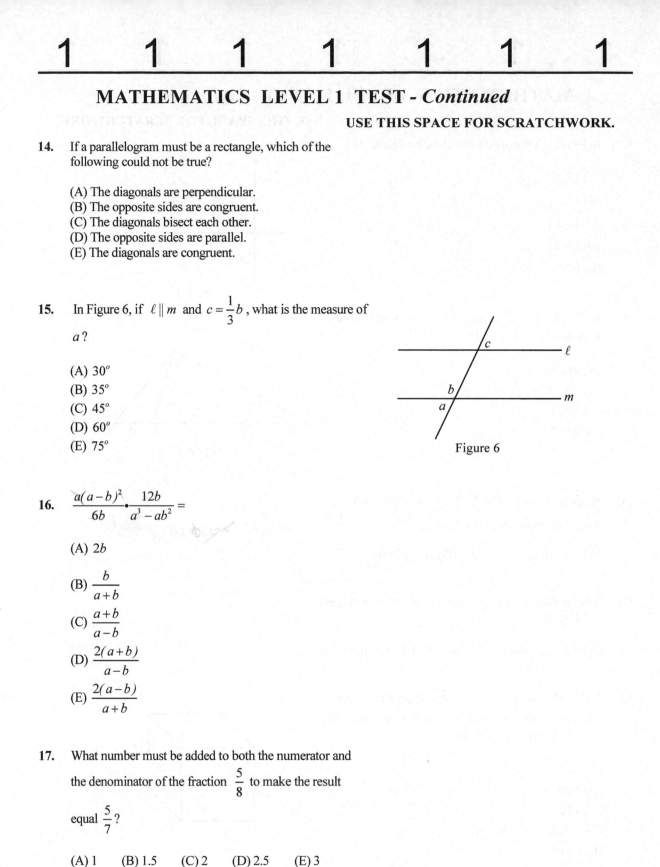

Figure 6

16. $\dfrac{a(a-b)^2}{6b} \cdot \dfrac{12b}{a^3 - ab^2} =$

(A) $2b$

(B) $\dfrac{b}{a+b}$

(C) $\dfrac{a+b}{a-b}$

(D) $\dfrac{2(a+b)}{a-b}$

(E) $\dfrac{2(a-b)}{a+b}$

17.   What number must be added to both the numerator and
the denominator of the fraction $\dfrac{5}{8}$ to make the result

equal $\dfrac{5}{7}$?

(A) 1   (B) 1.5   (C) 2   (D) 2.5   (E) 3

GO ON TO THE NEXT PAGE

MATHEMATICS LEVEL 1 TEST - *Continued*

USE THIS SPACE FOR SCRATCHWORK.

18. Which of the following could be the graph of the solution to the system of equations $y = x + 2$ and

$y = x^2 - 4x - 4$?

(A)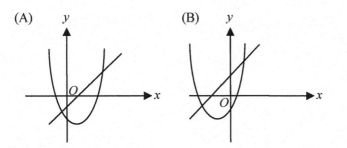

(B)

(C)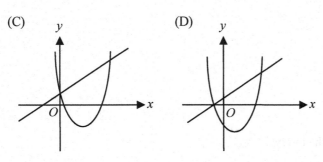

(D)

(E)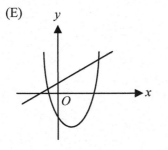

19. If Debby can clean the house in 6 hours and Steve can clean the house in 8 hours, how long would it take them to

clean $\frac{1}{3}$ of the house, in hours, if they worked together?

(A) 1.14
(B) 2.16
(C) 3.43
(D) 4.56
(E) 7.00

GO ON TO THE NEXT PAGE

MATHEMATICS LEVEL 1 TEST - *Continued*

USE THIS SPACE FOR SCRATCHWORK.

20. Which of the following is the solution to $\dfrac{9}{x-1} > 3$?

 (A) $x > 1$
 (B) $x \geq 1$
 (C) $x < 4$
 (D) $x > 4$
 (E) $1 < x < 4$

21. For which of the following value(s) of x is the rational expression $\dfrac{x^2 - 2x}{x^3 - 4x}$ undefined?

 (A) 0 only
 (B) -2 only
 (C) 0 and 4 only
 (D) 0 and -2 only
 (E) 0, -2, and 2

22. Which of the following is equivalent to the interval $-5 < x < 14$?

 (A) $|x - 4| \leq 10$
 (B) $|x + 4.5| < 4.5$
 (C) $|x - 4.5| < 9.5$
 (D) $|x - 4.5| > 9.5$
 (E) $|x + 4.5| > 9.5$

23. If $g^{-1}(x)$ is the inverse function of $g(x)$ and $g(x) = \sqrt[3]{2x - 3}$, then $g^{-1}(2) =$

 (A) 11
 (B) 5.5
 (C) 4.2
 (D) 2.5
 (E) 1

GO ON TO THE NEXT PAGE

MATHEMATICS LEVEL 1 TEST - *Continued*

USE THIS SPACE FOR SCRATCHWORK.

24. Which of the following does not have a domain for all real numbers?

(A) $f(x) = x^2 + 5$

(B) $f(x) = \dfrac{x}{x^2 + 1}$

(C) $f(x) = \dfrac{x^2 - 1}{x - 1}$

(D) $f(x) = \sin x$

(E) $f(x) = 3^x - 5$

25. If the discriminant of a quadratic equation equals 16, which of the following must be true for the roots?

(A) two real, unequal, irrational roots.
(B) two real, equal, rational roots.
(C) two imaginary roots.
(D) two real, equal, irrational roots.
(E) two real, unequal, rational roots.

26. In right triangle ABO shown in Figure 7, what is the value of k?

(A) 5
(B) $2\sqrt{10}$
(C) 8
(D) $3\sqrt{5}$
(E) $3\sqrt{10}$

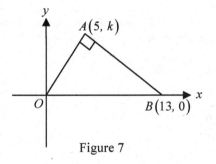

Figure 7

27. If $f(x) = 2x + 1$ and $f(g(x)) = 2x^2 - 1$, which of the following is the expression for $g(x)$?

(A) $x - 1$
(B) $x + 1$
(C) $x^2 - 1$
(D) $x^2 + 1$
(E) $4x^2$

GO ON TO THE NEXT PAGE

MATHEMATICS LEVEL 1 TEST - *Continued*

USE THIS SPACE FOR SCRATCHWORK.

28. If $9^{x-1} \cdot 3^{x^2} = 27^2$, what is the positive value of x?

    (A) 1   (B) 2   (C) 3   (D) 5   (E) 8

29. In Figure 8, $\overline{AE}$ and $\overline{BD}$ are the medians of $\triangle ABC$ and intersect at P. If $AE = 10$ and $BD = 8$, what is the value of $\dfrac{BP}{PE}$?

    (A) 1.2
    (B) 1.5
    (C) 1.6
    (D) 2.0
    (E) 2.5

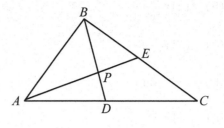

Figure 8

30. If two points P and Q are 10 inches apart, how many points are equidistant from P and Q, and 5 inches from the line passing through P and Q?

    (A) 0   (B) 1   (C) 2   (D) 3   (E) 4

31. In Figure 9, if the area of $\triangle POB$ is three times the area of $\triangle AOP$, then what is the value of a?

    (A) 3
    (B) 4
    (C) 5
    (D) 6
    (E) 8

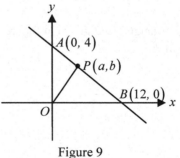

Figure 9

<u>Note:</u> Figure not drawn to scale.

32. If the vertex of $y = x^2 - ax + b$ has coordinates $(2, -5)$, what is the y-intercept of this parabola?

    (A) $(0, -2)$

    (B) $(0, -1)$

    (C) $(0, 0)$

    (D) $(0, 2)$

    (E) $(0, 4)$

GO ON TO THE NEXT PAGE

MATHEMATICS LEVEL 1 TEST - *Continued*

USE THIS SPACE FOR SCRATCHWORK.

33. If the graph of the exponential function $y = a^x$ passes through the points $(2, 16)$ and $(3, k)$, which of the following is the value(s) of k ?

    (A) $\{4, -4\}$

    (B) $\{16, -16\}$

    (C) $\{8, 64\}$

    (D) $\{64, -64\}$

    (E) $\{64\}$

34. A circle can be drawn inside square $ABCD$ shown in Figure 10. If the circle is inscribed in the square, what is the radius of the circle?

    (A) 2
    (B) $2\sqrt{2}$
    (C) $3\sqrt{2}$
    (D) 5
    (E) $5\sqrt{2}$

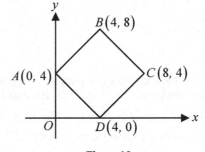

Figure 10

Note: Figure not drawn to scale.

35. Which of the following is the x-coordinate of the point of intersection in the graphs $y = \log(x-3)$ and $y = 1 - \log x$?

    (A) –2
    (B) 2
    (C) 3
    (D) 5
    (E) 10

36. In Figure 11, M and N are the midpoints of $\overline{AB}$ and $\overline{CD}$ respectively to trapezoid $ABCD$. If the area of the trapezoid $ABCD$ is 30 and the length of $\overline{EF}$ is 5, what is the length of $\overline{MN}$?

    (A) 6   (B) 8   (C) 10   (D) 12   (E) 14

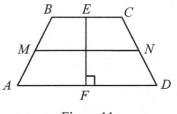

Figure 11

GO ON TO THE NEXT PAGE

MATHEMATICS LEVEL 1 TEST - *Continued*

USE THIS SPACE FOR SCRATCHWORK.

37. If the length of the diagonal of a cube is 12, what is the surface area of that cube?

(A) 24   (B) 72   (C) 144   (D) 288   (E) 576

38. If O is the center of the circle in Figure 12 and the area of the shaded region is 12, what is the length of minor arc AB?

(A) $\sqrt{\pi}$
(B) $2\sqrt{\pi}$
(C) $4\sqrt{\pi}$
(D) 2π
(E) 4π

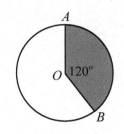

Figure 12

39. In Figure 13, a circle and a parabola have three points of intersection at P, Q, and R. If the equation of the parabola is defined by $y = x^2 - 4$, which of the following are the coordinates of point Q?

(A) $\left(\sqrt{6}, 2\right)$
(B) $\left(\sqrt{5}, 1\right)$
(C) $\left(\sqrt{7}, 3\right)$
(D) $(3, 5)$
(E) $(4, 12)$

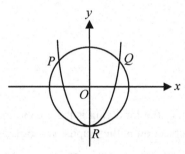

Figure 13
Note: Figure not drawn to scale.

40. If a recursive formula of a sequence is defined as $a_n = a_{n-1} - 3$ and $a_3 = 10$, what is the value of a_{100}?

(A) 313
(B) 270
(C) −135
(D) −281
(E) −313

GO ON TO THE NEXT PAGE

USE THIS SPACE FOR SCRATCHWORK.

41. In Figure 14, the lateral area of a regular circular cone is 100 square meters. If the height of the cone is $\sqrt{3}$ times the radius of the circular base, what is the value of the radius, in meters?

(A) 3.99
(B) 4.56
(C) 4.88
(D) 5.25
(E) 8.42

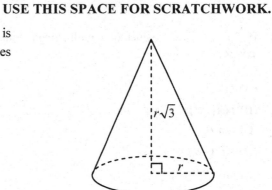

Figure 14

42. If the sum of the roots of $2x^2 - 8x = k$ is added to the product of the roots, the result is 5. What is the value of k?

(A) -2 (B) -1 (C) 0   (D) 1   (E) 2

43. If $z_1 = 5 - 6i$, then $|z_1 - 6i| =$

(A) 6   (B) 12   (C) 13   (D) 18   (E) 25

44. Which of the following shows the solution to the inequality $-x^2 + 14x - 48 < 0$?

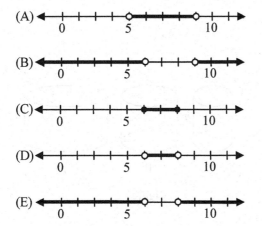

(A)

(B)

(C)

(D)

(E)

MATHEMATICS LEVEL 1 TEST - *Continued*

USE THIS SPACE FOR SCRATCHWORK.

45. If $90^\circ < \theta < 180^\circ$, which of the following is equivalent to $\cos \theta$?

    (A) $\sin \theta$
    (B) $\cos(-\theta)$
    (C) $\tan \theta$
    (D) $\sin(-\theta)$
    (E) $\cos(90 - \theta)$

46. If $\cos x = k$, then $\cos^2 x + \sin^2 x + \tan^2 x =$

    (A) k (B) $\dfrac{1}{k}$ (C) $\sqrt{k}$ (D) $\dfrac{1}{\sqrt{k}}$ (E) $\dfrac{1}{k^2}$

47. If $\cos\left(x^2\right)^\circ = \sin\left(2x - 30\right)^\circ$, which of the following is the solution set of the equation?

    (A) $\{-12, -10\}$
    (B) $\{-12, 12\}$
    (C) $\{10, 12\}$
    (D) $\{10, -12\}$
    (E) $\{10, 0\}$

48. In Figure 15, all of the right circular cylinders have the same height h. Cylinders I and II have the base radius a and $2a$, respectively. If the sum of the volumes of cylinders I and II is equal to the volume of cylinder III, what is the radius of cylinder III in terms of a ?

    (A) $5a$
    (B) $4a$
    (C) $3a$
    (D) $a\sqrt{5}$
    (E) $a\sqrt{3}$

I   II   III

Figure 15

GO ON TO THE NEXT PAGE

MATHEMATICS LEVEL 1 TEST - *Continued*

USE THIS SPACE FOR SCRATCHWORK.

49.   If $f(x) = \sqrt{x}$, which of the following could be the part
of the graph of $y = f(-x+2)$?

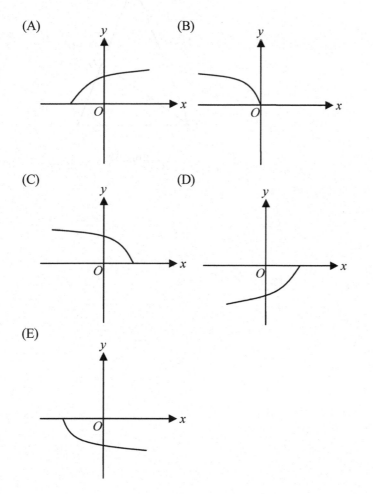

(A)

(B)

(C)

(D)

(E)

GO ON TO THE NEXT PAGE

MATHEMATICS LEVEL 1 TEST - *Continued*

USE THIS SPACE FOR SCRATCHWORK.

50. In Figure 16, $\triangle ABC$ is isosceles with $AB = BC$ and
$BD = AD = AC$. If $\angle BCA = \theta^o$, what is the value of θ?

(A) 36
(B) 72
(C) 80
(D) 82
(E) 84

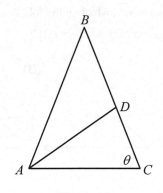

Figure 16

STOP
**IF YOU FINISH BEFORE TIME IS CALLED, YOU MAY CHECK YOUR WORK ON THIS TEST ONLY.
DO NOT TURN TO ANY OTHER TEST IN THIS BOOK.**

NO MATERIAL ON THIS PAGE

NO MATERIAL ON THIS PAGE

TEST 5   ANSWERS

#	answer	#	answer	#	answer	#	answer	#	answer
1	A	11	B	21	E	31	A	41	A
2	C	12	D	22	C	32	B	42	A
3	C	13	B	23	B	33	E	43	C
4	D	14	A	24	C	34	B	44	E
5	B	15	C	25	E	35	D	45	B
6	A	16	E	26	B	36	A	46	E
7	E	17	D	27	C	37	D	47	D
8	B	18	E	28	B	38	C	48	D
9	C	19	A	29	C	39	C	49	C
10	E	20	E	30	C	40	D	50	B

Explanations: Test 5

1. **(A)** 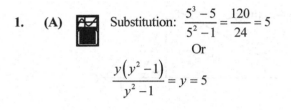 Substitution: $\dfrac{5^3 - 5}{5^2 - 1} = \dfrac{120}{24} = 5$

Or

$$\dfrac{y(y^2 - 1)}{y^2 - 1} = y = 5$$

2. **(C)** From the graph $\Rightarrow B(4,5)$

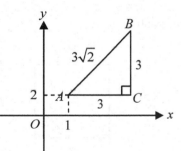

3. **(C)** Since $2^x = a$, $2^{x+3} = 2^3 \cdot 2^x = 8a$.

4. **(D)** Contrapositive: $p \rightarrow q$ is equivalent to $\sim q \rightarrow \sim p$.

5. **(B)** $\sqrt{x} = \dfrac{6}{3} = 2$, $x = 4$, $x^2 = 16$

6. **(A)** $\dfrac{1}{a} = 2 \Rightarrow a = 0.5$ and $\dfrac{2}{0.5} + \dfrac{1}{b} = 5 \Rightarrow \dfrac{1}{b} = 1 \Rightarrow b = 1$

$\therefore a + b = 1.5$

7. **(E)** 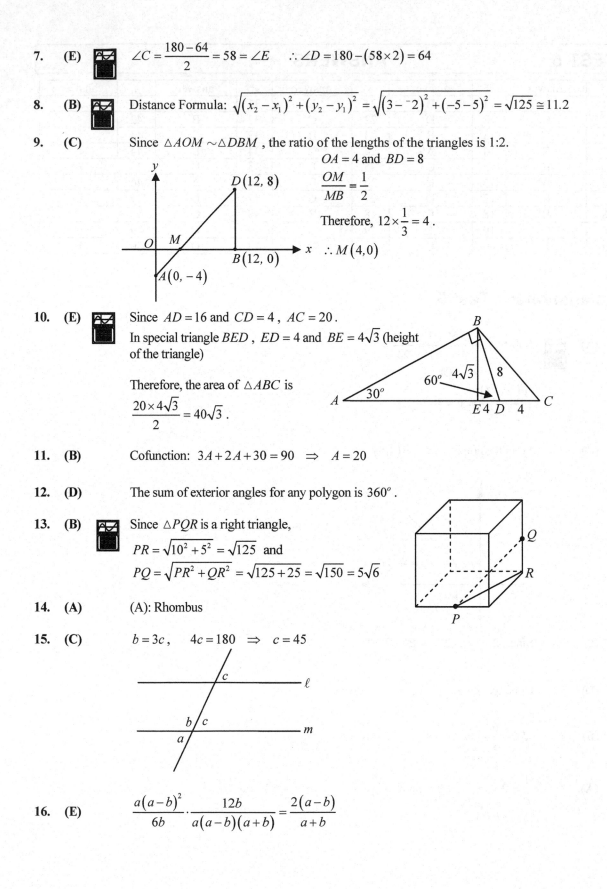 $\angle C = \dfrac{180-64}{2} = 58 = \angle E \quad \therefore \angle D = 180 - (58 \times 2) = 64$

8. **(B)** Distance Formula: $\sqrt{(x_2 - x_1)^2 + (y_2 - y_1)^2} = \sqrt{(3 - {}^-2)^2 + (-5 - 5)^2} = \sqrt{125} \cong 11.2$

9. **(C)** Since $\triangle AOM \sim \triangle DBM$, the ratio of the lengths of the triangles is 1:2.

$OA = 4$ and $BD = 8$

$\dfrac{OM}{MB} = \dfrac{1}{2}$

Therefore, $12 \times \dfrac{1}{3} = 4$.

$\therefore M(4, 0)$

10. **(E)** Since $AD = 16$ and $CD = 4$, $AC = 20$.

In special triangle BED, $ED = 4$ and $BE = 4\sqrt{3}$ (height of the triangle)

Therefore, the area of $\triangle ABC$ is

$\dfrac{20 \times 4\sqrt{3}}{2} = 40\sqrt{3}$.

11. **(B)** Cofunction: $3A + 2A + 30 = 90 \Rightarrow A = 20$

12. **(D)** The sum of exterior angles for any polygon is 360°.

13. **(B)** Since $\triangle PQR$ is a right triangle,

$PR = \sqrt{10^2 + 5^2} = \sqrt{125}$ and

$PQ = \sqrt{PR^2 + QR^2} = \sqrt{125 + 25} = \sqrt{150} = 5\sqrt{6}$

14. **(A)** (A): Rhombus

15. **(C)** $b = 3c$, $\quad 4c = 180 \Rightarrow c = 45$

16. **(E)** $\dfrac{a(a-b)^2}{6b} \cdot \dfrac{12b}{a(a-b)(a+b)} = \dfrac{2(a-b)}{a+b}$

17. (D) $\dfrac{5+x}{8+x}=\dfrac{5}{7} \;\Rightarrow\; x=2.5$

18. (E) $y=x^2-4x-4=(x-2)^2-8 \;\Rightarrow\;$ Axis of symmetry $x=2$ and the turning point is

$(2,-8)$.

You can use a graphic utility.

(D): point of intersection is not on x-axis.

19. (A)

	Hours	Rate	Sum of rate
Debby	6	$1\!/\!6$	$\dfrac{7}{24}$
Steve	8	$1\!/\!8$	

When they work together, it will take $\dfrac{24}{7}$ hours to complete the job.

Therefore, the time to finish $\dfrac{1}{3}$ of the job takes $\dfrac{1}{3}\times\dfrac{24}{7}\cong 1.14$ hours.

20. (E) From $\dfrac{9}{x-1}>3$, $x-1$ must be positive. therefore $x>1$.

$(x-1)\left(\dfrac{9}{x-1}\right)>3(x-1) \;\Rightarrow\; 9>3x-3 \;\Rightarrow\; 12<3x \;\Rightarrow\; 4<x$

Therefore, $1<x<4$

Or

(1) If $x-1>0$, $9>3x-3 \;\Rightarrow\; x<4$. $\;\therefore 1<x<4$

(2) If $x-1<0$, $9<3x-3 \;\Rightarrow\; x>4$. (No common interval) No solution

21. (E) Denominator:

If $x^3-4x=x(x+2)(x-2)=0$, undefined.

$\therefore x=0,\; x=-2,\; x=2$

22. (C) Midpoint $=\dfrac{14+(-5)}{2}=4.5$ and distance from the midpoint $=14-4.5=9.5$.

$\therefore |x-4.5|<9.5$

23. (B) Inverse: $g^{-1}(2)=y$

$x=\sqrt[3]{2y-3} \;\Rightarrow\; x^3=2y-3 \;\Rightarrow\; 2^3=2y-3 \;\Rightarrow\; y=5.5$

24. (C) (C) At $x=1$, f is undefined.

25. (E) $D=b^2-4ac=16>0$, roots: $r=\dfrac{-b\pm4}{2a}$

Two different real and rational roots.

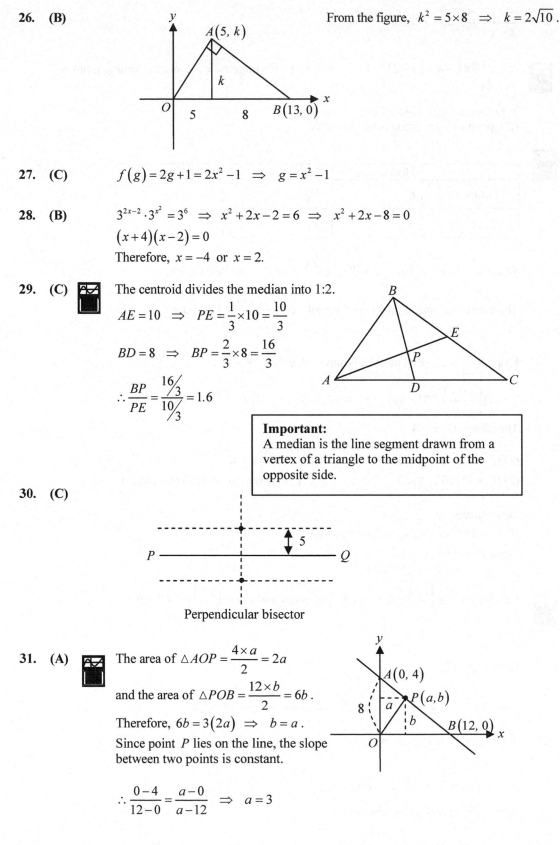

26. **(B)**

From the figure, $k^2 = 5 \times 8 \implies k = 2\sqrt{10}$.

27. **(C)**

$f(g) = 2g + 1 = 2x^2 - 1 \implies g = x^2 - 1$

28. **(B)**

$3^{2x-2} \cdot 3^{x^2} = 3^6 \implies x^2 + 2x - 2 = 6 \implies x^2 + 2x - 8 = 0$

$(x+4)(x-2) = 0$

Therefore, $x = -4$ or $x = 2$.

29. **(C)**

The centroid divides the median into 1:2.

$AE = 10 \implies PE = \dfrac{1}{3} \times 10 = \dfrac{10}{3}$

$BD = 8 \implies BP = \dfrac{2}{3} \times 8 = \dfrac{16}{3}$

$\therefore \dfrac{BP}{PE} = \dfrac{16/3}{10/3} = 1.6$

Important:
A median is the line segment drawn from a vertex of a triangle to the midpoint of the opposite side.

---

30. **(C)**

Perpendicular bisector

31. **(A)**

The area of $\triangle AOP = \dfrac{4 \times a}{2} = 2a$

and the area of $\triangle POB = \dfrac{12 \times b}{2} = 6b$.

Therefore, $6b = 3(2a) \implies b = a$.

Since point P lies on the line, the slope between two points is constant.

$\therefore \dfrac{0-4}{12-0} = \dfrac{a-0}{a-12} \implies a = 3$

32. **(B)** Axis of symmetry: $x = \dfrac{a}{2} = 2 \implies a = 4$

$f(2) = 2^2 - 4(2) + b = -5 \implies b = -1$

$\therefore y = x^2 - 4x - 1$ and y-intercept $f(0) = -1$

33. **(E)** Substitution: $(2, 16) \implies 16 = a^2 \implies a = 4, -4$ (a cannot be negative)

$(3, k) \implies k = 4^3 = 64$

> **Important:**
> $y = a^x$ is an exponential function
> where $a > 0$ and $a \neq 1$. x is any real number.

34. **(B)** $CD = \sqrt{(8-4)^2 + (4-0)^2} = 4\sqrt{2}$

radius $r = \dfrac{CD}{2} = 2\sqrt{2}$

35. **(D)** $\log(x-3) = 1 - \log x \implies \log(x-3) + \log x = 1 \implies \log x(x-3) = 1$

$x^2 - 3x = 10 \implies x^2 - 3x - 10 = 0 \implies (x-5)(x+2) = 0$

Therefore, $x = 5$. $x = -2$ cannot be a solution because $x > 3$.

36. **(A)** $\overline{MN}$ is a median: $MN = \dfrac{BC + AD}{2}$

$\dfrac{(BC + AD)5}{2} = 30$

Therefore,

$\dfrac{BC + AD}{2} = \dfrac{30}{5} = 6$

37. **(D)** If the length of an edge $= x$, then the length of the diagonal $= \sqrt{x^2 + x^2 + x^2} = x\sqrt{3}$

Since $x\sqrt{3} = 12 \implies x = \dfrac{12}{\sqrt{3}}$, and the surface area $= 6x^2 = 6\left(\dfrac{12}{\sqrt{3}}\right)^2 = 288$.

38. **(C)** The shaded region: $\pi r^2 \times \dfrac{120^o}{360^o} = \pi r^2 \times \dfrac{1}{3} = 12 \implies r^2 = \dfrac{36}{\pi} \implies r = \dfrac{6}{\sqrt{\pi}}$

$\overparen{AB} = 2\pi r \times \dfrac{1}{3} = 4\sqrt{\pi}$

39. (C) The equation of the circle: $x^2 + y^2 = 16$ because the radius $OR = 4$.

$y = x^2 - 4 \Rightarrow x^2 = y + 4$

Solve the system of equations.

$x^2 + y^2 = 16 \Rightarrow y + 4 + y^2 = 16 \Rightarrow (y+4)(y-3) = 0$

$y = -4$ and $y = 3$.

When $y = 3$, $x^2 = y + 4 = 7 \Rightarrow x = \pm\sqrt{7}$

Therefore, the intersections are $(\sqrt{7}, 3)$ and $(-\sqrt{7}, 3)$.

40. (D) $a_n - a_{n-1} = -3$: arithmetic sequence with $d = -3$.

$a_3 = a_1 + 2d = 10 \Rightarrow a_1 - 6 = 10 \Rightarrow a_1 = 16$

Therefore, $a_{100} = a_1 + 99d = 16 + 99(-3) = -281$.

41. (A)

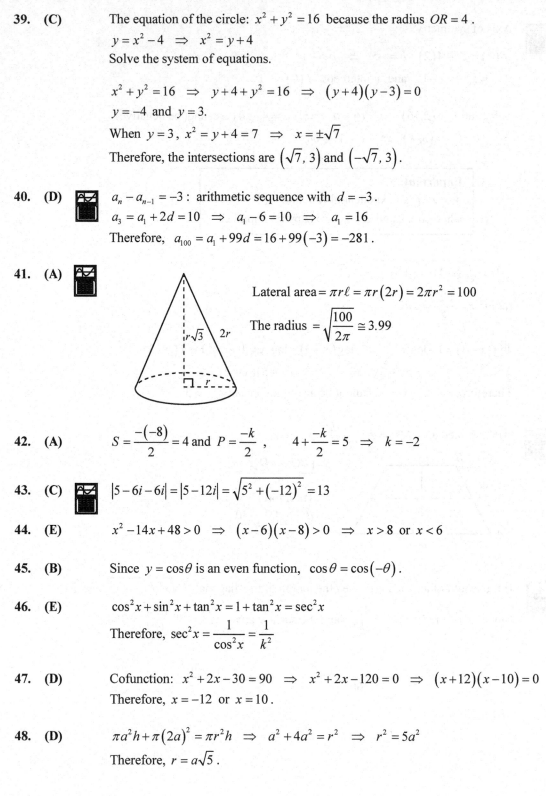

Lateral area $= \pi r \ell = \pi r(2r) = 2\pi r^2 = 100$

The radius $= \sqrt{\dfrac{100}{2\pi}} \cong 3.99$

42. (A) $S = \dfrac{-(-8)}{2} = 4$ and $P = \dfrac{-k}{2}$, $\qquad 4 + \dfrac{-k}{2} = 5 \Rightarrow k = -2$

43. (C) $|5 - 6i - 6i| = |5 - 12i| = \sqrt{5^2 + (-12)^2} = 13$

44. (E) $x^2 - 14x + 48 > 0 \Rightarrow (x-6)(x-8) > 0 \Rightarrow x > 8$ or $x < 6$

45. (B) Since $y = \cos\theta$ is an even function, $\cos\theta = \cos(-\theta)$.

46. (E) $\cos^2 x + \sin^2 x + \tan^2 x = 1 + \tan^2 x = \sec^2 x$

Therefore, $\sec^2 x = \dfrac{1}{\cos^2 x} = \dfrac{1}{k^2}$

47. (D) Cofunction: $x^2 + 2x - 30 = 90 \Rightarrow x^2 + 2x - 120 = 0 \Rightarrow (x+12)(x-10) = 0$

Therefore, $x = -12$ or $x = 10$.

48. (D) $\pi a^2 h + \pi(2a)^2 = \pi r^2 h \Rightarrow a^2 + 4a^2 = r^2 \Rightarrow r^2 = 5a^2$

Therefore, $r = a\sqrt{5}$.

49. **(C)** $f(x) = \sqrt{x} \Rightarrow f(-x+2) = \sqrt{-x+2} = \sqrt{-(x-2)}$

Therefore, (C) is the answer.

50. **(B)** $\triangle ABD$ and $\triangle ACD$ are isosceles.

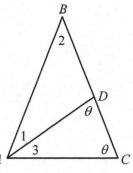

If $\angle ADC = \theta$, $\angle 1 = \angle 2 = \dfrac{\theta}{2}$ and $\angle 3 = 180 - 2\theta$.

Since $\triangle ABC$ is isosceles, $\angle BAC = \theta$.
Therefore,
$\angle 3 = 180 - 2\theta$ and $\angle 1 = \theta - (180 - 2\theta) = 3\theta - 180$

$\angle BAC = \angle 1 + \angle 3 = \theta$,
$\angle 2 = 180 - 2\theta$
Therefore, $\angle 1 \cong \angle 2$
$3\theta - 180 = 180 - 2\theta \Rightarrow 5\theta = 360 \Rightarrow \theta = 72$

END

NO MATERIAL ON THIS PAGE

Dr. John Chung's SAT II

Math Level 1

Test 6

MATHEMATICS LEVEL 1 TEST

TEST 6

REFERENCE INFORMATION

THE FOLLOWING INFORMATION IS FOR YOUR REFERENCE IN ANSWERING SOME OF THE QUESTIONS IN THIS TEST

Volume of a right circular cone with radius r and height h: $V = \dfrac{1}{3}\pi r^2 h$

Lateral Area of a right circular cone with circumference of the base c and slant height ℓ: $S = \dfrac{1}{2}c\ell$

Volume of a sphere with radius r: $V = \dfrac{4}{3}\pi r^3$

Surface Area of a sphere with radius r: $S = 4\pi r^2$

Volume of a pyramid with base area B and height h: $V = \dfrac{1}{3}Bh$

Answer Sheet

1	Ⓐ Ⓑ Ⓒ Ⓓ Ⓔ	26	Ⓐ Ⓑ Ⓒ Ⓓ Ⓔ
2	Ⓐ Ⓑ Ⓒ Ⓓ Ⓔ	27	Ⓐ Ⓑ Ⓒ Ⓓ Ⓔ
3	Ⓐ Ⓑ Ⓒ Ⓓ Ⓔ	28	Ⓐ Ⓑ Ⓒ Ⓓ Ⓔ
4	Ⓐ Ⓑ Ⓒ Ⓓ Ⓔ	29	Ⓐ Ⓑ Ⓒ Ⓓ Ⓔ
5	Ⓐ Ⓑ Ⓒ Ⓓ Ⓔ	30	Ⓐ Ⓑ Ⓒ Ⓓ Ⓔ
6	Ⓐ Ⓑ Ⓒ Ⓓ Ⓔ	31	Ⓐ Ⓑ Ⓒ Ⓓ Ⓔ
7	Ⓐ Ⓑ Ⓒ Ⓓ Ⓔ	32	Ⓐ Ⓑ Ⓒ Ⓓ Ⓔ
8	Ⓐ Ⓑ Ⓒ Ⓓ Ⓔ	33	Ⓐ Ⓑ Ⓒ Ⓓ Ⓔ
9	Ⓐ Ⓑ Ⓒ Ⓓ Ⓔ	34	Ⓐ Ⓑ Ⓒ Ⓓ Ⓔ
10	Ⓐ Ⓑ Ⓒ Ⓓ Ⓔ	35	Ⓐ Ⓑ Ⓒ Ⓓ Ⓔ
11	Ⓐ Ⓑ Ⓒ Ⓓ Ⓔ	36	Ⓐ Ⓑ Ⓒ Ⓓ Ⓔ
12	Ⓐ Ⓑ Ⓒ Ⓓ Ⓔ	37	Ⓐ Ⓑ Ⓒ Ⓓ Ⓔ
13	Ⓐ Ⓑ Ⓒ Ⓓ Ⓔ	38	Ⓐ Ⓑ Ⓒ Ⓓ Ⓔ
14	Ⓐ Ⓑ Ⓒ Ⓓ Ⓔ	39	Ⓐ Ⓑ Ⓒ Ⓓ Ⓔ
15	Ⓐ Ⓑ Ⓒ Ⓓ Ⓔ	40	Ⓐ Ⓑ Ⓒ Ⓓ Ⓔ
16	Ⓐ Ⓑ Ⓒ Ⓓ Ⓔ	41	Ⓐ Ⓑ Ⓒ Ⓓ Ⓔ
17	Ⓐ Ⓑ Ⓒ Ⓓ Ⓔ	42	Ⓐ Ⓑ Ⓒ Ⓓ Ⓔ
18	Ⓐ Ⓑ Ⓒ Ⓓ Ⓔ	43	Ⓐ Ⓑ Ⓒ Ⓓ Ⓔ
19	Ⓐ Ⓑ Ⓒ Ⓓ Ⓔ	44	Ⓐ Ⓑ Ⓒ Ⓓ Ⓔ
20	Ⓐ Ⓑ Ⓒ Ⓓ Ⓔ	45	Ⓐ Ⓑ Ⓒ Ⓓ Ⓔ
21	Ⓐ Ⓑ Ⓒ Ⓓ Ⓔ	46	Ⓐ Ⓑ Ⓒ Ⓓ Ⓔ
22	Ⓐ Ⓑ Ⓒ Ⓓ Ⓔ	47	Ⓐ Ⓑ Ⓒ Ⓓ Ⓔ
23	Ⓐ Ⓑ Ⓒ Ⓓ Ⓔ	48	Ⓐ Ⓑ Ⓒ Ⓓ Ⓔ
24	Ⓐ Ⓑ Ⓒ Ⓓ Ⓔ	49	Ⓐ Ⓑ Ⓒ Ⓓ Ⓔ
25	Ⓐ Ⓑ Ⓒ Ⓓ Ⓔ	50	Ⓐ Ⓑ Ⓒ Ⓓ Ⓔ

The number of right answers : ☐

The number of wrong answers : ☐

$$\underset{\text{\# of correct}}{\boxed{}} - \frac{1}{4} \times \underset{\text{\# of wrong}}{\boxed{}} = \underset{\text{Raw score}}{\boxed{}}$$

Score Conversion Table

Raw Score	Scaled Score	Raw Score	Scaled Score	Raw Score	Scaled Score
50	800	28	630	6	480
49	800	27	620	5	470
48	800	26	610	4	470
47	800	25	600	3	460
46	790	24	590	2	460
45	780	23	580	1	450
44	770	22	570	0	450
43	760	21	550		
42	750	20	540		
41	740	19	530		
40	740	18	520		
39	730	17	510		
38	720	16	500		
37	710	15	490		
36	710	14	480		
35	700	13	470		
34	690	12	460		
33	680	11	450		
32	670	10	440		
31	660	9	430		
30	650	8	420		
29	640	7	410		

MATHEMATICS LEVEL 1 TEST

For each of the following problems, decide which is the BEST of the choices given. If the exact numerical value is not one of the choices, select the choice that best approximates this value. Then fill in the corresponding circle on the answer sheet.

Notes: (1) A scientific or graphing calculator will be necessary for answering some (but not all) of the questions in this test. For each question you will have to decide whether or not you should use a calculator.

(2) For some questions in this test you may have to decide whether your calculator should be in the radian mode or the degree mode.

(3) Figures that accompany problems in this test are intended to provide information useful in solving the problems. They are drawn as accurately as possible EXCEPT when it is stated in a specific problem that its figure is not drawn to scale. All figures lie in a plane unless otherwise indicated.

(4) Unless otherwise specified, the domain of any function f is assumed to be the set of all real numbers x for which $f(x)$ is a real number. The range of f is assumed to be the set of all real numbers $f(x)$, where x is in the domain of f.

(5) Reference information that may be useful in answering the questions in this test can be found on the page preceding Question 1.

USE THIS SPACE FOR SCRATCHWORK.

1. If one of the roots of $x^2 + 3x - k = 0$ is 2, then $k =$

   (A) 3   (B) 5   (C) 10   (D) –10   (E) –5

2. If $2^{2x-3} = 8$, then $x =$

   (A) 3   (B) 6   (C) 9   (D) 12   (E) 15

3. If $x^{-1} = 3^{-1} + 5^{-1}$, what is the value of x ?

   (A) 8

   (B) $\dfrac{15}{8}$

   (C) $\dfrac{3}{2}$

   (D) $\dfrac{8}{15}$

   (E) $\dfrac{2}{5}$

GO ON TO THE NEXT PAGE

USE THIS SPACE FOR SCRATCHWORK.

4. For all $a^2 \neq b^2$, $\dfrac{\dfrac{1}{b-a}}{\dfrac{1}{a^2-b^2}} =$

(A) $\dfrac{1}{a-b}$

(B) $\dfrac{1}{a+b}$

(C) $b-a$

(D) $a-b$

(E) $-a-b$

5. If the line $y = mx + b$ is parallel to the line $y = 2x$ and passes through (2, 10), what is the value of b ?

(A) 3 (B) 6 (C) 8 (D) 10 (E) 12

6. If a parabola with the equation $y = x^2 + ax + b$ has a vertex at P, as shown in Figure 1, what are the coordinates of point P ?

(A) $(-2, -2)$

(B) $(2, -1)$

(C) $(2, -2)$

(D) $(2, -3)$

(E) $(2, -4)$

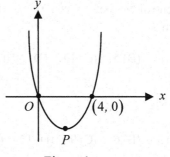

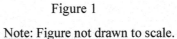

Figure 1

Note: Figure not drawn to scale.

7. If $a + \dfrac{1}{a} = 5$, then $a^2 + a^{-2} =$

(A) 3 (B) 5 (C) 23 (D) 25 (E) 27

GO ON TO THE NEXT PAGE

MATHEMATICS LEVEL 1 TEST - *Continued*

USE THIS SPACE FOR SCRATCHWORK.

8. If $\log_2 x = 5 + \log_2 y$, then $\dfrac{x}{y} =$

    (A) 32 (B) 64 (C) 128 (D) 512 (E) 10^5

9. If $x^2 - 2x + 1 = 3$, then $(x-1)^2 + 5 =$

    (A) 3 (B) 5 (C) 7 (D) 8 (E) 14

10. If $\log(AB) = 4$ and $\log\left(\dfrac{A}{B}\right) = -2$, what is the value of A?

    (A) 0.1 (B) 1 (C) 10 (D) 100 (E) 1000

11. In Figure 2, the graph of a parabola $y = x^2 + 4$ is tangent to the graph of the line $y = kx$ at point P. What is the value of k?

    (A) 4
    (B) 2
    (C) 1
    (D) −2
    (E) −4

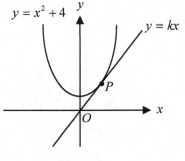

Figure 2

Note: Figure not drawn to scale.

12. In $\triangle ABC$ shown in Figure 3, $\sin C = \dfrac{3}{5}$ and the area of the triangle is 54. What is the length of $\overline{BC}$?

    (A) 10
    (B) 12
    (C) 15
    (D) 18
    (E) 25

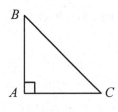

Figure 3

GO ON TO THE NEXT PAGE

MATHEMATICS LEVEL 1 TEST - *Continued*

USE THIS SPACE FOR SCRATCHWORK.

13. If Mr. Lee drives to work at an average speed of 20 miles per hour, and if he drives back home at an average speed of 30 miles per hour, Which of the following is his average speed for the entire trip?

(A) 24mph
(B) 24.5mph
(C) 25mph
(D) 25.5mph
(E) 26mph

14. The area of the rectangle in Figure 4 is $16\sqrt{3}$. If $\angle ACD = 60^o$, what is the length of $\overline{BC}$?

(A) $\sqrt{3}$
(B) $2\sqrt{3}$
(C) $3\sqrt{3}$
(D) $4\sqrt{3}$
(E) $6\sqrt{3}$

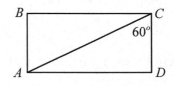

Figure 4

15. How many different four-digit numbers can be formed by rearranging the digits of 2010?

(A) 6   (B) 12   (C) 18   (D) 24   (E) 36

16. There are 8 girls and 6 boys in a Chess Club. In how many ways could 2 boys and 2 girls be selected to attend the state tournament?

(A) 210   (B) 420   (C) 840   (D) 1640   (E) 2520

17. In Figure 5, the length of a side of the square is s and points P and R are the midpoints of $\overline{AB}$ and $\overline{CD}$ respectively. Which of the following is the area of quadrilateral $PQRS$?

(A) $\dfrac{s^2}{2}$ (B) $\dfrac{s^2}{3}$ (C) $\dfrac{s^2}{4}$ (D) $\dfrac{s^2}{5}$ (E) $\dfrac{s^2}{6}$

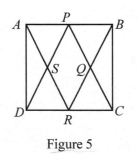

Figure 5

GO ON TO THE NEXT PAGE

MATHEMATICS LEVEL 1 TEST - *Continued*

USE THIS SPACE FOR SCRATCHWORK.

18. If $\dfrac{a-b}{a+b} = \dfrac{3}{2}$, then $\dfrac{a}{b} =$

(A) 5   (B) $\dfrac{2}{3}$ (C) $\dfrac{1}{5}$ (D) $-\dfrac{1}{5}$ (E) -5

19. If $5x^4 - 3x^2 + 7$ is divided by $(x+1)$, the remainder is

(A) 7   (B) 9   (C) 10   (D) 12   (E) 15

20. What is the product of all real solutions of
$8^{x^2+2x-4} = 16^{x^2-1}$?

(A) -8
(B) -4
(C) 4
(D) 8
(E) 16

21. If the measure of each interior angle of a regular polygon is five times that of an exterior angle of the polygon, what is the sum of all interior angles of the polygon?

(A) 30   (B) 150   (C) 900   (D) 1800   (E) 2700

22. How many different chords are determined by 10 distinct points lying on a circle?

(A) 90   (B) 45   (C) 30   (D) 20   (E) 10

23. In parallelogram $ABCD$ shown in Figure 6, $BE = \dfrac{1}{5}BC$ and $AF = FD$. What is the ratio of the area of $\triangle CEG$ to the area of $\triangle AGF$?

(A) $\dfrac{6}{5}$ (B) $\dfrac{8}{5}$ (C) $\dfrac{25}{16}$ (D) $\dfrac{36}{25}$ (E) $\dfrac{64}{25}$

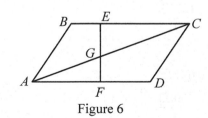

Figure 6

USE THIS SPACE FOR SCRATCHWORK.

24. If a point (x, y) is the circumcenter of the triangle with vertices $A(0, 0)$, $B(4, 2)$, and $C(6, 0)$, what is the point (x, y)?

(A) $(3, -1)$

(B) $(3, 0)$

(C) $(3, 1)$

(D) $(3, 2)$

(E) $(3, 3)$

25. If a regular hexagon prism has a base edge 4 and a height 5, what is the volume of the prism?

(A) 120

(B) $120\sqrt{3}$

(C) 240

(D) $240\sqrt{3}$

(E) $120(\sqrt{3} - 1)$

26. In isosceles triangle ABC shown in Figure 7, points $D, E,$ and M are the midpoints of $\overline{AB}$, $\overline{BC}$ and $\overline{AC}$ respectively. If the area of $\triangle ABC$ is 24, what is the area of quadrilateral $ADNM$?

(A) 6   (B) 9   (C) 10   (D) 12   (D) 15

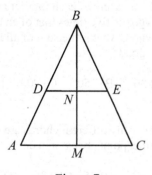

Figure 7

27. In the rhombus in Figure 8, $AC = 20$ and $\angle D = 120^o$. What is the area of the rhombus?

(A) $\dfrac{100\sqrt{3}}{3}$

(B) $80\sqrt{3}$

(C) $100\sqrt{3}$

(D) $\dfrac{200\sqrt{3}}{3}$

(E) $200\sqrt{3}$

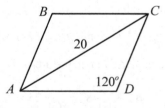

Figure 8

GO ON TO THE NEXT PAGE

MATHEMATICS LEVEL 1 TEST - *Continued*

USE THIS SPACE FOR SCRATCHWORK.

28. Which of the following is false?

(A) A plane is determined by three noncollinear points.
(B) A plane is determined by a line and a point not on the line.
(C) A plane is determined by two distinct intersecting lines.
(D) A plain is determined by two distinct parallel lines.
(E) A plain is determined by two nonintersecting lines.

29. A right circular cylinder is inscribed in a cube as shown in Figure 9. If the volume of the cylinder is 25 cubic meters, what is the volume of the cube, in cubic meters?

(A) 100π (B) 50π (C) $\dfrac{100}{\pi}$ (D) $\dfrac{50}{\pi}$ (E) $\dfrac{25}{\pi}$

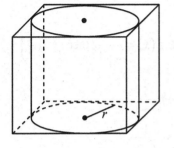

Figure 9

30. In right triangle ABC in Figure 10, $AD = BD$, $BC = 10\sqrt{3}$, and $\angle BAC = 30°$. What is the ratio of the area of $\triangle ABD$ to the area of $\triangle DBC$?

(A) 1:1
(B) 1:2
(C) 2:1
(D) 3:1
(E) 4:1

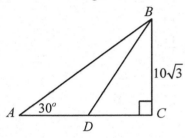

Figure 10

Note: Figure not drawn to sclae.

31. What is the sum of the roots in the equation $x^3 + 5x^2 - 4x = 0$?

(A) 5
(B) 4
(C) 0
(D) −4
(E) −5

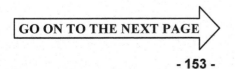
GO ON TO THE NEXT PAGE

MATHEMATICS LEVEL 1 TEST - *Continued*

32. In Figure 11, line ℓ is defined by the equation $3x + 4y = 12$ and $\overline{OP}$ is perpendicular to the line. Which of the following is the length of $\overline{OP}$?

    (A) 1.6
    (B) 2.0
    (C) 2.4
    (D) 3.5
    (E) 4.8

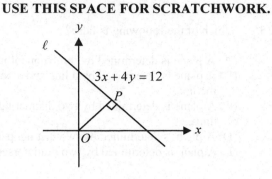

Figure 11

Note: Figure not drawn to scale.

33. If $f(x) = \dfrac{x-1}{x+1}$, then $f^{-1}\left(\dfrac{1}{t}\right) =$

    (A) $\dfrac{1}{t+1}$

    (B) $\dfrac{1}{t-1}$

    (C) $\dfrac{t-1}{t+1}$

    (D) $\dfrac{t+1}{t-1}$

    (E) $\dfrac{2t}{t-1}$

34. In Figure 12, $\overline{AB}$ is the diameter of the circle. Which of the following is the value of k ?

    (A) 4
    (B) 5
    (C) 6
    (D) 8
    (E) 9

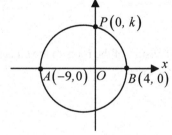

Figure 12

Note: Figure not drawn to scale.

35. Which of the following is the area enclosed by the graph of $\dfrac{|x|}{9} + \dfrac{|y|}{4} = 1$?

    (A) 36　(B) 72　(C) 144　(D) 216　(E) 288

GO ON TO THE NEXT PAGE

MATHEMATICS LEVEL 1 TEST - *Continued*

USE THIS SPACE FOR SCRATCHWORK.

36.   If $f(x) = 2^x$ and $f(x-1) = f(x) - 8$, then $x =$

(A) 4   (B) 6   (C) 8   (D) 10   (E) 12

37.   Which of the following is the value of $(1+i)^{20}$?

(A) 1024   (B) 512   (C) 1   (D) –512   (E) –1024

38.   If a recursive formula is defined as $a_n = na_{n-1}$ and
$a_1 = 2$, what is the 6th term of the sequence?

(A) 2
(B) 12
(C) 48
(D) 240
(E) 1440

39.   Which of the following could be the equation of the
graph shown in Figure 13?

(A) $y = \sin 2x$
(B) $y = 3\sin x + 3$
(C) $y = 3\cos x + 3$
(D) $y = 3\cos 2x + 3$
(E) $y = 3\cos 2x + 6$

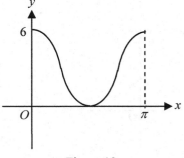

Figure 13

40.   If $f(x) = \dfrac{1}{x-2}$ and $0 < x < 2$, which of the following
is the range of $f(x)$?

(A) $0 < y < 2$
(B) $y < 0$
(C) $-2 < y < 0$
(D) $y < -0.5$
(E) All real numbers

GO ON TO THE NEXT PAGE

MATHEMATICS LEVEL 1 TEST - *Continued*

USE THIS SPACE FOR SCRATCHWORK.

41.   If the radius of a sphere is increased by 3 inches, the surface area becomes four times the original surface area. What is the radius of the original sphere, in inches?

(A) 3
(B) 5
(C) 8
(D) 10
(E) 12

42.   Which of the following could be the graph of
$f(x) = 2^{-|x|}$?

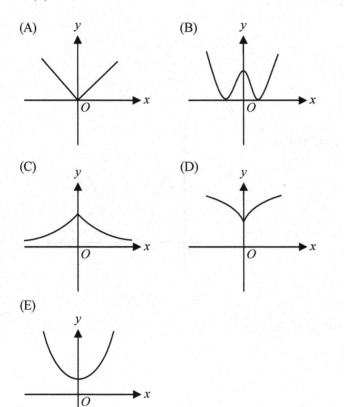

(A)
(B)
(C)
(D)
(E)

GO ON TO THE NEXT PAGE

MATHEMATICS LEVEL 1 TEST - *Continued*

USE THIS SPACE FOR SCRATCHWORK.

43. Which of the following must be true for the function
$f(x) = x|x|$?

    I.   The function is even.
    II. The function is odd.
    III. The graph of the function is symmetrical about the
           origin.

    (A) I only
    (B) II only
    (C) III only
    (D) I and III only
    (E) II and III only

44. If $f(x) = x + 3$, $g(x) = 3x$, and $g(f^{-1}(x)) = -3$,
what is the value of x ?

    (A) -2 (B) -1 (C) 1 (D) 2 (E) 3

45. If each digit is only used once, how many three-digit
even numbers can be formed from the digits 0, 1, 3, 8, 9 ?

    (A) 48   (B) 36   (C) 24   (D) 21   (E) 18

46. What is the maximum value of the function
$y = -5\cos x + 5$?

    (A) -10 (B) -5 (C) 0 (D) 5 (E) 10

47. What is the area of the region bounded by the graph of
$y = 2|x - 2| - 4$ and the x-axis?

    (A) 8   (B) 16   (C) 20   (D) 24   (E) 32

48. The area of rhombus $ABCD$ in Figure 14 is

    (A) 50
    (B) $50\sqrt{3}$
    (C) 75
    (D) $75\sqrt{3}$
    (E) 100

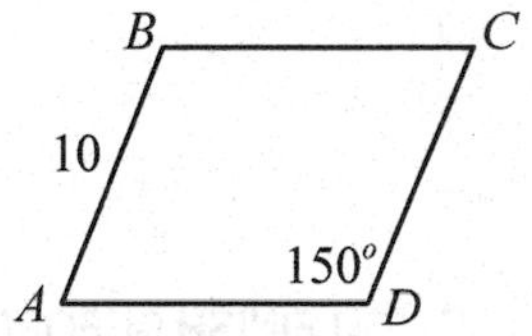

Figure 14

Note: Figure not drawn to scale.

GO ON TO THE NEXT PAGE

MATHEMATICS LEVEL 1 TEST - *Continued*

USE THIS SPACE FOR SCRATCHWORK.

49. If the graph of $y = x^2 - 2x + k$ intersects the line $y = 3$ at exactly two points, which of the following could not be the value of k ?

(A) 0   (B) 1   (C) 2   (D) 3   (E) 4

50. Car A and Car B are 150 miles apart. If they travel toward each other, they will meet in $1\frac{1}{2}$ hours. If Car A travels 20 miles per hour faster than Car B, what is the speed of Car A ?

(A) 40mph
(B) 50mph
(C) 60mph
(D) 75mph
(E) 80mph

STOP
**IF YOU FINISH BEFORE TIME IS CALLED, YOU MAY CHECK YOUR WORK ON THIS TEST ONLY.
DO NOT TURN TO ANY OTHER TEST IN THIS BOOK.**

NO MATERIAL ON THIS PAGE

NO MATERIAL ON THIS PAGE

#	answer	#	answer	#	answer	#	answer	#	answer
1	C	11	A	21	D	31	E	41	A
2	A	12	C	22	B	32	C	42	C
3	B	13	A	23	E	33	D	43	E
4	E	14	D	24	A	34	C	44	D
5	B	15	A	25	B	35	B	45	D
6	E	16	B	26	B	36	A	46	E
7	C	17	C	27	D	37	E	47	A
8	A	18	E	28	E	38	E	48	A
9	D	19	B	29	C	39	D	49	E
10	C	20	D	30	C	40	D	50	C

TEST 6 **ANSWERS**

Explanations: Test 6

1. **(C)** $\quad f(2)=0 \;\Rightarrow\; f(2)=4+6-k=0 \;\Rightarrow\; k=10$

2. **(A)** $\quad 2^{2x-3}=2^3 \;\Rightarrow\; 2x-3=3 \;\Rightarrow\; x=3$

3. **(B)** $\quad \dfrac{1}{x}=\dfrac{1}{3}+\dfrac{1}{5}=\dfrac{8}{15} \;\Rightarrow\; x=\dfrac{15}{8}$

4. **(E)** There are many ways to solve it.

$$\dfrac{1}{(b-a)}\times\dfrac{(a-b)(a+b)}{1}=-(a-b)=-a-b$$

5. **(B)** Since $m=2$, $y=2x+b$ passes through $(2,10)$.

Therefore, $10=4+b \;\Rightarrow\; b=6$.

6. **(E)** Axis of symmetry is $x=2$ and y-intercept is 0. Therefore, $b=0$.

$$\dfrac{-a}{2}=2 \;\Rightarrow\; a=-4, \qquad f(2)=2^2+(-4)(2)=-4$$

The coordinates are $(2,-4)$.

7. **(C)** $\quad \left(a+\dfrac{1}{a}\right)^2=a^2+\dfrac{1}{a^2}+2=25 \;\Rightarrow\; a^2+\dfrac{1}{a^2}=23$

8. **(A)** $\quad \log_2 x-\log_2 y=5 \;\Rightarrow\; \log_2\dfrac{x}{y}=5 \;\Rightarrow\; \dfrac{x}{y}=2^5=32$

9. **(D)** $\quad (x-1)^2+5=x^2-2x+1+5=x^2-2x+6$

Since $x^2-2x=2$, $(x^2-2x)+6=2+6=8$.

10. (C) $\log(AB) = 4 \implies \log A + \log B = 4$

$\log\dfrac{A}{B} = -2 \implies \log A - \log B = -2$

By addition: $2\log A = 2 \implies \log A = 1 \implies A = 10$

11. (A)   Since $y = kx$ is tangent to the parabola,
The discriminant of the equation
$x^2 + 4 = kx$ must be 0.
$x^2 - kx + 4 = 0 \implies D = k^2 - 4(1)(4) = 0$
$k^2 = 16 \implies k = \pm 4 \,(\text{but } k > 0)$

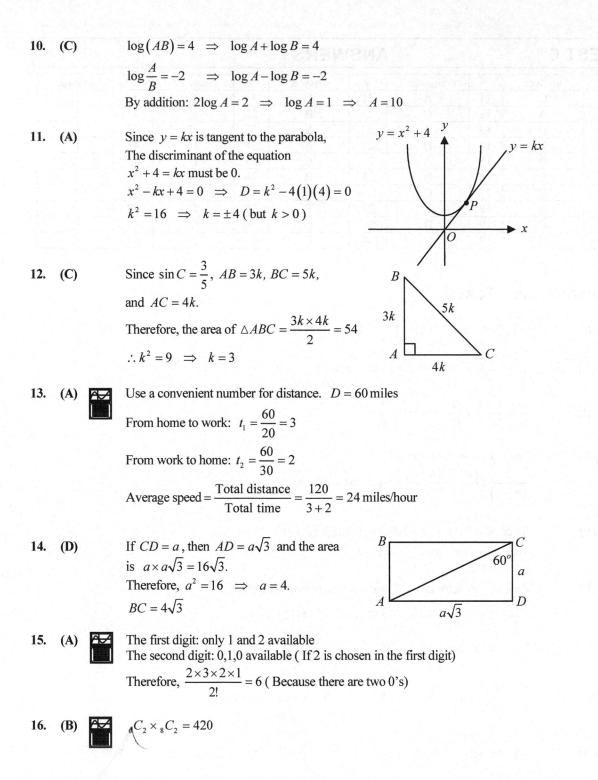

12. (C)   Since $\sin C = \dfrac{3}{5}$, $AB = 3k$, $BC = 5k$,

and $AC = 4k$.

Therefore, the area of $\triangle ABC = \dfrac{3k \times 4k}{2} = 54$

$\therefore k^2 = 9 \implies k = 3$

13. (A)   Use a convenient number for distance. $D = 60$ miles

From home to work: $t_1 = \dfrac{60}{20} = 3$

From work to home: $t_2 = \dfrac{60}{30} = 2$

Average speed $= \dfrac{\text{Total distance}}{\text{Total time}} = \dfrac{120}{3+2} = 24$ miles/hour

14. (D)   If $CD = a$, then $AD = a\sqrt{3}$ and the area
is $a \times a\sqrt{3} = 16\sqrt{3}$.
Therefore, $a^2 = 16 \implies a = 4$.
$BC = 4\sqrt{3}$

15. (A)   The first digit: only 1 and 2 available
The second digit: 0,1,0 available (If 2 is chosen in the first digit)

Therefore, $\dfrac{2 \times 3 \times 2 \times 1}{2!} = 6$ (Because there are two 0's)

16. (B) $_9C_2 \times _8C_2 = 420$

17. (C) $SQ = \dfrac{1}{2}(CD) = \dfrac{s}{2}$

The area of $\triangle PSQ = \dfrac{0.5s(0.5s)}{2} = \dfrac{0.25s^2}{2}$

Therefore, the area of $PQRS = 2\left(\dfrac{0.25s^2}{2}\right) = 0.25s^2$

$$\text{Or}$$

$$\dfrac{SQ \times BC}{2} = \dfrac{0.5s \times s}{2} = 0.25s^2$$

18. (E)   Cross-multiplication:

$2a - 2b = 3a + 3b \implies a = -5b$

Therefore, $\dfrac{a}{b} = \dfrac{-5b}{b} = -5$

19. (B)   Remainder theorem: $f(-1) = 5(1^4) - 3(1^2) + 7 = 9$ (Remainder)

> **Important:** Remainder theorem
> When polynomial $P(x)$ is divided by $(x-a)$, the remainder
> is $R = P(a)$.
> $\qquad P(x) = (x-a)Q(x) + R$ where R is the remainder.

20. (D) $2^{x^2+2x-4} = 2^{4(x^2-1)} \implies x^2 + 2x - 4 = 4x^2 - 4 \implies x^2 - 6x + 8 = 0$

$(x-4)(x-2) = 0$

Therefore, $x = 2$ or $x = 4$. $\implies$ $2 \times 4 = 8$

Or the product of the roots: $\dfrac{c}{a} = 8$.

21. (D)   If the measure of an exterior angle is x, then the measure of an interior angle is $5x$.
Therefore, $x + 5x = 180 \implies x = 30$ and $5x = 150$.

The number of sides (or angles) $= \dfrac{360}{30} = 12$.

Sum of interior angles $= 12 \times 150 = 1800$

22. (B)   When you choose two points, they form one diagonal.
Therefore, the number of choosing two points is equal to the number of the diagonals.
$\therefore\ _{10}C_2 = 45$

23. (E)   The ratio of area:
$\dfrac{\triangle EGC}{\triangle AGF} = \dfrac{4^2}{2.5^2} = \dfrac{64}{25}$ (Two triangles are similar)

24. (A) The circumcenter is the point of intersection of perpendicular bisectors.

line $\ell : x = 3$

line m :

midpoint $(2,1)$ and the slope of line $n = \dfrac{2}{4} = \dfrac{1}{2}$

the slope of line $m = -2$

Therefore, the equation of line m is

$y - 1 = -2(x - 2) \;\Rightarrow\; y = -2x + 5, \quad f(3) = -1$

$\therefore (x, y) = (3, -1)$

25. (B) The area of a regular hexagon: $B = 6\left(\dfrac{4 \times 4 \times \sin 60}{2}\right) = 24\sqrt{3}$

The volume of the prism: $V = Bh = 24\sqrt{3} \times 5 = 120\sqrt{3}$

26. (B) $\triangle BDE \sim \triangle BAC$: the ratio of the areas is $1 : 4$.

If the area of $\triangle BAC$ is 24, the area of $\triangle BDE$ is 6.

Therefore, the area of trapezoid $ADEC$ is $24 - 6 = 18$.

The area of $ADNM = \dfrac{18}{2} = 9$.

27. (D) $CE = 20\sin 60 = 10$ and $DE = 10\sqrt{3}$

$AD = CD = \dfrac{20}{\sqrt{3}}$

Therefore, the area of the rhombus is

$\dfrac{20}{\sqrt{3}} \times 10 = \dfrac{200}{\sqrt{3}} = \dfrac{200\sqrt{3}}{3}$.

Or, the diagonals perpendicularly bisect each other.

Therefore, The area is

$\dfrac{1}{2}\left(\dfrac{10}{\sqrt{3}} \times 20\right) \times 2 = \dfrac{200}{\sqrt{3}}$

28. (E)

> **Important:**
> A plane is determined by
> (1) three noncollinear points　　(2) a line and a point not on the line
> (3) two distinct intersecting lines　(4) two distinct parallel lines

29. (C)   The volume of the cylinder: $\pi r^2 h = \pi r^2 (2r) = 2\pi r^3 = 25$, $r^3 = \dfrac{25}{2\pi}$

The volume of the cube: $(2r)^3 = 8r^3$, $8r^3 = 8\left(\dfrac{25}{2\pi}\right) = \dfrac{100}{\pi}$

30. (C)   Since $AD = 20$ and $CD = 10$, the ratio of the areas will be 2:1. (Because they have the same height)

31. (E) $x^3 + 5x^2 - 4x = 0 \;\Rightarrow\; x(x^2 + 5x - 4) = 0 \;\Rightarrow\; x(x-4)(x-1) = 0$

The sum of the roots $= 0 + (-4) + (-1) = -5$. (Or you can use Vieta's formula)

32. (C)   Method 1)
The equation of $\overline{OP}$ is

$y = \dfrac{4}{3}x$ (Because the slope of line ℓ is $-\dfrac{3}{4}$)

When you solve the system of equations, you will get $(1.44, 1.92)$.

Distance from the origin is $\sqrt{1.44^2 + 1.92^2} = 2.4$

Method 2) Use distance formula from $(0, 0)$.

$D = \dfrac{|ax_1 + by_2 + c|}{\sqrt{a^2 + b^2}} = \dfrac{|3 \cdot 0 + 4 \cdot 0 - 12|}{\sqrt{3^2 + 4^2}} = \dfrac{12}{5} = 2.4$

33. (D)   Inverse: $y = \dfrac{x-1}{x+1} \Rightarrow$ Switch x and y $\Rightarrow x = \dfrac{y-1}{y+1}$ where $y = f^{-1}$.

$\dfrac{1}{t} = \dfrac{y-1}{y+1} \;\Rightarrow\; y+1 = ty - t \;\Rightarrow\; y(t-1) = 1+t \;\Rightarrow\; y = \dfrac{1+t}{t-1}$

34. (C)   Since $PO^2 = AO \times BO$,
$k^2 = 9 \times 4 \;\Rightarrow\; k = 6\,(k > 0)$

35. (B)   The graph of the figure is as follows.

The area is $\dfrac{18 \times 8}{2} = 72$.

36. (A) $f(x-1) = f(x) - 8 \implies 2^{x-1} = 2^x - 8$

$\dfrac{2^x}{2} = 2^x - 8 \implies 2^x = 2 \cdot 2^x - 16 \implies 2^x = 16 \implies x = 4$

37. (E) $(1+i)^{20} \implies \left((1+i)^2\right)^{10} \implies (2i)^{10} = 2^{10}(-1) = -1024$

38. (E) $a_1 = 2, \quad a_2 = 2a_1 = 4, \quad a_3 = 3a_2 = 12, \quad a_4 = 4a_3 = 48 \cdots$
Follow the pattern: $a_5 = 5 \times 48 = 240$ and $a_6 = 6 \times 240 = 1440$.

39. (D) The middle line $y = 3$, amplitude is 3, and the frequency is $f = \dfrac{2\pi}{\pi} = 2$.

40. (D) Use a graphic utility.

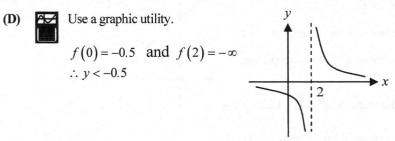

$f(0) = -0.5$ and $f(2) = -\infty$
$\therefore y < -0.5$

41. (A) The surface area of a sphere is $S = 4\pi r^2$ and the other surface area is $S' = 4\pi(r+3)$.

$S' = 4S \implies 4\pi(r+3)^2 = 4(4\pi r^2) \implies (r+3)^2 = 4r^2$

$\implies 3r^2 - 6r - 9 = 0 \implies 3(r-3)(r+1) = 0 \implies r = 3$ or $r = -1$.

$\therefore r = 3 \ (r > 0)$

42. (C) If $x \geq 0$, then $y = 2^{-x}$.
If $x < 0$, then $y = 2^x$.

43. (E) $f(x) = x|x|, \quad f(-x) = -x|-x| = -x|x|,$ and $-f(-x) = x|x|$.
Since $f(x) = -f(-x)$, f is an odd function which is symmetrical with respect to the origin.

44. (D) $f^{-1}(x) = x - 3 \implies g(f^{-1}) = 3(x-3) = -3 \implies 3x = 6 \implies x = 2$.

45. (D)   To be an even number, the last digit must be either 0 or 8.

Case 1 :   □ □ 0 $\Rightarrow$ $4 \times 3 \times 1 = 12$
        ↑

    1,3,8,9

Case 2 :   □ □ 8 $\Rightarrow$ $3 \times 3 = 9$
        ↑

    1,3,8

If number 1 is in the first digit, 3, 8, 0 are in the second digit.

46. (E)   Since amplitude is 5 and the middle line is 5, the maximum value is $5 + 5 = 10$.

47. (A)   Find x-intercept: $2|x-2| - 4 = 0$ $\Rightarrow$ $|x-2| = 2$
$x - 2 = 2, -2$ $\Rightarrow$ $x = 4$ or 0
The area of the triangle:
$A = \dfrac{4 \times 4}{2} = 8$ ($b = 4$ and $h = |-4| = 4$)

48. (A)   The area of rhombus $ABCD = 10 \times 10 \times \sin 30 = 10 \times 10 \times \dfrac{1}{2} = 50$.

49. (E)   To have two intersections, the minimum of y should be less than 3.

Axis of symmetry: $x = \dfrac{-(-2)}{2(1)} = 1$

Maximum: $y = f(1) = 1 - 2 + k = k - 1$

Therefore, $k - 1 < 3$ $\Rightarrow$ $k < 4$

50. (C)

Car	Speed	Time	Distance
A	$x+20$	1.5hr	$1.5(x+20)$
B	x	1.5hr	$1.5x$

Sum of distances is equal to 150miles.

$1.5x + 1.5(x+20) = 150$ $\Rightarrow$ $3x = 120$ $\Rightarrow$ $x = 40$ mph

Therefore, $x + 20 = 40 + 20 = 60$ mph

END

NO MATERIAL ON THIS PAGE

Dr. John Chung's SAT II

Math Level 1

Test 7

MATHEMATICS LEVEL 1 TEST

TEST 7

REFERENCE INFORMATION

THE FOLLOWING INFORMATION IS FOR YOUR REFERENCE IN ANSWERING SOME OF THE QUESTIONS IN THIS TEST

Volume of a right circular cone with radius r and height h: $V = \dfrac{1}{3}\pi r^2 h$

Lateral Area of a right circular cone with circumference of the base c and slant height ℓ: $S = \dfrac{1}{2}c\ell$

Volume of a sphere with radius r: $V = \dfrac{4}{3}\pi r^3$

Surface Area of a sphere with radius r: $S = 4\pi r^2$

Volume of a pyramid with base area B and height h: $V = \dfrac{1}{3}Bh$

Dr. John Chung's SAT II Math Level 1

Answer Sheet

1	Ⓐ Ⓑ Ⓒ Ⓓ Ⓔ		26	Ⓐ Ⓑ Ⓒ Ⓓ Ⓔ
2	Ⓐ Ⓑ Ⓒ Ⓓ Ⓔ		27	Ⓐ Ⓑ Ⓒ Ⓓ Ⓔ
3	Ⓐ Ⓑ Ⓒ Ⓓ Ⓔ		28	Ⓐ Ⓑ Ⓒ Ⓓ Ⓔ
4	Ⓐ Ⓑ Ⓒ Ⓓ Ⓔ		29	Ⓐ Ⓑ Ⓒ Ⓓ Ⓔ
5	Ⓐ Ⓑ Ⓒ Ⓓ Ⓔ		30	Ⓐ Ⓑ Ⓒ Ⓓ Ⓔ
6	Ⓐ Ⓑ Ⓒ Ⓓ Ⓔ		31	Ⓐ Ⓑ Ⓒ Ⓓ Ⓔ
7	Ⓐ Ⓑ Ⓒ Ⓓ Ⓔ		32	Ⓐ Ⓑ Ⓒ Ⓓ Ⓔ
8	Ⓐ Ⓑ Ⓒ Ⓓ Ⓔ		33	Ⓐ Ⓑ Ⓒ Ⓓ Ⓔ
9	Ⓐ Ⓑ Ⓒ Ⓓ Ⓔ		34	Ⓐ Ⓑ Ⓒ Ⓓ Ⓔ
10	Ⓐ Ⓑ Ⓒ Ⓓ Ⓔ		35	Ⓐ Ⓑ Ⓒ Ⓓ Ⓔ
11	Ⓐ Ⓑ Ⓒ Ⓓ Ⓔ		36	Ⓐ Ⓑ Ⓒ Ⓓ Ⓔ
12	Ⓐ Ⓑ Ⓒ Ⓓ Ⓔ		37	Ⓐ Ⓑ Ⓒ Ⓓ Ⓔ
13	Ⓐ Ⓑ Ⓒ Ⓓ Ⓔ		38	Ⓐ Ⓑ Ⓒ Ⓓ Ⓔ
14	Ⓐ Ⓑ Ⓒ Ⓓ Ⓔ		39	Ⓐ Ⓑ Ⓒ Ⓓ Ⓔ
15	Ⓐ Ⓑ Ⓒ Ⓓ Ⓔ		40	Ⓐ Ⓑ Ⓒ Ⓓ Ⓔ
16	Ⓐ Ⓑ Ⓒ Ⓓ Ⓔ		41	Ⓐ Ⓑ Ⓒ Ⓓ Ⓔ
17	Ⓐ Ⓑ Ⓒ Ⓓ Ⓔ		42	Ⓐ Ⓑ Ⓒ Ⓓ Ⓔ
18	Ⓐ Ⓑ Ⓒ Ⓓ Ⓔ		43	Ⓐ Ⓑ Ⓒ Ⓓ Ⓔ
19	Ⓐ Ⓑ Ⓒ Ⓓ Ⓔ		44	Ⓐ Ⓑ Ⓒ Ⓓ Ⓔ
20	Ⓐ Ⓑ Ⓒ Ⓓ Ⓔ		45	Ⓐ Ⓑ Ⓒ Ⓓ Ⓔ
21	Ⓐ Ⓑ Ⓒ Ⓓ Ⓔ		46	Ⓐ Ⓑ Ⓒ Ⓓ Ⓔ
22	Ⓐ Ⓑ Ⓒ Ⓓ Ⓔ		47	Ⓐ Ⓑ Ⓒ Ⓓ Ⓔ
23	Ⓐ Ⓑ Ⓒ Ⓓ Ⓔ		48	Ⓐ Ⓑ Ⓒ Ⓓ Ⓔ
24	Ⓐ Ⓑ Ⓒ Ⓓ Ⓔ		49	Ⓐ Ⓑ Ⓒ Ⓓ Ⓔ
25	Ⓐ Ⓑ Ⓒ Ⓓ Ⓔ		50	Ⓐ Ⓑ Ⓒ Ⓓ Ⓔ

The number of right answers : [   ]

The number of wrong answers : [   ]

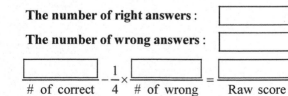

$$\underbrace{[\qquad]}_{\text{\# of correct}} - \frac{1}{4} \times \underbrace{[\qquad]}_{\text{\# of wrong}} = \underbrace{[\qquad]}_{\text{Raw score}}$$

Score Conversion Table

Raw Score	Scaled Score	Raw Score	Scaled Score	Raw Score	Scaled Score
50	800	28	630	6	480
49	800	27	620	5	470
48	800	26	610	4	470
47	800	25	600	3	460
46	790	24	590	2	460
45	780	23	580	1	450
44	770	22	570	0	450
43	760	21	550		
42	750	20	540		
41	740	19	530		
40	740	18	520		
39	730	17	510		
38	720	16	500		
37	710	15	490		
36	710	14	480		
35	700	13	470		
34	690	12	460		
33	680	11	450		
32	670	10	440		
31	660	9	430		
30	650	8	420		
29	640	7	410		

MATHEMATICS LEVEL 1 TEST

For each of the following problems, decide which is the BEST of the choices given. If the exact numerical value is not one of the choices, select the choice that best approximates this value. Then fill in the corresponding circle on the answer sheet.

Notes: (1) A scientific or graphing calculator will be necessary for answering some (but not all) of the questions in this test. For each question you will have to decide whether or not you should use a calculator.

(2) For some questions in this test you may have to decide whether your calculator should be in the radian mode or the degree mode.

(3) Figures that accompany problems in this test are intended to provide information useful in solving the problems. They are drawn as accurately as possible EXCEPT when it is stated in a specific problem that its figure is not drawn to scale. All figures lie in a plane unless otherwise indicated.

(4) Unless otherwise specified, the domain of any function f is assumed to be the set of all real numbers x for which $f(x)$ is a real number. The range of f is assumed to be the set of all real numbers $f(x)$, where x is in the domain of f.

(5) Reference information that may be useful in answering the questions in this test can be found on the page preceding Question 1.

USE THIS SPACE FOR SCRATCHWORK.

1. If $f(x) = x^2 - kx + 2$ and $f(1) = 5$, then $f(-1) =$

    (A) −5   (B) −1   (C) 1   (D) 2   (E) 5

2. $\dfrac{5}{2-\sqrt{3}} - \dfrac{5}{2+\sqrt{3}} =$

    (A) 20

    (B) 10

    (C) $20\sqrt{3}$

    (D) $10\sqrt{3}$

    (E) $\dfrac{10\sqrt{3}}{3}$

MATHEMATICS LEVEL 1 TEST - *Continued*

USE THIS SPACE FOR SCRATCHWORK.

3. If $x - 2y = 5$ and $x + 2y = 4$, then $x^2 - 4y^2 =$

(A) 16 (B) 20 (C) 25 (D) 30 (E) 36

4. In Figure 1, the area of the shaded region with center O is 3π. What is the perimeter of the shaded region?

(A) $\sqrt{6}$

(B) $4\sqrt{6}$

(C) $\pi\sqrt{6}$

(D) $\pi\left(\sqrt{6}+4\right)$

(E) $(\pi+4)\sqrt{6}$

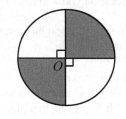

Figure 1

5. Which of the following could be the graph of a linear function $2x + 3y + 3 = 0$?

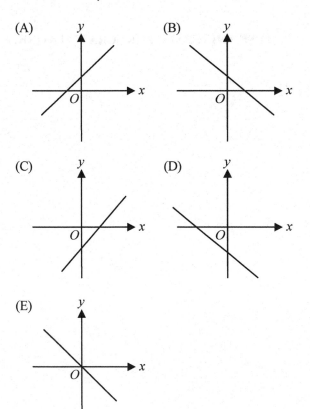

(A)

(B)

(C)

(D)

(E)

GO ON TO THE NEXT PAGE

MATHEMATICS LEVEL 1 TEST - *Continued*

USE THIS SPACE FOR SCRATCHWORK.

6. If $k(k^2 - 8) = k$, what are all possible values of k ?

(A) 0 only
(B) $2\sqrt{2}$ only
(C) $2\sqrt{2}$ and $-2\sqrt{2}$ only
(D) 0, $2\sqrt{2}$, and $-2\sqrt{2}$
(E) 0, 3, and -3

7. If $2^{2x-3} = 4^{2x-3}$, what is the value of x ?

(A) 0.5   (B) 0.75   (C) 1.5   (D) 2   (E) 4

8. Joan has a cellular phone that costs \$20.00 per month plus 25¢ per minute for each call. Kevin has a cellular phone that costs \$30.00 per month plus 15¢ per minute for each call. Which of the following equations could be used to find the number of minutes when the two plans cost the same?

(A) $20x + 25 = 30x + 15$
(B) $20 + 25x = 30 + 15x$
(C) $20 + 0.25x = 30 + 0.15x$
(D) $(20 + 0.25)x = (30 + 0.15)x$
(E) $20 - 0.15x = 30 - 0.25x$

9. If $k = x^{-3} - 1$, for what value of x is $k = 8$?

(A) 0.48
(B) 0.54
(C) 0.86
(D) 1.52
(E) 2.65

10. If two lines are parallel and the slope of one of the lines is $\dfrac{1}{k}$, then which of the following is the product of their slopes?

(A) k^{-2} (B) k^2 (C) 1   (D) -1 (E) $-k$

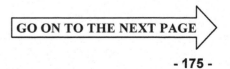

GO ON TO THE NEXT PAGE

USE THIS SPACE FOR SCRATCHWORK.

11. If a radioactive substance has an initial mass of 50 grams and its mass halves every 5 years, what is the number of grams remaining after 20 years?

(A) 25 grams
(B) 12.5 grams
(C) 6.25 grams
(D) 3.125 grams
(E) 1.56 grams

12. Tiffany tossed a ball in the air whose path of the ball was modeled by the equation $y = -x^2 + 10x$, where y is the height of the ball in feet and x is the time in seconds. Which of the following is the maximum height of the ball, in feet?

(A) 10   (B) 25   (C) 50   (D) 75   (E) 100

13. In Figure 2, $\sin \alpha = 0.4$, $\sin \beta = 0.5$, and $AB = 10$. What is the length of side CD?

(A) 4
(B) 6
(C) 8
(D) 10
(E) 12

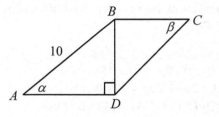

Figure 2

14. $\sqrt{\dfrac{x^2}{50} - \dfrac{x^2}{100}} =$

(A) $-\dfrac{x}{10}$ (B) $\dfrac{x}{5}$ (C) $\dfrac{x}{10}$ (D) $\dfrac{|x|}{5}$ (E) $\dfrac{|x|}{10}$

15. If a boy 1.3 meters tall casts a shadow 3 meters, how many meters tall is a building that casts a shadows 80 meters at the same time?

(A) 34.67
(B) 41.06
(C) 45.56
(D) 48.90
(E) 55.82

GO ON TO THE NEXT PAGE

MATHEMATICS LEVEL 1 TEST - *Continued*

USE THIS SPACE FOR SCRATCHWORK.

16. A person is standing at P on level ground x feet away from the foot of a 200-foot-tall building as shown in Figure 3. If $\sin k = 0.4$, what is the value of x?

   (A) 400
   (B) 458
   (C) 490
   (D) 525
   (E) 600

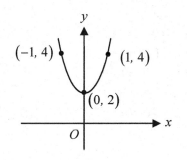

Figure 3

<u>Note</u>: Figure not drawn to scale.

17. For what value of x is $\dfrac{1}{1+\cos x^{o}}$ undefined?

   (A) 0   (B) 45   (C) 90   (D) 180   (E) 270

18. Which of the following is the equation represented by the graph in Figure 4?

   (A) $y = 3x^2 + 1$
   (B) $y = x^2 + 2$
   (C) $y = x^2 + 4$
   (D) $y = 2x^2 + 2$
   (E) $y = 3x^2 + 2$

Figure 4

19. What is the value of x in the equation $\dfrac{x}{3} + \dfrac{x}{5} = \dfrac{1}{3}$?

   (A) $\dfrac{1}{4}$ (B) $\dfrac{1}{3}$ (C) $\dfrac{1}{2}$ (D) $\dfrac{5}{8}$ (E) $\dfrac{8}{5}$

20. What are all values of x for which $|2x - 1| < 5$?

   (A) $x < -2$
   (B) $-2 < x < 0$
   (C) $-1 < x < 1$
   (D) $-1 < x < 3$
   (E) $-2 < x < 3$

MATHEMATICS LEVEL 1 TEST - *Continued*

USE THIS SPACE FOR SCRATCHWORK.

21. If $\log_3\left(9x^2\right) = \log_3(x) + 3$, then $x =$

    (A) 0　　(B) 1　　(C) 2　　(D) 3　　(E) 10

22. An exponential function is defined by $f(x) = ab^x$ where a and b represent constants. If ordered pairs $(2, 12)$ and $(5, 96)$ are the solutions of the function, then what is the value of a?

    (A) 3　　(B) 2　　(C) –1　　(D) –2　　(E) –3

23. If $a + bi = \dfrac{1-i}{1+i}$, then what are the values of a and b?

    (A) $a = 0$, $b = -1$
    (B) $a = 1$, $b = -1$
    (C) $a = 1$, $b = 1$
    (D) $a = -1$, $b = -1$
    (E) $a = -1$, $b = 1$

24. If $f(x) = \dfrac{2x+1}{x-1}$ and $f^{-1}(x)$ is the inverse of f, then $f^{-1}(-3) =$

    (A) $\dfrac{2}{7}$　　(B) $\dfrac{2}{5}$　　(C) $\dfrac{1}{2}$　　(D) $\dfrac{2}{3}$　　(E) $\dfrac{3}{4}$

25. A binary operation is defined by $a * b = a^b - a$ where a and b are positive integers. If $k * 2 = 12$, then $k =$

    (A) 1
    (B) 2
    (C) 3
    (D) 4
    (E) 5

GO ON TO THE NEXT PAGE

MATHEMATICS LEVEL 1 TEST - *Continued*

USE THIS SPACE FOR SCRATCHWORK.

26. Which of the following statements could not be true?

(A) Parallel lines are coplanar.
(B) Two intersecting lines are coplanar.
(C) Lines in parallel planes are parallel.
(D) Skew lines are non-coplanar.
(E) Two lines that are parallel to the third line are parallel.

27. In a regular pentagon shown in Figure 5, if $\overline{QP} \parallel \overline{AB}$, what is the value of $\angle PQR$?

(A) 20°
(B) 36°
(C) 45°
(D) 60°
(E) 72°

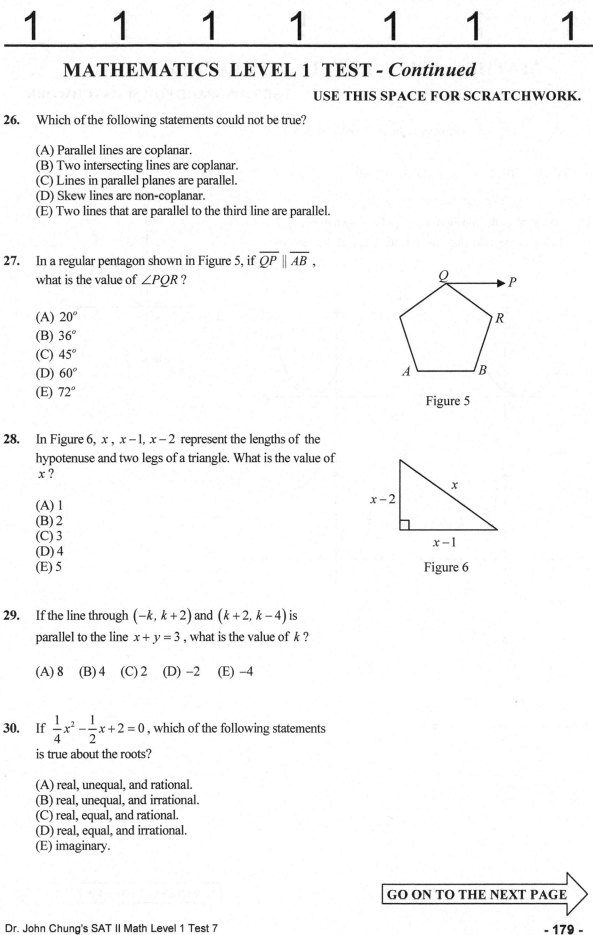

Figure 5

28. In Figure 6, x , $x-1$, $x-2$ represent the lengths of the hypotenuse and two legs of a triangle. What is the value of x ?

(A) 1
(B) 2
(C) 3
(D) 4
(E) 5

Figure 6

29. If the line through $(-k,\ k+2)$ and $(k+2,\ k-4)$ is parallel to the line $x+y=3$, what is the value of k ?

(A) 8   (B) 4   (C) 2   (D) –2   (E) –4

30. If $\frac{1}{4}x^2 - \frac{1}{2}x + 2 = 0$, which of the following statements is true about the roots?

(A) real, unequal, and rational.
(B) real, unequal, and irrational.
(C) real, equal, and rational.
(D) real, equal, and irrational.
(E) imaginary.

GO ON TO THE NEXT PAGE

MATHEMATICS LEVEL 1 TEST - *Continued*

USE THIS SPACE FOR SCRATCHWORK.

31.   If $\left(\dfrac{1}{x}\right)^2 + 3\left(\dfrac{1}{x}\right) = 10$, what is the positive value of x ?

(A) 0.5   (B) 1   (C) 2   (D) 5   (E) 10

32.   The graph of the function $y = f(x)$ is shown in Figure 7.
Which of the following could be the graph of the function
$y = 3f(x+2)$?

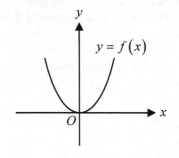

Figure 7

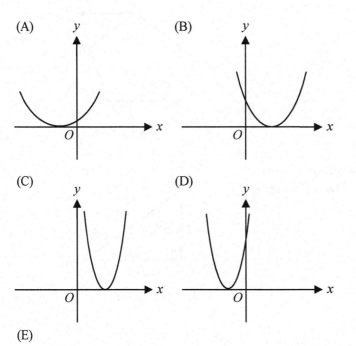

GO ON TO THE NEXT PAGE

MATHEMATICS LEVEL 1 TEST - *Continued*

USE THIS SPACE FOR SCRATCHWORK.

33. If n is a positive integer, which of the following must be true?

    I. $\sqrt{n}$ is a rational number.
    II. $\sqrt{n}$ is an integer.
    III. n^2 is a rational number.

(A) I only
(B) II only
(C) III only
(D) I and II only
(E) I, II, and III

34. $\dfrac{(n-1)!}{(n-3)!} =$

(A) n^2

(B) $n(n-1)$

(C) $n^2 - n + 2$

(D) $n^2 - 3n + 2$

(E) $n^2 - 5n - 2$

35. Merlyn walks at 5 miles per hour and runs at 8 miles per hour. If she can save 10 minutes by running instead of walking from home to her school, what is the distance from her home to school, in miles?

(A) 0.75
(B) 0.84
(C) 1.25
(D) 2.22
(E) 2.50

36. The average age of the students in both group A and group B is 15 years. If the average age of the students in group A is 12 years and the average age of the students in group B is 18, what is the ratio of the number of students in group A to the number of the students in group B?

(A) 1:1   (B) 1:2   (C) 2:3   (D) 2:5   (E) 3:5

GO ON TO THE NEXT PAGE

MATHEMATICS LEVEL 1 TEST - *Continued*

USE THIS SPACE FOR SCRATCHWORK.

37. If one of the roots of the quadratic equation
$x^2 - kx + 7 = 0$ is $3 - \sqrt{2}$, what is the value of k ?

(A) 2   (B) 3   (C) 4   (D) 6   (E) 8

38. In Figure 8, the circle with center $(5, 5)$ is tangent to
the x- and y-axis. If the equation of line ℓ is $y = 8$,
what are the x-coordinates of the points of intersection of
the line and the circle?

(A) 4 and 6
(B) 3 and 7
(C) 2 and 8
(D) 1 and 9
(E) 2.5 and 7.5

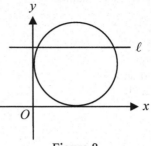

Figure 8

39. Segments CN and BM are the medians of triangle
ABC shown in Figure 9. If $BM = 15$, what is the length
of $\overline{EM}$?

(A) 3
(B) 5
(C) 8
(D) 10
(E) 12

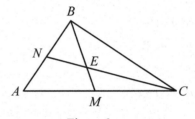

Figure 9

40. In Figure 10, $D, E,$ and F are the midpoints of
$\overline{AB}, \overline{BC}$, and $\overline{CA}$ respectively. If the area of $\triangle ABC$ is
64, which of the following is the area of $\triangle DEF$?

(A) 32
(B) 16
(C) 12
(D) 8
(E) 4

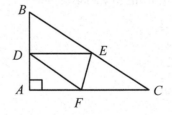

Figure 10

Note: Figure not drawn to scale.

GO ON TO THE NEXT PAGE

MATHEMATICS LEVEL 1 TEST - *Continued*

USE THIS SPACE FOR SCRATCHWORK.

41. If the shift of the graph of $y = x^2$ results in the graph of
$y = x^2 + 2x - 3$, which of the following is true?

(A) Left 2 units and down 3 units
(B) Right 2 units and down 3 units
(C) Left 1 unit and up 3 units
(D) Left 1 unit and down 4 units
(E) Left 1 unit and up 4 units

42. If the function $f(x) = -x^2 - 2x + 3$ is defined for
$-2 \le x \le 2$, what is the range of f?

(A) $3 \le f(x) \le 4$

(B) $-5 \le f(x) \le 3$

(C) $-5 \le f(x) \le 4$

(D) $-3 \le f(x) \le 5$

(E) $-3 \le f(x) \le 4$

43. If a cube is inscribed in a sphere with radius 5, then what
is the volume of the cube?

(A) 125
(B) 192.45
(C) 225
(D) 278.58
(E) 325

44. The value of $(\cos\theta + \sin\theta)^2 - 2\sin\theta\cos\theta$?

(A) 0
(B) $\sin\theta$
(C) $\cos\theta$
(D) 1
(E) 2

GO ON TO THE NEXT PAGE

USE THIS SPACE FOR SCRATCHWORK.

45. If a principal of $1000 is invested at 5% annual interest, what is the amount gained after 10 years if the interest is compounded quarterly?

   (A) 1643.62
   (B) 1865.28
   (C) 2025.56
   (D) 2125.85
   (E) 2200.02

46. Which of the following could be the graph of

   $f(x) = \dfrac{|x|}{x}$?

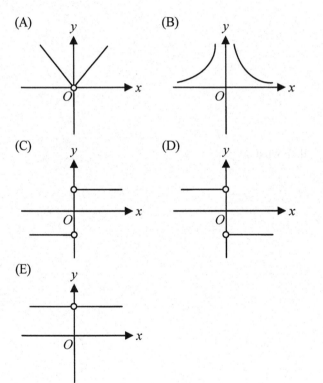

GO ON TO THE NEXT PAGE

USE THIS SPACE FOR SCRATCHWORK.

47.   A triangular patio is made of bricks shown in Figure 11.
      The first row has one brick and the second row has 3
      bricks, and so on. If the 20th row is the bottommost row,
      how many bricks are used in the patio?

      (A) 100
      (B) 200
      (C) 300
      (D) 400
      (E) 500

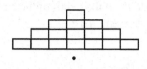

Figure 11

48.   If $f(x) = \sqrt{x-10}$ and $f^{-1}(x)$ is the inverse of f, then
      what is the domain of f^{-1}?

      (A) $x \leq 10$
      (B) $x = 10$
      (C) $0 \leq x \leq 10$
      (D) $x \geq 0$
      (E) $x \geq 10$

49.   In the rectangular box shown in Figure 12, if $AB = 12$,
      $BC = 4$, and $CD = 3$, what is the value of $\sin \angle BAD$?

      (A) $\dfrac{2}{5}$

      (B) $\dfrac{3}{5}$

      (C) $\dfrac{5}{13}$

      (D) $\dfrac{12}{13}$

      (E) $\dfrac{21}{25}$

Figure 12

GO ON TO THE NEXT PAGE

MATHEMATICS LEVEL 1 TEST - *Continued*

USE THIS SPACE FOR SCRATCHWORK.

50. In Figure 13, two identical circles are inscribed in square $ABCD$. If the radius of the circle is 10, what is the length of segment AB?

(A) 25

(B) $10 + 2\sqrt{10}$

(C) $20 + 10\sqrt{2}$

(D) $20 + 20\sqrt{2}$

(E) $30 + 5\sqrt{2}$

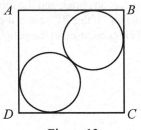

Figure 13

STOP
IF YOU FINISH BEFORE TIME IS CALLED, YOU MAY CHECK YOUR WORK ON THIS TEST ONLY.
DO NOT TURN TO ANY OTHER TEST IN THIS BOOK.

NO MATERIAL ON THIS PAGE

NO MATERIAL ON THIS PAGE

#	answer	#	answer	#	answer	#	answer	#	answer
1	C	11	D	21	D	31	A	41	D
2	D	12	B	22	A	32	D	42	C
3	B	13	C	23	A	33	C	43	B
4	E	14	E	24	B	34	D	44	D
5	D	15	A	25	D	35	D	45	A
6	E	16	B	26	C	36	A	46	C
7	C	17	D	27	B	37	D	47	D
8	C	18	D	28	E	38	D	48	D
9	A	19	D	29	C	39	B	49	C
10	A	20	E	30	E	40	B	50	C

Explanations: TEST 7

1. **(C)** Since $f(1) = 1 - k + 2 = 5 \implies k = -2$, then $f(x) = x^2 + 2x + 2$.

   $\therefore f(-1) = 1 - 2 + 2 = 1$

2. **(D)** $\dfrac{5(2+\sqrt{3}) - 5(2-\sqrt{3})}{(2-\sqrt{3})(2+\sqrt{3})} = \dfrac{10\sqrt{3}}{1}$

3. **(B)** $x^2 - 4y^2 = (x+2y)(x-2y) = 5 \times 4 = 20$

4. **(E)** Since $\dfrac{\pi r^2}{2} = 3\pi \implies r^2 = 6 \implies r = \sqrt{6}$ and a half of the circumference $\dfrac{2\pi r}{2} = \pi\sqrt{6}$, then

   the perimeter is $P = 4(\sqrt{6}) + \pi\sqrt{6} = (4+\pi)\sqrt{6}$.

5. **(D)** $2x + 3y + 3 = 0 \implies y = -\dfrac{2}{3}x - 1$

6. **(E)** $k(k^2 - 8) - k = 0 \implies k(k^2 - 9) = 0 \implies k(k+3)(k-3) = 0 \implies k = 0, 3, -3$

7. **(C)** $2^{2x-3} = 2^{2(2x-3)} \implies 2x - 3 = 4x - 6 \implies 2x = 3 \implies x = \dfrac{3}{2}$

8. **(C)** Linear equation: slope = rate

9. **(A)** $8 = \dfrac{1}{x^3} - 1 \implies x^3 = \dfrac{1}{9} \implies x = \left(\dfrac{1}{9}\right)^{\frac{1}{3}} \cong 0.48$

10. **(A)** $\quad \dfrac{1}{k} \times \dfrac{1}{k} = \dfrac{1}{k^2} = k^{-2}$

11. **(D)** $\quad P = 50\left(\dfrac{1}{2}\right)^{\frac{t}{5}} = 50\left(\dfrac{1}{2}\right)^{\frac{20}{5}} \cong 3.125$

12. **(B)** $\quad y = -x^2 + 10x$, Axis of symmetry: $x = \dfrac{-10}{2(-1)} = 5$

$\qquad f(5) = -25 + 50 = 25$

13. **(C)** $\quad BD = 10\sin\alpha = 10 \times 0.4 = 4$ and $\sin\beta = \dfrac{4}{CD}$

$\qquad CD = \dfrac{4}{\sin\beta} = \dfrac{4}{0.5} = 8$

14. **(E)** $\quad \sqrt{\dfrac{2x^2}{100} - \dfrac{x^2}{100}} = \sqrt{\dfrac{x^2}{100}} = \dfrac{|x|}{10}$

15. **(A)** $\quad$ Proportion: $\dfrac{1.3}{3} = \dfrac{x}{80} \implies x = \dfrac{1.3 \times 80}{3} \cong 34.67$

16. **(B)** $\quad$ Since $\sin k = \dfrac{4}{10}$, then $\tan k = \dfrac{2}{\sqrt{21}}$.

$\qquad$ Therefore, $x = \dfrac{200}{\tan k} = \dfrac{200}{\dfrac{2}{\sqrt{21}}} = 100\sqrt{21} \cong 458$.

17. **(D)** $\quad$ If $\cos x = -1$, the equation is undefined. $\tan 180 = -1$

18. **(D)** $\quad$ Let $y = ax^2 + 2$. For $(1, 4) \implies 4 = a + 2 \implies a = 2$

$\qquad \therefore y = 2x^2 + 2$

19. **(D)** $\quad 15\left(\dfrac{x}{3} + \dfrac{x}{5}\right) = 15\left(\dfrac{1}{3}\right) \implies 8x = 5 \implies x = \dfrac{5}{8}$

20. **(E)** $\quad |2x - 1| < 5 \implies -5 < 2x - 1 < 5 \implies -2 < x < 3$

21. **(D)** $\quad \log_3(9x^2) - \log_3 x = 3 \implies \log_3\left(\dfrac{9x^2}{x}\right) = \log_3 9x = 3$

$\qquad \therefore 9x = 3^3 = 27 \implies x = 3$

22. (A)   For $(2, 12)$: $12 = ab^2$, For $(5, 96)$: $96 = ab^5$

Therefore, $\dfrac{96}{12} = \dfrac{ab^5}{ab^2} = b^3 \;\Rightarrow\; 8 = b^3 \;\Rightarrow\; b = 2$

23. (A) $\dfrac{1-i}{1+i} = \dfrac{(1-i)(1-i)}{(1+i)(1-i)} = -i$, $a + bi = 0 + (-i) \;\Rightarrow\; a = 0$ and $b = -1$

24. (B)   Inverse f^{-1} : $x = \dfrac{2y+1}{y-1}$ where $y = f^{-1}$.

Substitution: $-3 = \dfrac{2y+1}{y-1} \;\Rightarrow\; y = \dfrac{2}{5}$

25. (D) $k * 2 = k^2 - k = 12 \;\Rightarrow\; k^2 - k - 12 = 0 \;\Rightarrow\; (k-4)(k+3) = 0 \;\Rightarrow\; k = 4, -3$

$\therefore k = 4 \ (k > 0)$

26. (C)   Planes are parallel, but the lines in those plane are not always parallel.
Skewed lines:

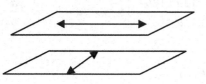

27. (B)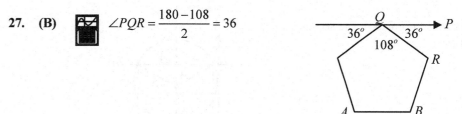

$\angle PQR = \dfrac{180 - 108}{2} = 36$

28. (E)   Pythagorean Theorem:

$(x-2)^2 + (x-1)^2 = x^2 \;\Rightarrow\; x^2 - 6x + 5 = 0 \;\Rightarrow\; (x-5)(x-1) = 0$

$\therefore x = 5 \ (x > 2)$

29. (C)   Slope: $\dfrac{(k-4)-(k+2)}{(k+2)-(-k)} = \dfrac{-6}{2k+2} \;\Rightarrow\; \dfrac{-6}{2k+2} = -1$

Therefore, $k = 2$.

30. (E) $\dfrac{1}{4}x^2 - \dfrac{1}{2}x + 2 = 0 \;\Rightarrow\; x^2 - 2x + 8 = 0$

Discriminant: $D = b^2 - 4ac = 4 - 31 < 0$: Imaginary roots

31. (A)   Let $Y = \dfrac{1}{x}$, then $Y^2 + 3Y - 10 = 0 \;\Rightarrow\; (Y+5)(Y-2) = 0$

$Y = 2 \;\Rightarrow\; \dfrac{1}{x} = 2 \;\Rightarrow\; x = \dfrac{1}{2} = 0.5$, $Y = -5 \;\Rightarrow\; \dfrac{1}{x} = -5 \;\Rightarrow\; x = -\dfrac{1}{5}$ (negative)

32. (D) Shift 2 units to the left and scale 3 (graph will be narrow).

33. (C)   I. $\sqrt{3}$ = irrational
    II. $\sqrt{2}$ is not an integer
    III. n^2 = integer (rational)

34. (D) $\dfrac{(n-1)!}{(n-3)!} = (n-1)(n-2) = n^2 - 3n + 2$

35. (D) D : distance
$$\frac{D}{5} - \frac{D}{8} = \frac{1}{6} \;\Rightarrow\; \frac{3D}{40} = \frac{1}{6} \;\Rightarrow\; D = \frac{40}{18} =\cong 2.22$$

36. (A) A = Sum of ages in group A and B = Sum of ages in group B

a = the number of students in group A and b = the number of students in group B

Therefore, $\dfrac{A}{a} = 12$, $\dfrac{B}{b} = 18$, and $\dfrac{A+B}{a+b} = 15$.

Since $A = 12a$ and $B = 18b$, then $\dfrac{12a+18b}{a+b} = 15 \;\Rightarrow\; a = b \;\Rightarrow\; \dfrac{a}{b} = 1$

37. (D)   Substitution or Vieta's formula:
$$S = \left(3+\sqrt{2}\right)\left(3-\sqrt{2}\right) = k \;\Rightarrow\; k = 6$$

38. (D)   From the graph, the points of intersection are $(1,8)$ and $(9,8)$.

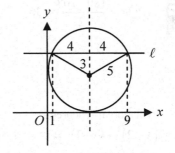

39. (B)   Centroid: $15 \times \dfrac{1}{3} = 5$

40. (B)   Since the ratio of the areas is 1:4, the area of $\triangle DEF = 64 \times \dfrac{1}{4} = 16$.

(The area of $\triangle BDE$ = the area of $\triangle DEF$)

41. (D) $y = x^2 + 2x - 3 \;\Rightarrow\; y = (x+1)^2 - 4$: left one unit and down 4 units

42. (C)   Axis of symmetry: $x = \dfrac{-(-2)}{2(-1)} = -1$

Since $f(-1) = 4$, $f(-2) = 3$, and $f(2) = -5$, the range of $f \;\Rightarrow\; -5 \le y \le 4$.

43. (B) The length of the diagonal of the cube: $\sqrt{x^2+x^2+x^2}=x\sqrt{3}$

$x\sqrt{3}=10 \implies x=\dfrac{10}{\sqrt{3}}$

The volume of the cube: $V=x^3=\left(\dfrac{10}{\sqrt{3}}\right)^3 \cong 192.45$

44. (D) $(\cos\theta+\sin\theta)^2-2\sin\theta\cos\theta=\cos^2\theta+\sin^2\theta+2\sin\theta\cos\theta-2\sin\theta\cos\theta=1$

45. (A) $1000\left(1+\dfrac{0.05}{4}\right)^{40} \cong 1643.62$

46. (C) If $x>0 \implies f(x)=\dfrac{x}{x}=1$

If $x<0 \implies f(x)=\dfrac{-x}{x}=-1$

47. (D) The pattern is as follows.

$S_1=1$, $S_2=1+3$, $S_3=1+3+5$, $\cdots$ $S_{20}=1+3+5+\cdots+39$ $\because a_{20}=1+(20-1)2=39$

Therefore, $S_{20}=\dfrac{20(1+39)}{2}=400$.

48. (D) Domain of $f:$ $x\ge 0$, Range of $f:$ $y\ge 0$
Therefore,
Domain of f^{-1} is the range of f . $\therefore x\ge 0$
Or use graph.

49. (C) $AB=12, BD=5, AD=13$, and $\angle ABD=90^o$

$\therefore \sin\angle BAD=\dfrac{5}{13}$

50 (C) $\triangle EFG$ is isosceles and $EF=\dfrac{20}{\sqrt{2}}=10\sqrt{2}$

$\therefore AB=10+10\sqrt{2}+10=20+10\sqrt{2}$

END

NO MATERIAL ON THIS PAGE

Dr. John Chung's SAT II

Math Level 1

Test 8

MATHEMATICS LEVEL 1 TEST

TEST 8

REFERENCE INFORMATION

THE FOLLOWING INFORMATION IS FOR YOUR REFERENCE IN ANSWERING SOME OF THE QUESTIONS IN THIS TEST

Volume of a right circular cone with radius r and height h: $V = \dfrac{1}{3}\pi r^2 h$

Lateral Area of a right circular cone with circumference of the base c and slant height ℓ: $S = \dfrac{1}{2}c\ell$

Volume of a sphere with radius r: $V = \dfrac{4}{3}\pi r^3$

Surface Area of a sphere with radius r: $S = 4\pi r^2$

Volume of a pyramid with base area B and height h: $V = \dfrac{1}{3}Bh$

Dr. John Chung's SAT II Math Level 1

Answer Sheet

1	Ⓐ Ⓑ Ⓒ Ⓓ Ⓔ	26	Ⓐ Ⓑ Ⓒ Ⓓ Ⓔ
2	Ⓐ Ⓑ Ⓒ Ⓓ Ⓔ	27	Ⓐ Ⓑ Ⓒ Ⓓ Ⓔ
3	Ⓐ Ⓑ Ⓒ Ⓓ Ⓔ	28	Ⓐ Ⓑ Ⓒ Ⓓ Ⓔ
4	Ⓐ Ⓑ Ⓒ Ⓓ Ⓔ	29	Ⓐ Ⓑ Ⓒ Ⓓ Ⓔ
5	Ⓐ Ⓑ Ⓒ Ⓓ Ⓔ	30	Ⓐ Ⓑ Ⓒ Ⓓ Ⓔ
6	Ⓐ Ⓑ Ⓒ Ⓓ Ⓔ	31	Ⓐ Ⓑ Ⓒ Ⓓ Ⓔ
7	Ⓐ Ⓑ Ⓒ Ⓓ Ⓔ	32	Ⓐ Ⓑ Ⓒ Ⓓ Ⓔ
8	Ⓐ Ⓑ Ⓒ Ⓓ Ⓔ	33	Ⓐ Ⓑ Ⓒ Ⓓ Ⓔ
9	Ⓐ Ⓑ Ⓒ Ⓓ Ⓔ	34	Ⓐ Ⓑ Ⓒ Ⓓ Ⓔ
10	Ⓐ Ⓑ Ⓒ Ⓓ Ⓔ	35	Ⓐ Ⓑ Ⓒ Ⓓ Ⓔ
11	Ⓐ Ⓑ Ⓒ Ⓓ Ⓔ	36	Ⓐ Ⓑ Ⓒ Ⓓ Ⓔ
12	Ⓐ Ⓑ Ⓒ Ⓓ Ⓔ	37	Ⓐ Ⓑ Ⓒ Ⓓ Ⓔ
13	Ⓐ Ⓑ Ⓒ Ⓓ Ⓔ	38	Ⓐ Ⓑ Ⓒ Ⓓ Ⓔ
14	Ⓐ Ⓑ Ⓒ Ⓓ Ⓔ	39	Ⓐ Ⓑ Ⓒ Ⓓ Ⓔ
15	Ⓐ Ⓑ Ⓒ Ⓓ Ⓔ	40	Ⓐ Ⓑ Ⓒ Ⓓ Ⓔ
16	Ⓐ Ⓑ Ⓒ Ⓓ Ⓔ	41	Ⓐ Ⓑ Ⓒ Ⓓ Ⓔ
17	Ⓐ Ⓑ Ⓒ Ⓓ Ⓔ	42	Ⓐ Ⓑ Ⓒ Ⓓ Ⓔ
18	Ⓐ Ⓑ Ⓒ Ⓓ Ⓔ	43	Ⓐ Ⓑ Ⓒ Ⓓ Ⓔ
19	Ⓐ Ⓑ Ⓒ Ⓓ Ⓔ	44	Ⓐ Ⓑ Ⓒ Ⓓ Ⓔ
20	Ⓐ Ⓑ Ⓒ Ⓓ Ⓔ	45	Ⓐ Ⓑ Ⓒ Ⓓ Ⓔ
21	Ⓐ Ⓑ Ⓒ Ⓓ Ⓔ	46	Ⓐ Ⓑ Ⓒ Ⓓ Ⓔ
22	Ⓐ Ⓑ Ⓒ Ⓓ Ⓔ	47	Ⓐ Ⓑ Ⓒ Ⓓ Ⓔ
23	Ⓐ Ⓑ Ⓒ Ⓓ Ⓔ	48	Ⓐ Ⓑ Ⓒ Ⓓ Ⓔ
24	Ⓐ Ⓑ Ⓒ Ⓓ Ⓔ	49	Ⓐ Ⓑ Ⓒ Ⓓ Ⓔ
25	Ⓐ Ⓑ Ⓒ Ⓓ Ⓔ	50	Ⓐ Ⓑ Ⓒ Ⓓ Ⓔ

The number of right answers :

The number of wrong answers :

$$\boxed{} - \frac{1}{4} \times \boxed{} = \boxed{}$$

\# of correct   \# of wrong   Raw score

Score Conversion Table

Raw Score	Scaled Score	Raw Score	Scaled Score	Raw Score	Scaled Score
50	800	28	630	6	480
49	800	27	620	5	470
48	800	26	610	4	470
47	800	25	600	3	460
46	790	24	590	2	460
45	780	23	580	1	450
44	770	22	570	0	450
43	760	21	550		
42	750	20	540		
41	740	19	530		
40	740	18	520		
39	730	17	510		
38	720	16	500		
37	710	15	490		
36	710	14	480		
35	700	13	470		
34	690	12	460		
33	680	11	450		
32	670	10	440		
31	660	9	430		
30	650	8	420		
29	640	7	410		

MATHEMATICS LEVEL 1 TEST

For each of the following problems, decide which is the BEST of the choices given. If the exact numerical value is not one of the choices, select the choice that best approximates this value. Then fill in the corresponding circle on the answer sheet.

Notes: (1) A scientific or graphing calculator will be necessary for answering some (but not all) of the questions in this test. For each question you will have to decide whether or not you should use a calculator.

(2) For some questions in this test you may have to decide whether your calculator should be in the radian mode or the degree mode.

(3) Figures that accompany problems in this test are intended to provide information useful in solving the problems. They are drawn as accurately as possible EXCEPT when it is stated in a specific problem that its figure is not drawn to scale. All figures lie in a plane unless otherwise indicated.

(4) Unless otherwise specified, the domain of any function f is assumed to be the set of all real numbers x for which $f(x)$ is a real number. The range of f is assumed to be the set of all real numbers $f(x)$, where x is in the domain of f.

(5) Reference information that may be useful in answering the questions in this test can be found on the page preceding Question 1.

USE THIS SPACE FOR SCRATCHWORK.

1. If $f(x) = |x-1| + |x-5|$, what is the value of $f(3)$?

   (A) -4
   (B) 0
   (C) 2
   (D) 4
   (E) 8

2. If $4x + 12 = \dfrac{k}{2}(x+3)$ for all x, then $k =$

   (A) 2
   (B) 4
   (C) 8
   (D) 12
   (E) 16

GO ON TO THE NEXT PAGE

MATHEMATICS LEVEL 1 TEST - *Continued*

USE THIS SPACE FOR SCRATCHWORK.

3. For all $x \neq 0$, $\dfrac{x - \dfrac{1}{x}}{\dfrac{1}{x}} =$

(A) $x - 1$
(B) $x^2 - 1$
(C) $1 - x$
(D) $1 - x^2$
(E) $x^3 - x$

4. If $f(x) = \dfrac{x-1}{2}$ and $g(x) = x + 2$, then

$f(g(1)) - g(f(1)) =$

(A) 3
(B) 2
(C) 1
(D) 0
(E) -1

5. What is the image of point $(5, 7)$ over a reflection of the line $x = -2$?

(A) $(-9, 7)$

(B) $(3, 7)$

(C) $(5, -9)$

(D) $(5, -11)$

(E) $(7, -11)$

6. In triangle PQR in Figure 1, $RP = 7$, and $PQ = 25$.
What is the value of $\sec \angle Q$?

(A) 0.96
(B) 1.04
(C) 1.25
(D) 1.36
(E) 1.68

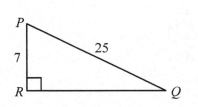

Figure 1

GO ON TO THE NEXT PAGE

MATHEMATICS LEVEL 1 TEST - *Continued*

USE THIS SPACE FOR SCRATCHWORK.

7.   In Figure 2, if $\ell \parallel m$, what is the value of $x + y$?

(A) 150
(B) 160
(C) 170
(D) 180
(E) 190

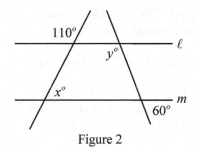

Figure 2

8.   If $2^{x+4} = 12$, then $4(2^x) =$

(A) 2   (B) 3   (C) 6   (D) 12   (E) 24

9.   If $\log_3 a$ is 25% of $\log_3 b$, then what is b in terms of a ?

(A) $\dfrac{a}{4}$ (B) $\dfrac{a}{3}$ (C) a^2 (D) a^4 (E) $4a$

10.   In trapezoid $ABCD$ in Figure 3, $AB = 4$, $BC = 4$, and $\angle BCD = 135^o$. What is the area of the trapezoid?

(A) 36
(B) 32
(C) 24
(D) 18
(E) 16

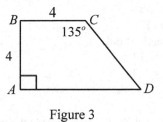

Figure 3

11. $\log_5 25\sqrt{5} =$

(A) 1.5   (B) 2   (C) 2.5   (D) 4   (E) 5

12.   In Figure 4, $AB = BC$, $\angle BAD = 50^o$, and $\angle ABC$ is 50° more than $\angle CBD$. Which of the following is the value of $\angle BDA$?

(A) 20° (B) 25° (C) 30° (D) 45° (E) 60°

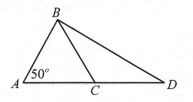

Figure 4

Note: Figure not drawn to scale.

GO ON TO THE NEXT PAGE

USE THIS SPACE FOR SCRATCHWORK.

13. In triangle ABC, if $AB = 5$ and $BC = 10$, what is the smallest integer value of CA?

    (A) 3   (B) 4   (C) 5   (D) 6   (E) 14

14. If the multiplicative inverse of $3 - 4i$ is $a + bi$, what is the value of $a + b$?

    (A) $\dfrac{7}{25}$ (B) $\dfrac{3}{4}$ (C) $\dfrac{4}{3}$ (D) 3   (E) 5

15. In Figure 5, if the area of isosceles trapezoid $OPQR$ is 128 square units, what is the value of a?

    (A) 8   (B) 10   (C) 12   (D) 14   (E) 16

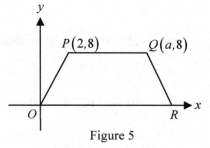

Figure 5

<u>Note</u>: Figure not drawn to scale.

16. For what value(s) of x is the expression $x\left(x^2 - 1\right)^{-2}$ undefined?

    (A) 0 only
    (B) 1 only
    (C) 1 and -1 only
    (D) 0 and 1 only
    (E) 0, 1, -1

17. Which of the following is not in the range of $y = 2^x - 3$?

    (A) 3   (B) 2   (C) -1 (D) -2 (E) -3

18. If $a^{\frac{3}{5}} - 10 = 17$, what is the value of a?

    (A) 9
    (B) 27
    (C) 81
    (D) 243
    (E) 729

GO ON TO THE NEXT PAGE ⟩

MATHEMATICS LEVEL 1 TEST - *Continued*

USE THIS SPACE FOR SCRATCHWORK.

19. What are all values of x for which $\left|5 - \dfrac{x}{3}\right| \le 4$?

    (A) $x \le -4$ or $x \ge 4$
    (B) $x < -9$ or $x \ge 9$
    (C) $x \le 9$ or $x \ge 15$
    (D) $1 \le x \le 9$
    (E) $3 \le x \le 27$

20. If the line $y = mx + b$ is perpendicular to the line $2x - y = 12$ and passes through the point $(1, 4)$, what is the value of b ?

    (A) $\dfrac{9}{2}$ (B) 4 (C) $\dfrac{7}{2}$ (D) 3 (E) $\dfrac{5}{2}$

21. In circle O shown in Figure 6, the area of $\triangle ABC$ is 10. What is the area of circle O ?

    (A) 27
    (B) 31.4
    (C) 36.3
    (D) 40.5
    (E) 62.8

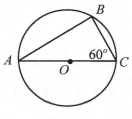

Figure 6

22. If the circumference of a circle is twice the perimeter of a square, what is the ratio of the area of the circle to the area of the square?

    (A) $2 : 1$
    (B) $4 : \pi$
    (C) $16 : \pi$
    (D) $4\pi : 3$
    (E) $25 : 9$

GO ON TO THE NEXT PAGE

USE THIS SPACE FOR SCRATCHWORK.

23. In Figure 7, $\triangle ABC$ is equilateral and $\overline{EF} \parallel \overline{DG} \parallel \overline{AC}$.
If $AD = 2$, $DE = 4$, and $BE = 2$, then what is the area of quadrilateral $DEFG$?

(A) 4
(B) 6
(C) $6\sqrt{3}$
(D) $8\sqrt{3}$
(E) $16\sqrt{3}$

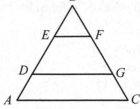

Figure 7

24. A projectile is fired from ground level shown in Figure 8. If the height is defined by $h(t) = 160t - 16t^2$ feet after t seconds, how long does the projectile stay higher than 336 feet, in seconds?

(A) 3
(B) 4
(C) 5
(D) 6
(E) 10

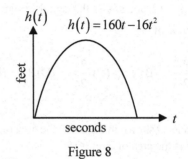

Figure 8

Note: Figure not drawn to scale.

25. If $i = \sqrt{-1}$, what is the value of $(1 - i)^4$?

(A) -4
(B) -2
(C) -1
(D) 2
(E) 4

26. If the first three positive numbers x, $x + 4$, and $3x + 4$ form a geometric progression in which $x > 0$, what is the fourth term?

(A) 8
(B) 12
(C) 16
(D) 24
(E) 32

GO ON TO THE NEXT PAGE

MATHEMATICS LEVEL 1 TEST - *Continued*

USE THIS SPACE FOR SCRATCHWORK.

27. If a square pyramid has a base that measures 10 feet on a side and an altitude of 12 feet, which of the following is the total surface area of the pyramid?

(A) 120
(B) 240
(C) 360
(D) 480
(E) 600

28. In Figure 9, a circle with radius 5 is tangent to the *x*- and *y*-axis. If line ℓ is tangent to the circle and passes through point $(-7, 0)$, what is the length of $\overline{PQ}$?

(A) 10
(B) 12
(C) 13
(D) 14.5
(E) 16

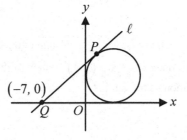

Figure 9

29. In Figure 10, what is the value of x ?

(A) 5
(B) 6
(C) 7
(D) 8
(E) 9

Figure 10

Note: Figure not drawn to scale.

30. If the diagonals of a parallelogram are congruent, then the parallelogram is

(A) a rectangle
(B) a square
(C) a rhombus
(D) a trapezoid
(E) an isosceles trapezoid

31. If the measure of angles in a quadrilateral are in the ratio 3:4:5:6, which of the following cannot be the measure of an exterior angle of the quadrilateral?

(A) 120° (B) 100° (C) 80° (D) 60° (E) 40°

GO ON TO THE NEXT PAGE

MATHEMATICS LEVEL 1 TEST - *Continued*

USE THIS SPACE FOR SCRATCHWORK.

32. If the coordinates of the turning point of the graph of $y = x^2 + px + q$ are $(-2, 8)$, what are the values of p and q?

(A) $p = 2, q = 10$
(B) $p = 2, q = 12$
(C) $p = 4, q = 10$
(D) $p = 4, q = 12$
(E) $p = -2, q = 10$

33. A circle has a center $(-2, 3)$ and diameter $\overline{AB}$. If the coordinates of A are $(1, 7)$, which of the following is the equation of the circle?

(A) $x^2 + y^2 = 5$
(B) $(x-2)^2 + (y+3)^2 = 5$
(C) $(x+2)^2 + (y-3)^2 = 5$
(D) $(x+2)^2 + (y-3)^2 = 25$
(E) $(x+2)^2 + (y-3)^2 = 36$

34. If $f(x) = 5x - 3$ and $g(x) = \sqrt[3]{x^2}$, then $f(g(-8)) =$

(A) –23   (B) –13   (C) 13   (D) 17   (E) 24

35. If the roots of the equation $x^2 - 4x + k = 0$ are a and b such that $b = 3a$, what is the value of k?

(A) $\dfrac{1}{3}$ (B) 2   (C) 3   (D) $\dfrac{9}{2}$ (E) $\dfrac{13}{3}$

36. What is the period of the graph of the equation $y = 5\tan\dfrac{x}{3}$, in degrees?

(A) 60   (B) 120   (C) 240   (D) 360   (E) 540

GO ON TO THE NEXT PAGE

MATHEMATICS LEVEL 1 TEST - *Continued*

USE THIS SPACE FOR SCRATCHWORK.

37. If the radius of a sphere decreases by 20% , by what percent of the volume of the sphere is decreased?

(A) 20.4
(B) 40.2
(C) 48.8
(D) 51.2
(E) 60.6

38. In how many ways can the letters of the word CAREER be rearranged ?

(A) 60   (B) 120   (C) 180   (D) 360   (E) 720

39. A line with equation $y = x$ and a circle are graphed in Figure 11. What is the length of $\overline{OP}$?

(A) 10.5
(B) 10.8
(C) 11.3
(D) 11.8
(E) 12.1

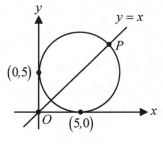

Figure 11

40. If $\dfrac{1}{x^2 - 4} = \dfrac{a}{x-2} - \dfrac{b}{x+2}$, then $a =$

(A) 4   (B) 2   (C) $\dfrac{1}{2}$ (D) $\dfrac{1}{4}$ (E) $\dfrac{1}{8}$

41. In Figure 12, the radius of the top circle is 1 and the radius of the bottom circle is 4. If $AC = BD = 5$, what is the length of $\overline{BC}$?

(A) 6.1
(B) 6.4
(C) 7.2
(D) 7.5
(E) 8.4

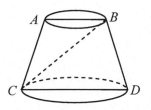

Figure 12

Note: Figure not drawn to scale.

GO ON TO THE NEXT PAGE

MATHEMATICS LEVEL 1 TEST - *Continued*

USE THIS SPACE FOR SCRATCHWORK.

42. Which of the following could be not true?

    (A) All equilateral triangles are similar.
    (B) All squares are similar.
    (C) All regular pentagons are similar.
    (D) All rectangles are similar.
    (E) All circles are similar.

43. Which of the following is equivalent to the statement " If $x = 3$, then $x^2 = 9$ " ?

    (A) If $x \neq 3$, then $x^2 \neq 9$.
    (B) If $x \neq 3$, then $x^2 > 9$.
    (C) If $x^2 = 9$, then $x = 3$.
    (D) If $x^2 \neq 9$, then $x \neq -3$.
    (E) If $x^2 \neq 9$, then $x \neq 3$.

44. In Figure 13, $\ell \parallel m$, $\overline{AC}$ is the angle bisector of $\angle BAD$, and $\overline{CD}$ is the angle bisector of $\angle ADE$. What is the measure of $\angle ACD$?

    (A) 30°
    (B) 45°
    (C) 60°
    (D) 75°
    (E) 90°

Figure 13
Note: Figure not drawn to scale.

45. If $4^x - 2^x = 6$, what is the value of x ?

    (A) 1
    (B) $\log_2 3$
    (C) $\log 5$
    (D) 2
    (E) 5

46. If $2x^2 - 4x + 7 = 2(x-a)^2 + b$, what is the value of b ?

    (A) 2   (B) 3   (C) 4   (D) 5   (E) 7

MATHEMATICS LEVEL 1 TEST - *Continued*

USE THIS SPACE FOR SCRATCHWORK.

47. Alex painted one-third of his house in three hours and his brother Kevin took over and finished the job in 5 hours. If they both paint the entire house working together, how long would it take, in hours?

 (A) 3   (B) 3.51   (C) 4.09   (D) 5.63   (E) 6

48. A solution is made by mixing concentrate with water. How many gallons of acid must be added to 40 gallons of a 20% acid solution to get a 50% acid solution?

 (A) 24   (B) 18   (C) 12   (D) 10   (E) 8

49. Figure 14 shows the graph of $f(x) = 3|x - 5| - 6$. What is the area of the shaded region?

 (A) 3
 (B) 6
 (C) 12
 (D) 18
 (E) 24

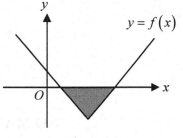

Figure 14

50. Figure 15 shows the graph of $y = f(x)$. What is the length of $\overline{PQ}$?

 (A) 4
 (B) 8
 (C) $2\sqrt{11}$
 (D) $4\sqrt{10}$
 (E) 9.5

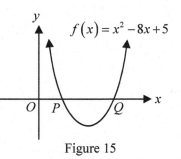

Figure 15

STOP

**IF YOU FINISH BEFORE TIME IS CALLED, YOU MAY CHECK YOUR WORK ON THIS TEST ONLY.
DO NOT TURN TO ANY OTHER TEST IN THIS BOOK.**

NO MATERIAL ON THIS PAGE

TEST 8   ANSWERS

#	answer	#	answer	#	answer	#	answer	#	answer
1	D	11	C	21	C	31	E	41	B
2	C	12	A	22	C	32	D	42	D
3	B	13	D	23	D	33	D	43	E
4	E	14	A	24	B	34	D	44	E
5	A	15	E	25	A	35	C	45	B
6	B	16	C	26	E	36	E	46	D
7	E	17	E	27	C	37	C	47	C
8	B	18	D	28	B	38	C	48	A
9	D	19	E	29	C	39	E	49	C
10	C	20	A	30	A	40	D	50	C

Explanations: Test 8

1.   **(D)** $f(3) = |3-1| + |3-5| = 2 + 2 = 4$

2.   **(C)** $4x + 12 = \dfrac{k}{3}(x+3) \implies 4(x+3) = \dfrac{k}{3}(x+3) \implies 4 = \dfrac{k}{3} \implies k = 12$

3.   **(B)** $\dfrac{\left(x - \dfrac{1}{x}\right)x}{\left(\dfrac{1}{x}\right)x} = \dfrac{x^2 - 1}{1} = x^2 - 1$

4.   **(E)**   Since $g(1) = 3$ and $f(1) = 0$,

                 $f\big(g(1)\big) - g\big(f(1)\big) = f(3) - g(0) = 1 - 2 = -1$

5.   **(A)** $(5,7) \xrightarrow{\;r_{x=-2}\;} (-9, 7)$

6.   **(B)** $RQ = 24$, $\sec \angle Q = \dfrac{hyp}{adj} = \dfrac{25}{24} \cong 1.04$

7.   **(E)**   Vertical angle: $x + y = 360 - (110 + 60) = 190$

8.   **(B)** $2^{x+4} = 12 \implies 16 \cdot 2^x = 12 \implies 2^x = \dfrac{12}{16} = \dfrac{3}{4}$

                 $\therefore 4(2^x) = 4\left(\dfrac{3}{4}\right) = 3$

9.   **(D)** $\log_3 a = \dfrac{1}{4}(\log_3 b) \implies \log_3 b = 4\log_3 a \implies b = a^4$

10. (C) $AD = 8$ and $CE = 4$

The area of the trapezoid is

$$\frac{(4+8)4}{2} = 24$$

11. (C) $\log_5 25\sqrt{5} = \log_5 5^{\frac{5}{2}} = \frac{5}{2}\log_5 5 = \frac{5}{2}$

12. (A) $\angle CBD = 80 - 50 = 30$ and $\angle BCD = 130$

$\therefore \angle BDA = 20^o$

13. (D) Triangular inequality:

$10 - 5 < CA < 10 + 5 \implies 5 < CA < 15 \implies$ The smallest integer is 6.

14. (A) Multiplicative inverse:

$$\frac{1}{3-4i} = a + bi \implies \frac{1(3+4i)}{(3-4i)(3+4i)} = \frac{3}{25} + \frac{4}{25}i$$

Therefore, $a + b = \frac{3}{25} + \frac{3}{25} + \frac{4}{25} = \frac{7}{25}$.

15. (E) Because $OR = a + 2$ and $PQ = a - 2$,

The area of the trapezoid is

$$\frac{(a-2+a+2)8}{2} = 128 \implies 8a = 128$$

$\therefore a = 16$

16. (C) $x(x^2 - 1)^{-2} = \frac{x}{(x^2-1)^2} \implies x = 1 \text{ or } -1$

17. (E) The range of f is $y > -3$.

18. (D) $a^{\frac{3}{5}} - 10 = 17 \implies a^{\frac{3}{5}} = 27 \implies \left(5^{\frac{3}{5}}\right)^{\frac{5}{3}} = 27^{\frac{5}{3}} = 243$

19. (E) $\left|5 - \frac{x}{3}\right| \le 4 \implies \left|\frac{x}{3} - 5\right| \le 4 \implies -4 \le \frac{x}{3} - 5 \le 4 \implies 1 \le \frac{x}{3} \le 9 \implies 3 \le x \le 27$

20. (A) $2x - y = 12 \implies y = 2x - 12$: slope $= 2$

$m = -\frac{1}{2}$ and the perpendicular line $y = -\frac{1}{2}x + b$.

For $(1, 4)$: $4 = -\frac{1}{2} + b \implies b = \frac{9}{2}$

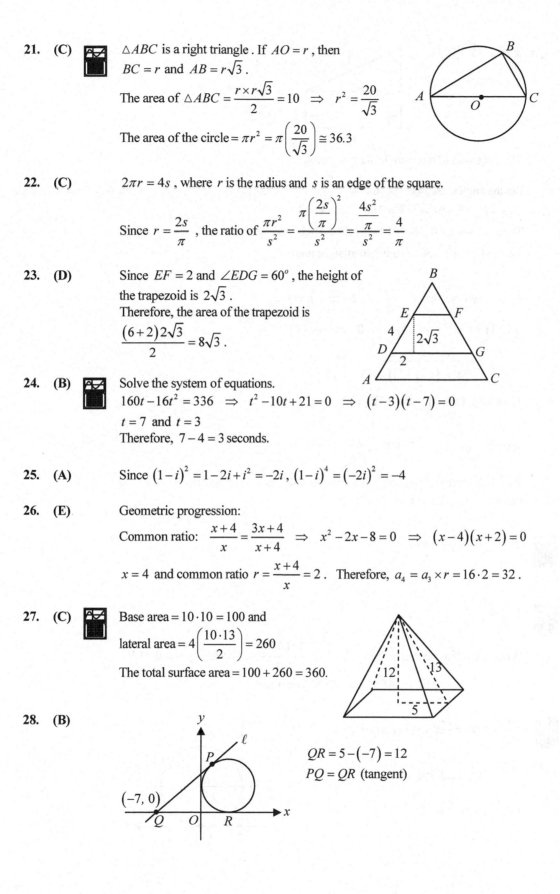

21. (C) $\triangle ABC$ is a right triangle. If $AO = r$, then $BC = r$ and $AB = r\sqrt{3}$.

The area of $\triangle ABC = \dfrac{r \times r\sqrt{3}}{2} = 10 \;\Rightarrow\; r^2 = \dfrac{20}{\sqrt{3}}$

The area of the circle $= \pi r^2 = \pi\left(\dfrac{20}{\sqrt{3}}\right) \cong 36.3$

22. (C) $2\pi r = 4s$, where r is the radius and s is an edge of the square.

Since $r = \dfrac{2s}{\pi}$, the ratio of $\dfrac{\pi r^2}{s^2} = \dfrac{\pi\left(\dfrac{2s}{\pi}\right)^2}{s^2} = \dfrac{\dfrac{4s^2}{\pi}}{s^2} = \dfrac{4}{\pi}$

23. (D) Since $EF = 2$ and $\angle EDG = 60^o$, the height of the trapezoid is $2\sqrt{3}$.
Therefore, the area of the trapezoid is
$\dfrac{(6+2)2\sqrt{3}}{2} = 8\sqrt{3}$.

24. (B) Solve the system of equations.
$160t - 16t^2 = 336 \;\Rightarrow\; t^2 - 10t + 21 = 0 \;\Rightarrow\; (t-3)(t-7) = 0$
$t = 7$ and $t = 3$
Therefore, $7 - 4 = 3$ seconds.

25. (A) Since $(1-i)^2 = 1 - 2i + i^2 = -2i$, $(1-i)^4 = (-2i)^2 = -4$

26. (E) Geometric progression:
Common ratio: $\dfrac{x+4}{x} = \dfrac{3x+4}{x+4} \;\Rightarrow\; x^2 - 2x - 8 = 0 \;\Rightarrow\; (x-4)(x+2) = 0$

$x = 4$ and common ratio $r = \dfrac{x+4}{x} = 2$. Therefore, $a_4 = a_3 \times r = 16 \cdot 2 = 32$.

27. (C) Base area $= 10 \cdot 10 = 100$ and
lateral area $= 4\left(\dfrac{10 \cdot 13}{2}\right) = 260$

The total surface area $= 100 + 260 = 360$.

28. (B) $QR = 5 - (-7) = 12$
$PQ = QR$ (tangent)

29. (C) $\qquad x = 12 - 5 = 7$

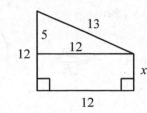

30. (A) The diagonals of a rectangle are congruent.

31. (E) Let the angles: $3k,\ 4k,\ 5k,\ 6k$

$3k + 4k + 5k + 6k = 18k = 360 \quad \Rightarrow \quad k = 20$

The angles are $60^o,\ 80^o,\ 100^o,\ 120^o$. Their exterior angles are

$120^o,\ 100^o,\ 80^o,\ 60^o$ (supplementary angle)

32. (D) Axis of symmetry: $x = \dfrac{-p}{2} = -2 \quad \Rightarrow \quad p = 4$

$f(-2) = (-2)^2 + 4(-2) + q = 8 \quad \Rightarrow \quad q = 12$

33. (D) $r = \sqrt{(7-3)^2 + (1 - (-2))^2} = 5$

Therefore, $(x+2)^2 + (y-3)^2 = 25$.

34. (D) $g(-8) = \sqrt[3]{(-8)^2} = 4$ and $f(4) = 5 \cdot 4 - 3 = 7$

35. (C) Vieta's Formula: $S = a + b = a + 3a = 4a = 4 \quad \Rightarrow \quad a = 1$ and $b = 3$

Product: $P = 3 \times 1 = 3$

36. (E) $P = \dfrac{180}{b} = \dfrac{180}{\dfrac{1}{3}} = 540$

37. (C) $V = \dfrac{4\pi r^3}{3}$

When the radius decreases by 20%, $V' = \dfrac{4\pi (0.8r)^3}{3} = 0.512 \dfrac{4\pi r^3}{3} = 0.512 V$

Therefore, $1 - 0.512 = 0.488 \quad \Rightarrow \quad 48.8\%$ decrease

38. (C) $\dfrac{6!}{2!2!} = 180$ (repetition in permutation)

39. (E) $OR = 5\sqrt{2}$ and $PR = 5$

$OP = 5 + 5\sqrt{2} \cong 12.1$

40. **(D)** $\dfrac{a(x+2)-b(x-2)}{(x-2)(x+2)} = \dfrac{(a-b)x+2a+2b}{(x-2)(x+2)} = \dfrac{1}{x^2-4}$

Therefore, $a-b=0$ and $2a+2b=1$. $\therefore a = \dfrac{1}{4}$

41. **(B)** $BC = \sqrt{4^2+5^2} = \sqrt{41} \cong 6.4$

42. **(D)** All rectangles are not similar.

43. **(E)** Contrapositive: Equivalent

44. **(E)** $2a+2b=180 \Rightarrow a+b=90$

Therefore, the angle $C = 90^o$

45. **(B)** $2^{2x} - 2^x = 6$

Let $Y = 2^x$. $Y^2 - Y - 6 = 0 \Rightarrow (Y-3)(Y+2) = 0 \Rightarrow Y = 3$ and $\cancel{Y=-2}$

$2^x = 3 \Rightarrow x = \log_2 3$

46. **(D)** $2x^2 - 4x + 7 = 2(x-1)^2 + 5 \Rightarrow b = 5$

47. **(C)** Rate: $\dfrac{1}{9} + \dfrac{1}{7.5} = \dfrac{1}{9} + \dfrac{2}{15} = \dfrac{1}{x} \Rightarrow x = \dfrac{45}{11} = 4.09090 \cong 4.09$

48. **(A)** Solute: $0.2 \times 40 = 8$ gallons

If the amount of acid is x, then $\dfrac{8+x}{40+x} = \dfrac{50}{100} \Rightarrow x = 24$

49. **(C)** $3|x-5| - 6 = 0 \Rightarrow x = 3$ and $x = 7$

The area $= \dfrac{4 \times 6}{2} = 12$

50. **(C)** If r and s are the zeros of the equation,

$r+s = 8$ and $rs = 5$.

$PQ^2 = |r-s|^2 = (r+s)^2 - 4rs = 8^2 - 4 \cdot 5 = 44$

Therefore, $PQ = \sqrt{44} = 2\sqrt{11}$.

End

NO MATERIAL ON THIS PAGE

Dr. John Chung's SAT II

Math Level 1

Test 9

MATHEMATICS LEVEL 1 TEST

TEST 9

REFERENCE INFORMATION

THE FOLLOWING INFORMATION IS FOR YOUR REFERENCE IN ANSWERING SOME OF THE QUESTIONS IN THIS TEST

Volume of a right circular cone with radius r and height h: $V = \dfrac{1}{3}\pi r^2 h$

Lateral Area of a right circular cone with circumference of the base c and slant height ℓ: $S = \dfrac{1}{2}c\ell$

Volume of a sphere with radius r: $V = \dfrac{4}{3}\pi r^3$

Surface Area of a sphere with radius r: $S = 4\pi r^2$

Volume of a pyramid with base area B and height h: $V = \dfrac{1}{3}Bh$

Dr. John Chung's SAT II Math Level 1

Answer Sheet

1	Ⓐ Ⓑ Ⓒ Ⓓ Ⓔ	26	Ⓐ Ⓑ Ⓒ Ⓓ Ⓔ
2	Ⓐ Ⓑ Ⓒ Ⓓ Ⓔ	27	Ⓐ Ⓑ Ⓒ Ⓓ Ⓔ
3	Ⓐ Ⓑ Ⓒ Ⓓ Ⓔ	28	Ⓐ Ⓑ Ⓒ Ⓓ Ⓔ
4	Ⓐ Ⓑ Ⓒ Ⓓ Ⓔ	29	Ⓐ Ⓑ Ⓒ Ⓓ Ⓔ
5	Ⓐ Ⓑ Ⓒ Ⓓ Ⓔ	30	Ⓐ Ⓑ Ⓒ Ⓓ Ⓔ
6	Ⓐ Ⓑ Ⓒ Ⓓ Ⓔ	31	Ⓐ Ⓑ Ⓒ Ⓓ Ⓔ
7	Ⓐ Ⓑ Ⓒ Ⓓ Ⓔ	32	Ⓐ Ⓑ Ⓒ Ⓓ Ⓔ
8	Ⓐ Ⓑ Ⓒ Ⓓ Ⓔ	33	Ⓐ Ⓑ Ⓒ Ⓓ Ⓔ
9	Ⓐ Ⓑ Ⓒ Ⓓ Ⓔ	34	Ⓐ Ⓑ Ⓒ Ⓓ Ⓔ
10	Ⓐ Ⓑ Ⓒ Ⓓ Ⓔ	35	Ⓐ Ⓑ Ⓒ Ⓓ Ⓔ
11	Ⓐ Ⓑ Ⓒ Ⓓ Ⓔ	36	Ⓐ Ⓑ Ⓒ Ⓓ Ⓔ
12	Ⓐ Ⓑ Ⓒ Ⓓ Ⓔ	37	Ⓐ Ⓑ Ⓒ Ⓓ Ⓔ
13	Ⓐ Ⓑ Ⓒ Ⓓ Ⓔ	38	Ⓐ Ⓑ Ⓒ Ⓓ Ⓔ
14	Ⓐ Ⓑ Ⓒ Ⓓ Ⓔ	39	Ⓐ Ⓑ Ⓒ Ⓓ Ⓔ
15	Ⓐ Ⓑ Ⓒ Ⓓ Ⓔ	40	Ⓐ Ⓑ Ⓒ Ⓓ Ⓔ
16	Ⓐ Ⓑ Ⓒ Ⓓ Ⓔ	41	Ⓐ Ⓑ Ⓒ Ⓓ Ⓔ
17	Ⓐ Ⓑ Ⓒ Ⓓ Ⓔ	42	Ⓐ Ⓑ Ⓒ Ⓓ Ⓔ
18	Ⓐ Ⓑ Ⓒ Ⓓ Ⓔ	43	Ⓐ Ⓑ Ⓒ Ⓓ Ⓔ
19	Ⓐ Ⓑ Ⓒ Ⓓ Ⓔ	44	Ⓐ Ⓑ Ⓒ Ⓓ Ⓔ
20	Ⓐ Ⓑ Ⓒ Ⓓ Ⓔ	45	Ⓐ Ⓑ Ⓒ Ⓓ Ⓔ
21	Ⓐ Ⓑ Ⓒ Ⓓ Ⓔ	46	Ⓐ Ⓑ Ⓒ Ⓓ Ⓔ
22	Ⓐ Ⓑ Ⓒ Ⓓ Ⓔ	47	Ⓐ Ⓑ Ⓒ Ⓓ Ⓔ
23	Ⓐ Ⓑ Ⓒ Ⓓ Ⓔ	48	Ⓐ Ⓑ Ⓒ Ⓓ Ⓔ
24	Ⓐ Ⓑ Ⓒ Ⓓ Ⓔ	49	Ⓐ Ⓑ Ⓒ Ⓓ Ⓔ
25	Ⓐ Ⓑ Ⓒ Ⓓ Ⓔ	50	Ⓐ Ⓑ Ⓒ Ⓓ Ⓔ

The number of right answers : ☐

The number of wrong answers : ☐

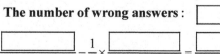

$$\boxed{}_{\text{\# of correct}} - \frac{1}{4} \times \boxed{}_{\text{\# of wrong}} = \boxed{}_{\text{Raw score}}$$

Score Conversion Table

Raw Score	Scaled Score	Raw Score	Scaled Score	Raw Score	Scaled Score
50	800	28	630	6	480
49	800	27	620	5	470
48	800	26	610	4	470
47	800	25	600	3	460
46	790	24	590	2	460
45	780	23	580	1	450
44	770	22	570	0	450
43	760	21	550		
42	750	20	540		
41	740	19	530		
40	740	18	520		
39	730	17	510		
38	720	16	500		
37	710	15	490		
36	710	14	480		
35	700	13	470		
34	690	12	460		
33	680	11	450		
32	670	10	440		
31	660	9	430		
30	650	8	420		
29	640	7	410		

MATHEMATICS LEVEL 1 TEST

For each of the following problems, decide which is the BEST of the choices given. If the exact numerical value is not one of the choices, select the choice that best approximates this value. Then fill in the corresponding circle on the answer sheet.

Notes: (1) A scientific or graphing calculator will be necessary for answering some (but not all) of the questions in this test. For each question you will have to decide whether or not you should use a calculator.

(2) For some questions in this test you may have to decide whether your calculator should be in the radian mode or the degree mode.

(3) Figures that accompany problems in this test are intended to provide information useful in solving the problems. They are drawn as accurately as possible EXCEPT when it is stated in a specific problem that its figure is not drawn to scale. All figures lie in a plane unless otherwise indicated.

(4) Unless otherwise specified, the domain of any function f is assumed to be the set of all real numbers x for which $f(x)$ is a real number. The range of f is assumed to be the set of all real numbers $f(x)$, where x is in the domain of f.

(5) Reference information that may be useful in answering the questions in this test can be found on the page preceding Question 1.

USE THIS SPACE FOR SCRATCHWORK.

1.   If $x = 3$ and $y = -2$, then what is the value of

$$\frac{(x+y)^{-1}}{x^{-1}+y^{-1}}?$$

(A) 6   (B) 3   (C) 1   (D) –3   (E) –6

2.   If $10-(2x-3) = 6+(2x-3)$, then $2x-3 =$

(A) –4   (B) –2   (C) 1   (D) 2   (E) 4

3. $\dfrac{\left(a^2 b^{-1}\right)^3}{\left(a^2 b^3\right)^2} =$

(A) $a^2 b^7$ (B) $a^2 b^9$ (C) $\dfrac{b^9}{a^2}$ (D) $\dfrac{a^2}{b^9}$ (E) $\dfrac{1}{a^2 b^9}$

GO ON TO THE NEXT PAGE

USE THIS SPACE FOR SCRATCHWORK.

4. In Figure 1, the diameter of the sphere is $10cm$ and the shaded cross-section is $4cm$ from the center of the sphere. What is the area of the shaded cross section, in squared centimeters?

(A) 3π
(B) 6π
(C) 9π
(D) 16π
(E) 25π

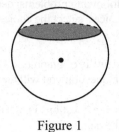

Figure 1

5. If $f(x)=|x-3|$ and $g(x)=f(x-1)$, then $g(-2)=$

(A) -6 (B) -3 (C) 3 (D) 6 (E) 9

6. In Figure 2, If $\overline{OM}$ is the median of $\triangle OAB$, what is the area of $\triangle OBM$?

(A) 24
(B) 18
(C) 15
(D) 12
(E) 9

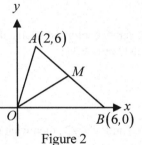

Figure 2

Note: Figure not drawn to scale.

7. If one root of the equation $x^2+8x+k=0$ is -5, what is the value of k ?

(A) -15 (B) -10 (C) 8 (D) 10 (E) 15

8. If $|x-4|>3$, which of the following represents the solution of the inequality?

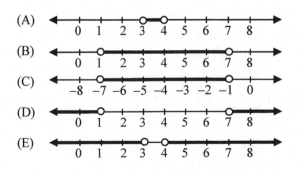

GO ON TO THE NEXT PAGE

MATHEMATICS LEVEL 1 TEST - *Continued*

USE THIS SPACE FOR SCRATCHWORK.

9. In Figure 3, M is the midpoint of $\overline{AB}$. What is the length of $\overline{OM}$?

    (A) 5
    (B) 6
    (C) $\sqrt{41}$
    (D) 7
    (E) $2\sqrt{13}$

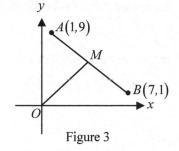

Figure 3

Note: Figure not drawn to scale.

10. In the xy-coordinate plane, the points $(0,5),(1,8)$, and $(2, k)$ lies on a straight line. Which of the following is the value of k?

    (A) 10   (B) 11   (C) 12   (C) 15   (D) 20

11. If the line $4x - ky = 9$ is perpendicular to the line passing through the points $(4,-7)$ and $(2,-2)$, what is the value of k?

    (A) −10   (B) −8   (C) 6   (D) 8   (E) 10

12. How many diagonals can be drawn from all of the vertices of a 20-sided polygon?

    (A) 85
    (B) 170
    (C) 190
    (D) 360
    (E) 380

13. If the radius of a sphere is tripled, then its volume is multiplied by what factor?

    (A) 2   (B) 3   (C) 9   (D) 18   (E) 27

14. The length of the diagonal of a rectangle is 6 and the length of the rectangle is 5 more than the width. What is the area of the rectangle?

    (A) 5.5   (B) 11   (C) 16.5   (D) 18   (E) 20.5

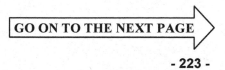

GO ON TO THE NEXT PAGE

MATHEMATICS LEVEL 1 TEST - *Continued*

USE THIS SPACE FOR SCRATCHWORK.

15. In Figure 4, square *EFGH* is inscribed in square *ABCD*.
If $\dfrac{CF}{BC} = \dfrac{1}{4}$, what is the ratio of the area of square
EFGH to the area of square *ABCD*?

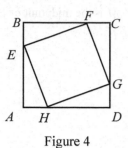

Figure 4

(A) $\dfrac{1}{2}$

(B) $\dfrac{2}{3}$

(C) $\dfrac{5}{8}$

(D) $\dfrac{3}{4}$

(E) $\dfrac{7}{8}$

16. The equation $x^2 + ax - x + 4 = 0$ has only one solution
for x, where $a > 0$. What is the value of a?

(A) 1   (B) 2   (C) 3   (D) 4   (E) 5

17. How many of the first 200 positive integers are multiples
of 4 or multiples of 10?

(A) 50   (B) 60   (C) 70   (D) 80   (E) 100

18. If the fifth term of an arithmetic sequence is 20 and the
20th term is 80, what is the 25th term of the sequence?

(A) 80   (B) 83   (C) 92   (D) 100   (E) 112

19. If $y = x^3 - 5x - 2$ for $0 \le x \le 5$, for what value of
x does the function have the maximum value of y?

(A) 0
(B) 1.29
(C) 2.5
(D) 2.41
(E) 5

GO ON TO THE NEXT PAGE

MATHEMATICS LEVEL 1 TEST - *Continued*

USE THIS SPACE FOR SCRATCHWORK.

20. Figure 5 shows the graph of $f(x) = x^2 - 6x$. Which of the following could be the graph of $y = -f(-x)$?

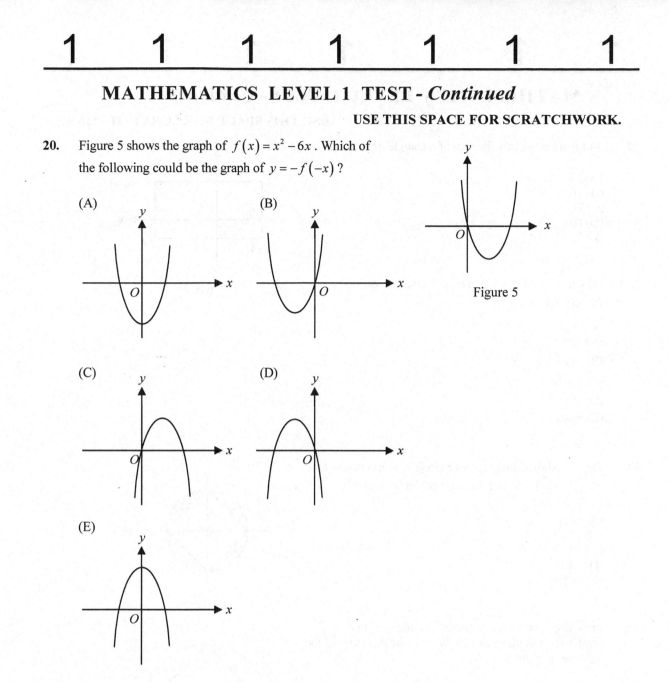

(A)

(B)

Figure 5

(C)

(D)

(E)

21. If $\log_3(x^2 - 1) - \log_3(x+1) = 2$, then $x =$

(A) 1
(B) 9
(C) 10
(D) 100
(E) 101

GO ON TO THE NEXT PAGE

MATHEMATICS LEVEL 1 TEST - *Continued*

USE THIS SPACE FOR SCRATCHWORK.

22.   In Figure 6, what is the area of rectangle *ABCD* ?

(A) 35
(B) 40
(C) 70
(D) 80
(E) 95

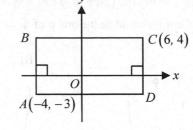

Figure 6

23.   Which of the following is equal to the expression $(1-\sin^2\theta)\sec\theta$?

(A) $\cos\theta$

(B) $\sin\theta$

(C) $\cos^2\theta$

(D) $\sin^2\theta$

(E) $\tan\theta$

24.   Figure 7 shows the graph of a circle whose equation is $x^2 + y^2 = 25$. What is the area of shaded region?

(A) 28.54
(B) 31.25
(C) 57.08
(D) 84.56
(E) 342.7

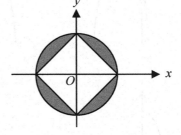

Figure 7

25.   In Figure 8, an isosceles triangle is inscribed in a semicircle with diameter 10. What is the perimeter of the isosceles triangle?

(A) $10 + 5\sqrt{2}$
(B) $10 + 5\sqrt{3}$
(C) 20
(D) $10 + 10\sqrt{2}$
(E) $20 + 5\sqrt{2}$

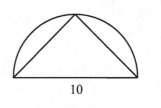

10

Figure 8

GO ON TO THE NEXT PAGE

MATHEMATICS LEVEL 1 TEST - *Continued*

USE THIS SPACE FOR SCRATCHWORK.

26.   The graph of the parabola $y = x^2 - 6x + 2$ intersects the graph of the line $y = x + 1$ at exactly two points. What is the sum of the x-coordinates of these two points?

(A) 3   (B) 4   (C) 5   (D) 6   (E) 7

27.   In Figure 9, a circle is inscribed in equilateral triangle ABC. If $AB = 4\sqrt{3}$, what is the area of the circle?

(A) 2π
(B) 3π
(C) 4π
(D) 5π
(E) 6π

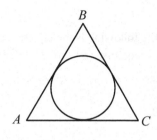

Figure 9

28.   If a and b are the roots of the equation $x^2 - k^2x - k = 0$. If $a + b - ab = 6$, then which of the following could be the value of k?

(A) -4 (B) -2 (C) 2   (D) 4   (E) 6

29.   Which of the following has the greatest number of lines of symmetry?

(A) square
(B) rhombus
(C) rectangle
(D) equilateral triangle
(E) isosceles trapezoid

30.   A total of $1,000 is invested at an annual interest rate of 6%. If it is compounded quarterly, what is the balance after 5 years?

(A) 1077.28
(B) 1338.23
(C) 1346.86
(D) 1425.82
(E) 1520.05

GO ON TO THE NEXT PAGE

USE THIS SPACE FOR SCRATCHWORK.

31. If $(x-2)^{\frac{2}{3}} = 9$, what are all the values of x?

(A) 27 only
(B) 27 and −27
(C) 29 only
(D) 29 and −25
(E) 64 only

32. Which of the following is the equation of the locus of points that is equidistant from $x^2 + y^2 = 4$ and $x^2 + y^2 = 36$?

(A) $x = 20$
(B) $y = x$
(C) $x^2 + y^2 = 20$
(D) $x^2 + y^2 = 16$
(E) $x^2 + y^2 = 9$

33. In Figure 10, $AE = 18$, $DE = 9$, and $CD = 15$. What is the length of $\overline{AB}$?

(A) 15
(B) 18
(C) 21
(D) 24
(E) 27

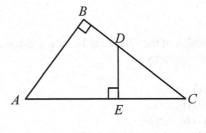

Figure 10

34. The 5th term of an arithmetic sequence is 20 and the 11th term is 5. What is the sum of the first 30 terms of the arithmetic sequence?

(A) −225
(B) −187.5
(C) −150
(D) 150
(E) 225

GO ON TO THE NEXT PAGE

MATHEMATICS LEVEL 1 TEST - *Continued*

USE THIS SPACE FOR SCRATCHWORK.

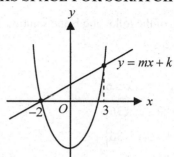

35. In Figure 11, the graphs of $y = x^2 - 4$ and $y = mx + k$ intersect at $x = -2$ and $x = 3$. What is the value of k?

(A) 1
(B) 2
(C) 3
(D) 4
(E) 5

36. If $4^x - 4^{x-1} = 15$, what is the value of x?

(A) 4.5
(B) $\log_2 10$
(C) $\log_4 20$
(D) 2^5
(E) 5^2

Figure 11
<u>Note</u>: Figure not drawn to scale.

37. If the probability that team A wins the first game is $\dfrac{1}{3}$ and the probability that team A wins the second game is $\dfrac{3}{4}$, what is the probability that team A wins only one game out of the two games?

(A) $\dfrac{1}{4}$ (B) $\dfrac{1}{3}$ (C) $\dfrac{7}{12}$ (D) $\dfrac{3}{4}$ (E) $\dfrac{5}{6}$

38. For which of the following equations is the sum of the real roots equal to the product of the real roots?

(A) $x^2 + 5x + 5 = 0$
(B) $x^2 - 5x - 5 = 0$
(C) $2x^2 + 6x + 6 = 0$
(D) $2x^2 + 6x - 6 = 0$
(E) $3x^2 - 6x - 6 = 0$

GO ON TO THE NEXT PAGE

MATHEMATICS LEVEL 1 TEST - *Continued*

USE THIS SPACE FOR SCRATCHWORK.

39. Which of the following is the solution set for x in which $\left| \sqrt{x} - 2 \right| \le 4$?

    (A) $\{ x \mid -4 \le x \le 6 \}$

    (B) $\{ x \mid 0 \le x \le 36 \}$

    (C) $\{ x \mid 4 \le x \le 36 \}$

    (D) $\{ x \mid 16 \le x \le 36 \}$

    (E) $\{ x \mid x \ge 36 \text{ or } x \le 0 \}$

40. What is the range of the function $f(x) = 5 - 3e^x$?

    (A) $y > 0$
    (B) $y < 2$
    (C) $y < 5$
    (D) $-3 < y < 5$
    (E) $y > 5$

41. If $f(x) = ax^3 + bx - 2$ and $f(-5) = 10$, then what is the value of $f(5)$?

    (A) 14   (B) 10   (C) 8   (D) –8   (E) –14

42. If $f(x) = \sqrt{4 - x^2}$ and $g(x) = x - 3$, then what is the domain of $f(g(x))$?

    (A) $x \ge 3$
    (B) $1 \le x \le 5$
    (C) $x \le 1$ or $x \ge 5$
    (D) $-2 \le x \le 2$
    (E) $x \ge 2$ or $x \le -2$

GO ON TO THE NEXT PAGE

MATHEMATICS LEVEL 1 TEST - *Continued*

USE THIS SPACE FOR SCRATCHWORK.

43. If a six-sided die is rolled twice, what is the probability that the number on the first roll is greater than the number on the second roll?

(A) $\frac{1}{4}$ (B) $\frac{1}{3}$ (C) $\frac{5}{12}$ (D) $\frac{1}{2}$ (E) $\frac{2}{3}$

44. How many ways can 4 students be seated in a row of 7 chairs?

(A) $_7C_4$ (B) $\frac{_7C_4}{7!}$ (C) $_4P_7$ (D) $_7P_4$ (E) $\frac{_7P_4}{7!}$

45. If $f(x) = 2x$ and $g(x) = 2x - 4k$ when k is a positive, which of the following is true?

(A) The graph of g is the graph of f shifted $4k$ units up.
(B) The graph of g is the graph of f shifted $2k$ units up.
(C) The graph of g is the graph of f shifted $4k$ units to the right.
(D) The graph of g is the graph of f shifted $2k$ units to the left.
(E) The graph of g is the graph of f shifted $2k$ units to the right.

46. In Figure 12, $BD = CD = a$ and $\angle BCA = \theta^o$, which of the following is the expression for the area of $\triangle BCD$?

(A) $a^2\sin\theta$

(B) $a^2(1+\cos\theta)\sin\theta$

(C) $a^2(1+\cos2\theta)\sin\theta$

(D) $a^2\cos2\theta$

(E) $\dfrac{a^2\sin2\theta}{2}$

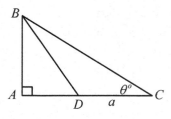

FIgure 12
Note: Figure not drawn to scale.

GO ON TO THE NEXT PAGE

USE THIS SPACE FOR SCRATCHWORK.

47. Which of the following functions has a period of 90° ?

   (A) $y = 2\sin2x$
   (B) $y = 2\cos3x$
   (C) $y = 5\tan2x$
   (D) $y = 3\tan4x$
   (E) $y = -3\cos6x$

48. The height, $h(n)$, of a bouncing ball after n bounces is

   defined by $h(n) = 100\left(\dfrac{1}{3}\right)^{n}$. How many times higher is

   the first bounce than the fifth bounce?

   (A) 3   (B) 9   (C) 27   (D) 81   (E) 243

49. In Figure 13, a regular hexagon is inscribed in a circle
   with a radius of 10. What is the value of the shaded area?

   (A) 9.06
   (B) 12.89
   (C) 15.45
   (D) 20.25
   (E) 25.04

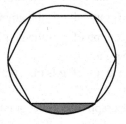

FIgure 13

50. Which of the following statements must be true?

   (A) If $n > 0$, then $n^2 > n$.
   (B) If $n^2 > 0$, then $n > 0$.
   (C) If $n^2 < n$, then $n < 0$.
   (D) If $n < 0$, then $n^2 > n$.
   (E) If $n < 1$, then $n^2 < n$.

STOP
**IF YOU FINISH BEFORE TIME IS CALLED, YOU MAY CHECK YOUR WORK ON THIS TEST ONLY.
DO NOT TURN TO ANY OTHER TEST IN THIS BOOK.**

NO MATERIAL ON THIS PAGE

NO MATERIAL ON THIS PAGE

#	answer	#	answer	#	answer	#	answer	#	answer
1	E	11	E	21	C	31	D	41	E
2	D	12	B	22	C	32	D	42	B
3	D	13	E	23	A	33	B	43	C
4	C	14	A	24	A	34	B	44	D
5	D	15	C	25	D	35	B	45	E
6	E	16	E	26	E	36	C	46	E
7	E	17	B	27	C	37	C	47	C
8	D	18	D	28	C	38	D	48	D
9	C	19	E	29	A	39	B	49	A
10	B	20	D	30	C	40	C	50	D

Explanations: Test 9

1.   (E) $\dfrac{(x+y)^{-1}}{x^{-1}+y^{-1}} = \dfrac{(3-2)^{-1}}{\dfrac{1}{3}+\dfrac{1}{-2}} = \dfrac{1}{-\dfrac{1}{6}} = -6$

2.   (D) $2(2x-3)=4 \;\Rightarrow\; 2x-3=2$

3.   (D) $\dfrac{\left(a^2b^{-1}\right)^3}{\left(a^2b^3\right)^2} = \dfrac{a^6b^{-3}}{a^4b^6} = \dfrac{a^2}{b^9}$

4.   (C)   Since the radius of the circle is 3, the area is
$\pi r^2 = 9\pi$

5.   (D) $g(-2)=f(-2-1)=f(-3) \;\Rightarrow\; f(-3)=|-3-3|=6$

6.   (E)   Midpoint $\left(\dfrac{2+6}{2},\dfrac{6+0}{2}\right)=(4,3)$ Since base $=6$ and height $=3$, the area is $\dfrac{6\times 3}{2}=9$.

7.   (E)   The other root: α
Sum $= -5+\alpha=-8 \;\Rightarrow\; \alpha=-3$
Product $=(-5)(-3)=k \;\Rightarrow\; k=15$
Or, because -5 is the root, $f(-5)=0 \;\Rightarrow\; 25-40+k=0 \;\Rightarrow\; k=15$

8.   (D) $|x-4|>3 \;\Rightarrow\; x-4>3$ or $x-4<-3 \;\Rightarrow\; x>7$ or $x<1$

9.   (C)   Midpoint: $M\left(\dfrac{1+7}{2},\dfrac{9+1}{2}\right)=(4,5)$
$OM=\sqrt{4^2+5^2}=\sqrt{41}$

10. **(B)**   Slopes between any two points on the line are constant.

$$\frac{8-5}{1-0} = \frac{k-5}{2-0} \implies k = 11$$

11. **(E)** $y = \frac{4}{k}x - \frac{9}{k} \implies m_1 = \frac{4}{k}$

Slope of the other line $= \frac{-2-(-7)}{2-4} = -\frac{5}{2}$ should be the negative reciprocal.

Therefore, $\frac{4}{k} = \frac{2}{5} \implies k = 10$

12. **(B)** $_{20}C_2 = \frac{20 \cdot 19}{2!} = 190$ segments.   Because 20 sides are not diagonals, the number of diagonals is

$190 - 20 = 170$.

13. **(E)** $V = \frac{4\pi r^3}{3} \implies V' = \frac{4\pi (3r)^3}{3} = 27\left(\frac{4\pi r^3}{3}\right) = 27V$

14. **(A)** $(w+5)^2 + w^2 = 6^2 \implies 2w^2 + 10w - 11 = 0 \implies 2w^2 + 10w = 11 \implies w^2 + 5w = \frac{11}{2} = 5.5$

The area of the rectangle: $(w+5)w = w^2 + 5w = 5.5$.

15. **(C)**   If $FC = k$, then $BF = 3k$ and $EF = \sqrt{(3k)^2 + k^2} = \sqrt{10k^2}$.

The area of $EFGH = \left(\sqrt{10k^2}\right)^2 = 10k^2$ and the area of $ABCD = (4k)^2 = 16k^2$

Therefore, the ratio is $\frac{10k^2}{16k^2} = \frac{5}{8}$.   (You can use $k = 1$)

16. **(E)** $x^2 + (a-1)x + 4 = 0 \implies$ Discriminant should be $0 \implies (a-1)^2 - 4(1)(4) = 0$

$a^2 - 2a - 15 = 0 \implies (a-5)(a+3) = 0 \implies a = 5, \cancel{a = -3}$

17. **(B)** $\left\lfloor \frac{200}{4} \right\rfloor = 50, \quad \left\lfloor \frac{200}{10} \right\rfloor = 20, \quad \left\lfloor \frac{200}{20} \right\rfloor = 10$

The number is $50 + 20 - 10 = 60$.

> **Important:**
> The number of multiples of 6 from 1 to 200 is
> $\left\lfloor \dfrac{200}{6} \right\rfloor = 33$, where $\lfloor \ \rfloor$ is the floor integer function.

18. **(D)** $a_5 = a + 4d = 20$, $a_{20} = a + 19d = 80$

From those two equations: $a = 4$ and $d = 4$.

Therefore, $a_{25} = a + (n-1)d = 4 + 24 \cdot 4 = 100$

19. (E) Use a graphic utility: At $x = 5$, y is maximum.

$$x = 1.2909935 \quad y = -6.303315$$

20. (D) Symmetry with respect to the origin. $\Rightarrow$ Odd function

21. (C) $\log_3\left(x^2 - 1\right) - \log_3\left(x+1\right) = 2 \Rightarrow \log_3 \dfrac{x^2-1}{x+1} = 2 \Rightarrow x - 1 = 3^2$

$x = 10$

22. (C) Since $BC = 10$ and $CD = 7$, then the area $= 10 \times 7 = 70$.

23. (A) $\left(1 - \sin^2\theta\right)\sec\theta = \cos^2\theta \times \dfrac{1}{\cos\theta} = \cos\theta$

24. (A) The area of the circle $= \pi r^2 = 25\pi$, and the area of the square $= \left(\dfrac{10 \times 10}{2}\right) = 50$.

The area of the shaded region $= 25\pi - 50 \cong 28.54$

25. (D) The triangle is an isosceles right triangle. Each leg has the length of $\dfrac{10}{\sqrt{2}} = 5\sqrt{2}$.

$10 + 5\sqrt{2} + 5\sqrt{2} = 10 + 10\sqrt{2}$

26. (E) $x^2 - 6x + 2 = x + 1 \Rightarrow x^2 - 7x + 1 = 0$

Therefore, the sum of the two zeros is 7.

27. (C) The radius of the circle is 2.

Area $= \pi r^2 = 4\pi$

28. (C) $S = a + b = k^2$ and $P = ab = -k$

$a + b - ab = 6 \Rightarrow k^2 + k - 6 = 0 \Rightarrow (k+3)(k-2) = 0$

Therefore, $k = 2 \ (k > 0)$

29. (A) Square (4) Rhombus (2) Rectangle (2) Equilateral triangle (3)
Isosceles trapezoid (1)

30. (C) 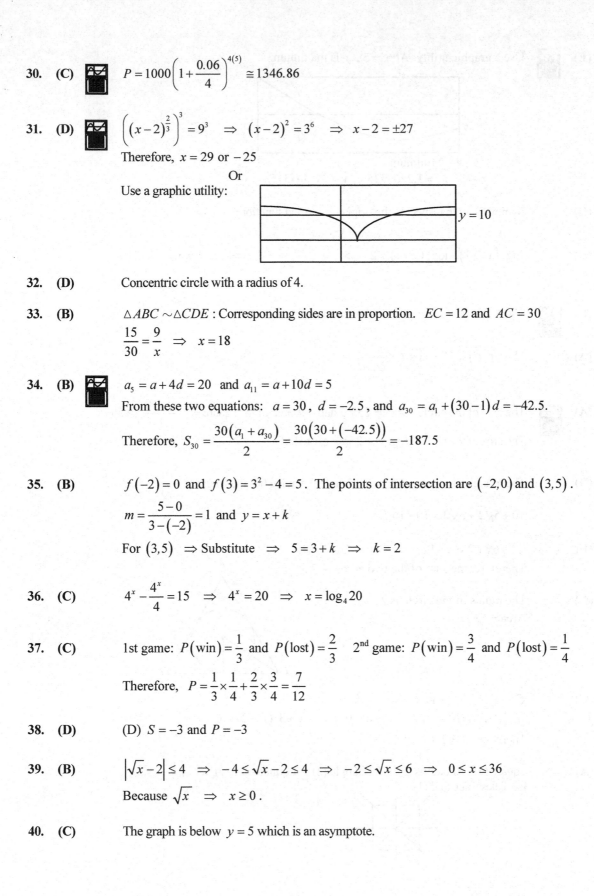 $P = 1000\left(1 + \dfrac{0.06}{4}\right)^{4(5)} \cong 1346.86$

31. (D) $\left(\left(x-2\right)^{\frac{2}{3}}\right)^3 = 9^3 \;\Rightarrow\; \left(x-2\right)^2 = 3^6 \;\Rightarrow\; x-2 = \pm 27$

Therefore, $x = 29$ or -25

Or

Use a graphic utility:

$y = 10$

32. (D) Concentric circle with a radius of 4.

33. (B) $\triangle ABC \sim \triangle CDE$: Corresponding sides are in proportion. $EC = 12$ and $AC = 30$

$\dfrac{15}{30} = \dfrac{9}{x} \;\Rightarrow\; x = 18$

34. (B) $a_5 = a + 4d = 20$ and $a_{11} = a + 10d = 5$

From these two equations: $a = 30$, $d = -2.5$, and $a_{30} = a_1 + (30-1)d = -42.5$.

Therefore, $S_{30} = \dfrac{30\left(a_1 + a_{30}\right)}{2} = \dfrac{30\left(30 + (-42.5)\right)}{2} = -187.5$

35. (B) $f(-2) = 0$ and $f(3) = 3^2 - 4 = 5$. The points of intersection are $(-2, 0)$ and $(3, 5)$.

$m = \dfrac{5-0}{3-(-2)} = 1$ and $y = x + k$

For $(3, 5) \;\Rightarrow\;$ Substitute $\;\Rightarrow\; 5 = 3 + k \;\Rightarrow\; k = 2$

36. (C) $4^x - \dfrac{4^x}{4} = 15 \;\Rightarrow\; 4^x = 20 \;\Rightarrow\; x = \log_4 20$

37. (C) 1st game: $P(\text{win}) = \dfrac{1}{3}$ and $P(\text{lost}) = \dfrac{2}{3}$ 2nd game: $P(\text{win}) = \dfrac{3}{4}$ and $P(\text{lost}) = \dfrac{1}{4}$

Therefore, $P = \dfrac{1}{3} \times \dfrac{1}{4} + \dfrac{2}{3} \times \dfrac{3}{4} = \dfrac{7}{12}$

38. (D) (D) $S = -3$ and $P = -3$

39. (B) $\left|\sqrt{x} - 2\right| \le 4 \;\Rightarrow\; -4 \le \sqrt{x} - 2 \le 4 \;\Rightarrow\; -2 \le \sqrt{x} \le 6 \;\Rightarrow\; 0 \le x \le 36$

Because $\sqrt{x} \;\Rightarrow\; x \ge 0$.

40. (C) The graph is below $y = 5$ which is an asymptote.

41. **(E)** $f(-5) = -125a - 5b - 2 = 10 \implies 125a + 5b = -12$

$f(5) = 125a + 5b - 2 = -12 - 2 = -14$

42. **(B)** $f(x) = \sqrt{4 - g^2} = \sqrt{4 - (x-3)^2} = \sqrt{-x^2 + 6x - 5}$

$-x^2 + 6x - 5 \geq 0 \implies (x-5)(x-1) \leq 1 \implies 1 \leq x \leq 5$

43. **(C)** $(2,1)\ (3,1)\ (3,2)\ (4,1)\ (4,2)\ (4,3)\ \cdots\ 15$ pairs

$P = \dfrac{15}{36} = \dfrac{5}{12}$

44. **(D)** First choose 4 chairs out of 7: $\ _7C_4$

Second: Assign 4 students to these 4 chairs. $\ _7C_4 \times 4! = \ _7P_4$

Or

Assign the chairs to 4 students: $7 \times 6 \times 5 \times 4 = \ _7P_4$

45. **(E)** $g(x) = 2(x - 2k) \implies g(x) = f(x - 2k)$

46. **(E)** The area of $\triangle ABC = \dfrac{a(a\sin 2\theta)}{2} = \dfrac{a^2 \sin 2\theta}{2}$

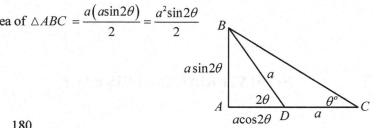

47. **(C)** (C) $p = \dfrac{180}{2} = 90$

48. **(D)** $h(1) = 100\left(\dfrac{1}{3}\right) = \dfrac{100}{3}$ and $h(5) = 100\left(\dfrac{1}{3}\right)^5 = \dfrac{100}{243}$

$\dfrac{h(1)}{h(5)} = \dfrac{100}{3} \div \dfrac{100}{243} = 81$

49. **(A)** The area of a sector with central angle of $60^0 = \dfrac{100\pi}{6}$.

The area of an equilateral triangle $= \dfrac{10 \cdot 10 \cdot \sin 60}{2} = 25\sqrt{3}$

The area of the shaded region $= \dfrac{100\pi}{6} - 25\sqrt{5} \cong 9.06$

50. **(D)** (A) If $n = \dfrac{1}{2}$, it is false.   (B) If $n = -2$, it is false   (C) If $n = \dfrac{1}{2}$, it is false

(E) If $n = -2$, it is false   (D) If $n < 0$, $n^2 > 0$, it is always true.

END

NO MATERIAL ON THIS PAGE

Dr. John Chung's SAT II

Math Level 1

Test 10

MATHEMATICS LEVEL 1 TEST

TEST 10

REFERENCE INFORMATION

THE FOLLOWING INFORMATION IS FOR YOUR REFERENCE IN ANSWERING SOME OF THE QUESTIONS IN THIS TEST

Volume of a right circular cone with radius r and height h: $V = \frac{1}{3}\pi r^2 h$

Lateral Area of a right circular cone with circumference of the base c and slant height ℓ: $S = \frac{1}{2}c\ell$

Volume of a sphere with radius r: $V = \frac{4}{3}\pi r^3$

Surface Area of a sphere with radius r: $S = 4\pi r^2$

Volume of a pyramid with base area B and height h: $V = \frac{1}{3}Bh$

Dr. John Chung's SAT II Math Level 1

Answer Sheet

1	Ⓐ Ⓑ Ⓒ Ⓓ Ⓔ		26	Ⓐ Ⓑ Ⓒ Ⓓ Ⓔ
2	Ⓐ Ⓑ Ⓒ Ⓓ Ⓔ		27	Ⓐ Ⓑ Ⓒ Ⓓ Ⓔ
3	Ⓐ Ⓑ Ⓒ Ⓓ Ⓔ		28	Ⓐ Ⓑ Ⓒ Ⓓ Ⓔ
4	Ⓐ Ⓑ Ⓒ Ⓓ Ⓔ		29	Ⓐ Ⓑ Ⓒ Ⓓ Ⓔ
5	Ⓐ Ⓑ Ⓒ Ⓓ Ⓔ		30	Ⓐ Ⓑ Ⓒ Ⓓ Ⓔ
6	Ⓐ Ⓑ Ⓒ Ⓓ Ⓔ		31	Ⓐ Ⓑ Ⓒ Ⓓ Ⓔ
7	Ⓐ Ⓑ Ⓒ Ⓓ Ⓔ		32	Ⓐ Ⓑ Ⓒ Ⓓ Ⓔ
8	Ⓐ Ⓑ Ⓒ Ⓓ Ⓔ		33	Ⓐ Ⓑ Ⓒ Ⓓ Ⓔ
9	Ⓐ Ⓑ Ⓒ Ⓓ Ⓔ		34	Ⓐ Ⓑ Ⓒ Ⓓ Ⓔ
10	Ⓐ Ⓑ Ⓒ Ⓓ Ⓔ		35	Ⓐ Ⓑ Ⓒ Ⓓ Ⓔ
11	Ⓐ Ⓑ Ⓒ Ⓓ Ⓔ		36	Ⓐ Ⓑ Ⓒ Ⓓ Ⓔ
12	Ⓐ Ⓑ Ⓒ Ⓓ Ⓔ		37	Ⓐ Ⓑ Ⓒ Ⓓ Ⓔ
13	Ⓐ Ⓑ Ⓒ Ⓓ Ⓔ		38	Ⓐ Ⓑ Ⓒ Ⓓ Ⓔ
14	Ⓐ Ⓑ Ⓒ Ⓓ Ⓔ		39	Ⓐ Ⓑ Ⓒ Ⓓ Ⓔ
15	Ⓐ Ⓑ Ⓒ Ⓓ Ⓔ		40	Ⓐ Ⓑ Ⓒ Ⓓ Ⓔ
16	Ⓐ Ⓑ Ⓒ Ⓓ Ⓔ		41	Ⓐ Ⓑ Ⓒ Ⓓ Ⓔ
17	Ⓐ Ⓑ Ⓒ Ⓓ Ⓔ		42	Ⓐ Ⓑ Ⓒ Ⓓ Ⓔ
18	Ⓐ Ⓑ Ⓒ Ⓓ Ⓔ		43	Ⓐ Ⓑ Ⓒ Ⓓ Ⓔ
19	Ⓐ Ⓑ Ⓒ Ⓓ Ⓔ		44	Ⓐ Ⓑ Ⓒ Ⓓ Ⓔ
20	Ⓐ Ⓑ Ⓒ Ⓓ Ⓔ		45	Ⓐ Ⓑ Ⓒ Ⓓ Ⓔ
21	Ⓐ Ⓑ Ⓒ Ⓓ Ⓔ		46	Ⓐ Ⓑ Ⓒ Ⓓ Ⓔ
22	Ⓐ Ⓑ Ⓒ Ⓓ Ⓔ		47	Ⓐ Ⓑ Ⓒ Ⓓ Ⓔ
23	Ⓐ Ⓑ Ⓒ Ⓓ Ⓔ		48	Ⓐ Ⓑ Ⓒ Ⓓ Ⓔ
24	Ⓐ Ⓑ Ⓒ Ⓓ Ⓔ		49	Ⓐ Ⓑ Ⓒ Ⓓ Ⓔ
25	Ⓐ Ⓑ Ⓒ Ⓓ Ⓔ		50	Ⓐ Ⓑ Ⓒ Ⓓ Ⓔ

The number of right answers : ☐

The number of wrong answers : ☐

$$\underbrace{\boxed{}}_{\text{\# of correct}} - \frac{1}{4} \times \underbrace{\boxed{}}_{\text{\# of wrong}} = \underbrace{\boxed{}}_{\text{Raw score}}$$

Score Conversion Table

Raw Score	Scaled Score	Raw Score	Scaled Score	Raw Score	Scaled Score
50	800	28	630	6	480
49	800	27	620	5	470
48	800	26	610	4	470
47	800	25	600	3	460
46	790	24	590	2	460
45	780	23	580	1	450
44	770	22	570	0	450
43	760	21	550		
42	750	20	540		
41	740	19	530		
40	740	18	520		
39	730	17	510		
38	720	16	500		
37	710	15	490		
36	710	14	480		
35	700	13	470		
34	690	12	460		
33	680	11	450		
32	670	10	440		
31	660	9	430		
30	650	8	420		
29	640	7	410		

MATHEMATICS LEVEL 1 TEST

For each of the following problems, decide which is the BEST of the choices given. If the exact numerical value is not one of the choices, select the choice that best approximates this value. Then fill in the corresponding circle on the answer sheet.

Notes: (1) A scientific or graphing calculator will be necessary for answering some (but not all) of the questions in this test. For each question you will have to decide whether or not you should use a calculator.

(2) For some questions in this test you may have to decide whether your calculator should be in the radian mode or the degree mode.

(3) Figures that accompany problems in this test are intended to provide information useful in solving the problems. They are drawn as accurately as possible EXCEPT when it is stated in a specific problem that its figure is not drawn to scale. All figures lie in a plane unless otherwise indicated.

(4) Unless otherwise specified, the domain of any function f is assumed to be the set of all real numbers x for which $f(x)$ is a real number. The range of f is assumed to be the set of all real numbers $f(x)$, where x is in the domain of f.

(5) Reference information that may be useful in answering the questions in this test can be found on the page preceding Question 1.

USE THIS SPACE FOR SCRATCHWORK.

1. If $\dfrac{12}{2+\sqrt{x}} - \dfrac{3}{2+\sqrt{x}} = 2$, what is the value of x?

    (A) 4   (B) 4.96   (C) 6.25   (D) 7.5   (E) 10.25

2. $\dfrac{3x+6y}{4} \cdot \dfrac{2xy}{x^2+2xy} =$

    (A) $3y$

    (B) $\dfrac{y}{3}$

    (C) $\dfrac{3y}{2}$

    (D) $\dfrac{3x}{2}$

    (E) $\dfrac{3y}{2x}$

GO ON TO THE NEXT PAGE

USE THIS SPACE FOR SCRATCHWORK.

3.   If $x = 6$ and $y = -4$, what is the value of $\dfrac{x^2 - 4y}{y}$?

(A) 15   (B) 12   (C) 5   (D) –5   (E) –13

4.   If $-2x - 5 = 11$ and $3x - 1 = 5 - y$, what is the value of y ?

(A) 30   (B) 25   (C) 20   (D) –25   (E) –30

5.   A truck leaves City A traveling at an average speed of 40miles per hour. Three hours later, a car leaves City A, on the same route, traveling at an average speed of 50 miles per hour. How many hours after the car leaves City A will the car catch up to the truck?

(A) 6
(B) 8
(C) 10
(D) 12
(E) 15

6.   In the graph of $y \le -x + 2$, which quadrant is completely shaded?

(A) I   (B) II   (C) III   (D) IV   (E) II and III

7.   Two numbers are in the ratio of $5 : 3$. If 8 is subtracted from the sum of the two numbers, the result is 40. What is the larger number?

(A) 15   (B) 18   (C) 24   (D) 30   (E) 36

8.   If $(x - 5)$ is a factor of $x^2 - 3x - k = 0$, then what is the value of k ?

(A) 4   (B) 10   (C) –4   (D) –10   (E) –18

MATHEMATICS LEVEL 1 TEST - *Continued*

USE THIS SPACE FOR SCRATCHWORK.

9. In Figure 1, if $\ell \parallel m$ and $\angle MAB = 125^o$, what is the measure of $\angle BCN$?

(A) 35°
(B) 40°
(C) 45°
(D) 55°
(E) 60°

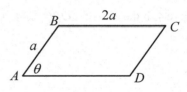

Figure 1

Note: Figure not drawn to scale.

10. If $16^x = 8$, then $x =$

(A) $\dfrac{1}{2}$ (B) $\dfrac{3}{4}$ (C) $\dfrac{4}{3}$ (D) 2   (E) 3

11. In parallelogram $ABCD$ in Figure 2, $AB = a$, $BC = 2a$, and $\sin\theta = 0.5$. Which of the following is the area of the parallelogram?

(A) $3a$
(B) a^2
(C) $2a^2$
(D) $a^2 + a$
(E) $a^2 - a$

Figure 2

12. If $f(x-2) = 2x - 5$, then what is $f(x)$?

(A) $2x + 1$
(B) $2x + 3$
(C) $2x + 5$
(D) $2x - 1$
(E) $2x - 3$

13. Which of the following is not a factor of $x^5 - 16x$?

(A) x
(B) $x + 2$
(C) $x^2 - 4$
(D) $x^2 + 4$
(E) $2x + 4$

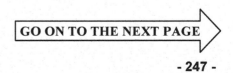

GO ON TO THE NEXT PAGE

MATHEMATICS LEVEL 1 TEST - *Continued*

USE THIS SPACE FOR SCRATCHWORK.

14. In Figure 3, $\triangle ABC$ is inscribed in a semicircle. If $BD = 6$ and $CD = 4$, what is the area of $\triangle ABC$?

 (A) 78
 (B) 39
 (C) 36
 (D) 32
 (E) 25

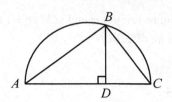

Figure 3

15. $\sin x + \cot x \cos x =$

 (A) $\sin x$
 (B) $\cos x$
 (C) $\sec x$
 (D) $\csc x$
 (E) $\tan x$

16. In Figure 4, if the area of $\triangle OPQ$ is 24, what is the slope of $\overline{OP}$?

 (A) $\dfrac{3}{4}$

 (B) $\dfrac{1}{2}$

 (C) $\dfrac{3}{8}$

 (D) $\dfrac{1}{4}$

 (E) $\dfrac{2}{7}$

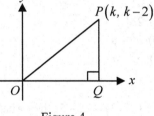

Figure 4

17. For which of the following values of x is
 $$\frac{1}{\sin x^o - \cos x^o}$$ undefined?

 (A) 30
 (B) 45
 (C) 60
 (D) 90
 (E) 180

GO ON TO THE NEXT PAGE

USE THIS SPACE FOR SCRATCHWORK.

18.   In Figure 5, M and N are the midpoints of $\overline{AB}$ and $\overline{BC}$ respectively. If the area of $\triangle ABC$ is 36, then what is the area of $\triangle AMN$?

(A) 4.5
(B) 6
(C) 9
(D) 12
(E) 15

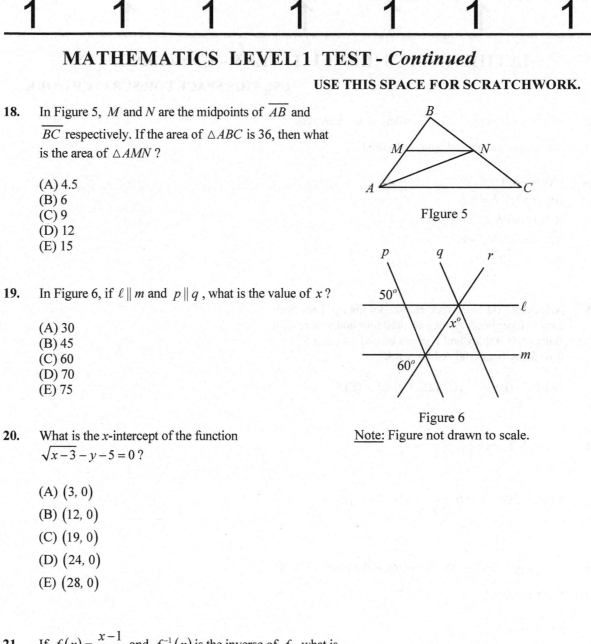

FIgure 5

19.   In Figure 6, if $\ell \parallel m$ and $p \parallel q$, what is the value of x ?

(A) 30
(B) 45
(C) 60
(D) 70
(E) 75

Figure 6

Note: Figure not drawn to scale.

20.   What is the x-intercept of the function $\sqrt{x-3} - y - 5 = 0$?

(A) $(3, 0)$

(B) $(12, 0)$

(C) $(19, 0)$

(D) $(24, 0)$

(E) $(28, 0)$

21.   If $f(x) = \dfrac{x-1}{x-4}$ and $f^{-1}(x)$ is the inverse of f , what is the value of $f^{-1}(4)$?

(A) 5
(B) 6
(C) 8
(D) 10
(E) 15

GO ON TO THE NEXT PAGE

MATHEMATICS LEVEL 1 TEST - *Continued*

USE THIS SPACE FOR SCRATCHWORK.

22. If $z = a + bi$ and $\dfrac{z - i}{z + 1} = 3$, where a and b are real numbers, what are the values of a and b ?

(A) $a = 1, b = 2$
(B) $a = 1.5, b = 0.5$
(C) $a = -1.5, b = -0.5$
(D) $a = -2, b = -3$
(E) $a = -12.5, b = -3$

23. Ashley and Barbara work at a school library. They each earn \$10 per hour. Ashley worked four hours more than Barbara. If Ashley and Barbara earned a total of \$240, how many hours did Ashley work?

(A) 16   (B) 14   (C) 12   (D) 10   (E) 8

24. If $i = \sqrt{-1}$, then $\left(i - \dfrac{1}{i} \right)^{-2} =$

(A) i (B) $-i$ (C) $\dfrac{1}{2}$ (D) $-\dfrac{1}{4}$ (E) $-\dfrac{1}{2}$

25. If $\dfrac{1}{x} > \dfrac{1}{5}$, which of the following is the solution set of the inequality?

(A) $\{x \,|\, x > 5\}$
(B) $\{x \,|\, x < 5\}$
(C) $\{x \,|\, x > 0\}$
(D) $\{x \,|\, x < 0\}$
(E) $\{x \,|\, 0 < x < 5\}$

GO ON TO THE NEXT PAGE

MATHEMATICS LEVEL 1 TEST - *Continued*

USE THIS SPACE FOR SCRATCHWORK.

26. Which of the following represents the graph shown in Figure 7?

(A) $|x-1| < 1$

(B) $|x-1| > 1$

(C) $|x-0.5| < 1.5$

(D) $|x+0.5| < 1.5$

(E) $|x+0.5| > 1.5$

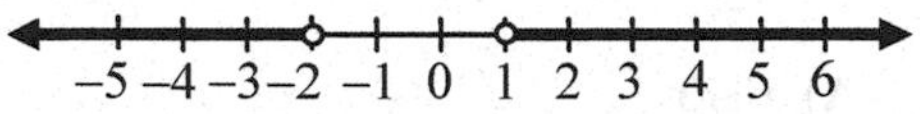

$$\begin{array}{c}\longleftrightarrow\\ -5\;-4\;-3\;-2\;-1\;\;0\;\;1\;\;2\;\;3\;\;4\;\;5\;\;6\end{array}$$

Figure 7

27. If $3^{2x} - 2(3^x) = 15$, what is the value of x?

(A) $\log 3$

(B) $\log_3 5$

(C) $\log_5 3$

(D) $\log 8$

(E) $\log 3 + \log 5$

28. A rectangular box is inscribed in a cylinder shown in Figure 8. If $AB = 3$, $BC = 4$, and the volume of the rectangular box is 60, what is the volume of the cylinder?

(A) 46.4
(B) 56.2
(C) 78.5
(D) 82.5
(E) 98.2

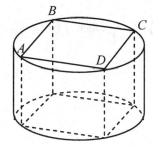

Figure 8

29. If $|x^2 - 5x| = 6$, which of the following must be true?

(A) It has two real solutions.
(B) It has two real and two imaginary solutions.
(C) It has three real solutions.
(D) It has four real solutions.
(E) It has four imaginary solutions.

GO ON TO THE NEXT PAGE

MATHEMATICS LEVEL 1 TEST - *Continued*

USE THIS SPACE FOR SCRATCHWORK.

30. If $x^2 - 9 \le x - 3$, which of the following is the complete solution to the inequality?

    (A) $x \le 3$
    (B) $x \ge -2$
    (C) $-2 \le x \le 3$
    (D) $-3 \le x \le 2$
    (E) $0 \le x \le 9$

31. If $a^2 - b^2 = 15$ and $a - b = 3$, then $3a + 2b =$

    (A) 10　(B) 12　(C) 14　(D) 18　(E) 24

32. If $f(g(x)) = 3x^2 - 10$ and $g(x) = x^2 - 4$, then $f(0) =$

    (A) 0　(B) 2　(C) 4　(D) 10　(E) -10

33. If $f(x) = \dfrac{x}{x+1}$, then $f(f(x)) =$

    (A) $\dfrac{x}{x+2}$

    (B) $\dfrac{x}{2x+1}$

    (C) $\dfrac{x+1}{x}$

    (D) $\dfrac{2x+1}{x}$

    (E) $\dfrac{x^2}{2x+1}$

34. If $\dfrac{(n+2)!}{n!} = 56$, what is the value of n?

    (A) 2　(B) 4　(C) 6　(D) 8　(E) 10

- 252 -

USE THIS SPACE FOR SCRATCHWORK.

35.   Figure 9 shows the graph of $y = f(x)$. Which of the following best describe the graph of $y = -f(-x) + 2$?

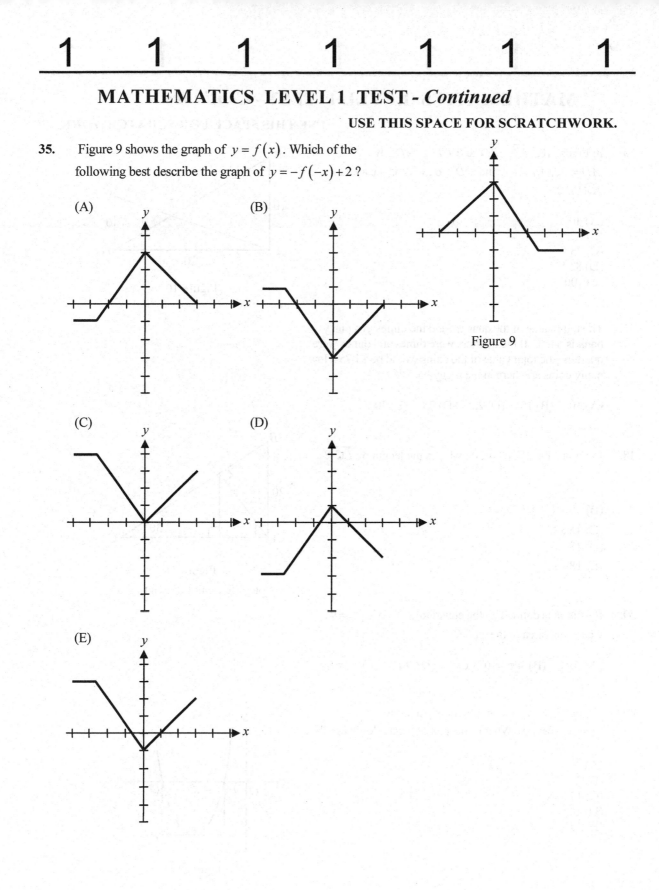

(A)

(B)

(C)

(D)

(E)

Figure 9

GO ON TO THE NEXT PAGE

USE THIS SPACE FOR SCRATCHWORK.

36. In Figure 10, $\overline{AB} \perp \overline{AD}$ and $\overline{CD} \perp \overline{AD}$. If
$AD = 20, AB = 10$, and $CD = 6$, what is the area of
$\triangle AEB$?

    (A) 40
    (B) 62.5
    (C) 75
    (D) 82.5
    (E) 100

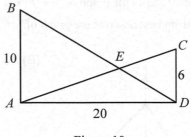

Figure 10

37. The total value of the quarters and the dimes in a piggy
bank is $4.00. If the quarters were dimes and dimes were
quarters, the total value of the coins would be $4.75. How
many coins are there in the piggy bank?

    (A) 10   (B) 15   (D) 20   (D) 25   (E) 30

38. In Figure 11, If $AB = 20$, what is the length of $\overline{EC}$?

    (A) $12\sqrt{3}$
    (B) 15
    (C) $15\sqrt{3}$
    (D) 18
    (E) $18\sqrt{3}$

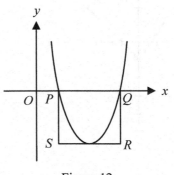

Figure 11

<u>Note:</u> Figure not drawn to scale.

39. If a circle is defined by the equation $x^2 - 2x + y^2 = 9$,
what is the area of the circle?

    (A) 3π (B) 4π (C) 6π (D) 9π (E) 10π

40. Figure 12 shows the graph of the parabola
$y = x^2 - 6x + 5$. What is the area of rectangle $PQRS$?

    (A) 4
    (B) 8
    (C) 12
    (D) 16
    (E) 20

Figure 12

GO ON TO THE NEXT PAGE

MATHEMATICS LEVEL 1 TEST - *Continued*

USE THIS SPACE FOR SCRATCHWORK.

41.   If the equation of a line is given by $5x - 8y = 20$, what is the distance between the x-intercept and y-intercept?

(A) 2.63   (B) 3.21   (C) 4.72   (D) 11.13   (E) 22.25

42.   A triangular cone is cut off from a cube shown in Figure 13. If the length of a side of the cube is 4, what is the volume of the remainder of the cube?

(A) 10.7
(B) 32
(C) 53.3
(D) 60
(E) 75.8

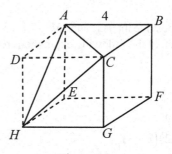

Figure 13

43.   If the line $y = 2x + k$ passes through the center of circle $x^2 - 4x + y^2 - 2y = 5$, then what is the value of k?

(A) −3   (B) −2   (C) 2   (D) 3   (E) 4

44.   How many lines in a space are perpendicular to a line at a point on the same line?

(A) 0   (B) 1   (C) 2   (D) 3   (E) Infinitely many

45.   The vertices of $\triangle PQR$ are $P(2, 8)$, $Q(6, 0)$, and $R(1, -1)$. What is the equation of the line containing the altitude through vertex R?

(A) $y = -2x + 10$

(B) $y = -2x - 10$

(C) $y = \frac{1}{2}x - \frac{3}{2}$

(D) $y = \frac{1}{2}x + \frac{2}{3}$

(E) $y = -\frac{1}{2}x + \frac{3}{2}$

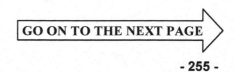

GO ON TO THE NEXT PAGE

MATHEMATICS LEVEL 1 TEST - *Continued*

USE THIS SPACE FOR SCRATCHWORK.

46. Five straight lines are drawn in a plane. If no two lines are parallel and no three lines are concurrent, into how many regions do the lines divide the plane?

    (A) 4　(B) 7　(C) 11　(D) 16　(E) 22

47. If k is a positive integer, and $3k + 7$ is an even integer, then which of the following expressions represents an odd integer?

    (A) $2k - 4$

    (B) $k^2 + 3$

    (C) $(k + 2)(k + 3)$

    (D) $(k + 1)(k - 1)$

    (E) $k^2(k + 2)$

48. If $\log 2 = a$, $\log 7 = b$, and $4^x = 49$, then what is x in terms of a and b?

    (A) $\dfrac{b}{a}$　(B) $\dfrac{a}{b}$　(C) $\dfrac{a+b}{2}$　(D) $\dfrac{ab}{2}$　(E) $\dfrac{a-b}{2}$

49. In Figure 14, the area of rectangle $ABCD$ is 21, $BF = 2$, and $CF = 5$. What is the value of $\tan\theta$?

    (A) $\dfrac{3}{2}$

    (B) 1

    (C) $\dfrac{2}{5}$

    (D) $\dfrac{2}{3}$

    (E) $\dfrac{4}{5}$

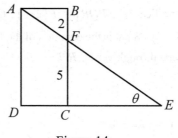

Figure 14

GO ON TO THE NEXT PAGE

MATHEMATICS LEVEL 1 TEST - *Continued*

USE THIS SPACE FOR SCRATCHWORK.

50. If $g(x) = x^2 + 2$ and $f(x) = \sqrt{x-2}$, which of the following could be a portion of the graph of $g(f(x))$?

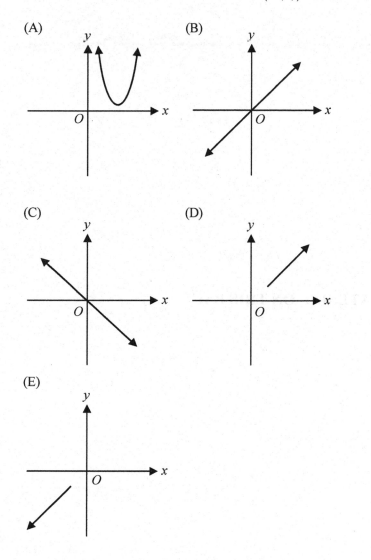

(A)

(B)

(C)

(D)

(E)

STOP
IF YOU FINISH BEFORE TIME IS CALLED, YOU MAY CHECK YOUR WORK ON THIS TEST ONLY.
DO NOT TURN TO ANY OTHER TEST IN THIS BOOK.

NO MATERIAL ON THIS PAGE

#	answer	#	answer	#	answer	#	answer	#	answer
1	C	11	B	21	A	31	C	41	C
2	C	12	D	22	C	32	B	42	C
3	E	13	E	23	B	33	B	43	A
4	A	14	B	24	D	34	C	44	E
5	D	15	D	25	E	35	E	45	C
6	C	16	A	26	E	36	B	46	D
7	D	17	B	27	B	37	E	47	E
8	B	18	C	28	E	38	C	48	A
9	A	19	D	29	D	39	E	49	D
10	B	20	E	30	C	40	D	50	D

Explanations: Test 10

1. (C) $\text{Equation} = \dfrac{9}{2+\sqrt{x}} = 2 \;\Rightarrow\; 2+\sqrt{x} = 4.5 \;\Rightarrow\; \sqrt{x} = 2.5 \;\Rightarrow\; x = 6.25$

2. (C) $\text{Expression} \Rightarrow \dfrac{3(x+2y)}{4} \cdot \dfrac{2xy}{x(x+2y)} = \dfrac{3y}{2}$

3. (E) Substitution: $\dfrac{x^2-4y}{y} = \dfrac{x^2}{y} - 4 = \dfrac{36}{(-4)} - 4 = -13$

4. (A) $-2x - 5 = 11 \;\Rightarrow\; x = -8 \quad \text{and} \quad 3(-8) - 1 = 5 - y \;\Rightarrow\; y = 30$

5. (D)

	Traveling hour	Speed	Traveled distance
Car	t	50mph	$50t$
Truck	$t+3$	40mph	$40t+120$

They traveled the same distance.
$50t = 40t + 120 \;\Rightarrow\; t = 12$

6. (C)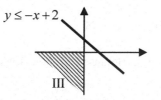
$y \le -x + 2$

7. (D) Let the two numbers be $5k$ and $3k$.
$8k - 8 = 40 \;\Rightarrow\; k = 6 \;\Rightarrow\; 5k = 5 \cdot 6 = 30$

8. (B) $f(5) = 25 - 3 \cdot 5 - k = 0 \;\Rightarrow\; k = 10$

9. **(A)** Since $\angle MAB = 125^\circ$, $\angle ABC = 55^\circ$ and
$\angle CBA = 25^\circ$.
Therefore, $\angle BCN \simeq \angle CBA = 35^\circ$

10. **(B)** $16^x = 8 \;\Rightarrow\; 2^{4x} = 2^3 \;\Rightarrow\; 4x = 3 \;\Rightarrow\; x = \dfrac{3}{4}$

11. **(B)** $BE = a\sin\theta = 0.5a$
Area $= 2a(0.5a) = a^2$

12. **(D)** Substitute $x \to (x+2)$.
$f(x) = 2(x+2) - 5 = 2x - 1$

13. **(E)** $x^5 - 16x = x(x^2+4)(x-2)(x+2)$
$2x + 4$ is not a factor.

14. **(B)** Since $BD^2 = AD \times DC$, $\;\Rightarrow\; 6^2 = AD \times 4 \;\Rightarrow\; AD = 9$.
Therefore, the area of $\triangle ABC = \dfrac{13 \times 6}{2} = 39$.

15. **(D)** $\sin x + \cot x \cos x = \sin x + \dfrac{\cos x}{\sin x} \cdot \cos x = \dfrac{\sin^2 x + \cos^2 x}{\sin x} = \dfrac{1}{\sin x} = \csc x$

16. **(A)** Slope $= \dfrac{k-2}{k}$ and the area $= \dfrac{k(k-2)}{2} = 24 \;\Rightarrow\; k^2 - 2k - 48 = 0$
$\Rightarrow\; (k+6)(k-8) = 0 \;\Rightarrow\; k = 8$
Therefore, slope $= \dfrac{k-2}{k} = \dfrac{3}{4}$

17. **(B)** If $\sin x = \cos x$, it is undefined.
Cofunction: If $\sin x = \cos x$, then $x + x = 90 \;\Rightarrow\; x = 45$.

18. **(C)** $\triangle BMN \sim \triangle BAC$ and the ratio of the areas is 1:4. (Because the ratio of the corresponding sides is 1:2)
Therefore, the area of $\triangle BMN$ is $36 \times \dfrac{1}{4} = 9$ and the area of $AMNC = 36 - 9 = 27$.
Since $\dfrac{\text{area of } \triangle AMN}{\text{area of } \triangle ACN} = \dfrac{1}{2}$, the area of $AMN = 27 \times \dfrac{1}{3} = 9$.

19. (D) $x = 180 - (60 + 50) = 70$

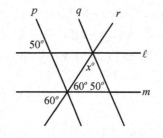

20. (E)   Since $y = 0$, $\sqrt{x-3} = 5$ $\Rightarrow$ $x - 3 = 25$ $\Rightarrow$ $x = 28$

21. (A)   Inverse: Switch x and y : $x = \dfrac{y-1}{y-4}$ $\Rightarrow$ $4 = \dfrac{y-1}{y-4}$ $\Rightarrow$ $y = 5$

22. (C) $\dfrac{z-i}{z+1} = 3$ $\Rightarrow$ $3z + 3 = z - i$ $\Rightarrow$ $3(a+bi) + 3 = a + bi - i$
$\Rightarrow$ $(3a+3) + (3b)i = a + (b-1)i$
$3a + 3 = a$ $\Rightarrow$ $a = -1.5$ and $3b = b - 1$ $\Rightarrow$ $b = -0.5$

23. (B)

	Working hours	Rate	Amount
Barbara	x	\$10	$10x$
Ashley	$x+4$	\$10	$10x + 40$

Therefore, the total amount is equal .
$20x + 40 = 240$ $\Rightarrow$ $x = 10$

24. (D) $i - \dfrac{1}{i} = \dfrac{i^2 - 1}{i} = \dfrac{-2}{i}$ $\Rightarrow$ $\left(\dfrac{-2}{i}\right)^{-2} = \dfrac{i^2}{4} = -\dfrac{1}{4}$

25. (E) x must be positive : $x > 0$.
$\dfrac{1}{x} > \dfrac{1}{5}$ $\Rightarrow$ $5 < x$ and $x > 0$ $\Rightarrow$ $0 < x < 5$

26. (E)   Midpoint $= -0.5$ and distance from the end point $= 1 - (-0.5) = 1.5$.
Therefore, $|x - (-0.5)| > 1.5$ $\Rightarrow$ $|x + 0.5| > 1.5$

27. (B)   If $3^x = K$, then $K^2 - 2K - 15 = 0$ $\Rightarrow$ $(K-5)(K+3) = 0$ $\Rightarrow$ $K = 5$ ($K \neq -3$).
Therefore, $3^x = 5$ $\Rightarrow$ $x = \log_3 5$.

28. (E) $60 = 3 \times 4 \times h$ $\Rightarrow$ $h = 5$
Diameter of the cylinder $AC = 5$, and the volume is $\pi(2.5^2)5 \cong 98.2$

29. **(D)** $\quad x^2 - 5x = 6 \quad$ or $\quad x^2 - 5x = -6$

(1) $x^2 - 5x + 6 = 0 \;\Rightarrow\; (x-2)(x-3) = 0 \;\Rightarrow\; x = 2$ or 3

(2) $x^2 - 5x - 6 = 0 \;\Rightarrow\; (x-6)(x+1) = 0 \;\Rightarrow\; x = 6$ or $x = -1$

30. **(C)** $\quad x^2 - 9 \le x - 3 \;\Rightarrow\; x^2 - x - 6 \le 0 \;\Rightarrow\; (x-3)(x+2) \le 0 \;\Rightarrow\; -2 \le x \le 3$

31. **(C)** $\quad a^2 - b^2 = 15 \;\Rightarrow\; (a+b)(a-b) = 15 \;\Rightarrow\; a+b = 5$ and $a - b = 3$

From these equations: $a = 4$ and $b = 1 \;\Rightarrow\; 3a + 2b = 14$

32. **(B)** $\quad$ Since $g(x) = 0, \;\Rightarrow\; x^2 - 4 = 0 \;\Rightarrow\; x^2 = 4$.

Therefore, $f(0) = 3(4) - 10 = 2$.

33. **(B)** $\quad f(f) = \dfrac{\left(\dfrac{x}{x+1}\right)(x+1)}{\left(\dfrac{x}{x+1} + 1\right)(x+1)} = \dfrac{x}{2x+1}$

34. **(C)** $\quad \dfrac{(n+2)!}{n!} = 56 \;\Rightarrow\; (n+2)(n+1) = 56 \;\Rightarrow\; n^2 + 3n - 54 = 0 \;\Rightarrow\; (n+9)(n-6) = 0$

Therefore, $n = 6 \;(n > 0)$

35. **(E)** $\quad$ Reflect with respect to origin and shift 2 units upward.

36. **(B)** $\quad \triangle ABE \sim \triangle CDE$ and the ratio of similitude is $5 : 3$.

$EF = 20 \times \dfrac{5}{8} = 12.5$

The area of $\triangle ABE = \dfrac{10 \times 12.5}{2} = 62.5$

37. **(D)** $\quad q = \#$ of quarters and $d = \#$ of dimes

Set up equations:

$25q + 10d = 400$ and $25d + 10q = 475$

When you add these two equations,

$35q + 35d = 875 \;\Rightarrow\; q + d = 25$.

38. **(C)** $\quad$ In the figure, $EC = 15\sqrt{3}$

39. **(E)** Equation $\Rightarrow$ $(x-1)^2 + y^2 = 10$ $\Rightarrow$ $r^2 = 10$

Area $= \pi r^2 = \pi(10) = 10\pi$

40. **(D)** Find the zeros: $x^2 - 6x + 5 = 0$ $\Rightarrow$ $(x-5)(x-1) = 0$ $\Rightarrow$ $x = 5, x = 1$

Find the height: $f(3) = -4$ $\Rightarrow$ $|-4| = 4$ (Axis of symmetry $\Rightarrow$ $x = 3$)

Area of $PQRS = 4 \times 4 = 16$

41. **(C)** x-intercept: $(4, 0)$ y-intercept: $(0, -2.5)$

$D = \sqrt{(2.5)^2 + (4)^2} \cong 4.72$

42. **(C)** The volume of the triangular cone $= \dfrac{Bh}{3} = \dfrac{\left(\frac{4 \times 4}{2}\right)4}{3} = \dfrac{32}{3}$

The volume of the cube $= 4^3 = 64$

Therefore, the volume of the remainder $= 64 - \dfrac{32}{3} \cong 53.3$

43. **(A)** $x^2 - 4x + y^2 - 2y = 5$ $\Rightarrow$ $(x-2)^2 + (y-1)^2 = 10$

Center: $(2, 1)$

$1 = 2(2) + b$ $\Rightarrow$ $b = -3$

44. **(E)** In a space, there are infinitely many perpendicular lines.

45. **(C)** $RM \perp PQ$, slope of $\overline{PQ} = \dfrac{8-0}{2-6} = -2$

Slope of $\overline{RM} = \dfrac{1}{2}$

The equation of line RM is

$y - (-1) = \dfrac{1}{2}(x-1)$ $\Rightarrow$ $y = \dfrac{1}{2}x - \dfrac{3}{2}$ $(1,-1)$

46. **(D)**

# of lines	# of regions
1	2
2	2+2
3	2+2+3
4	2+2+3+4
5	2+2+3+4+5 = 16

47. **(E)** If $3k + 7$ is even, then k must be odd number.

Use any odd number to check

48. **(A)** $x = \log_4 49 = \dfrac{\log 49}{\log 4} = \dfrac{\cancel{2}\log 7}{\cancel{2}\log 2} = \dfrac{b}{a}$

49. **(D)** 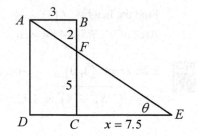 Since $BC = 7$, $AB = \dfrac{21}{7} = 3$.

$\dfrac{3}{x} = \dfrac{2}{5} \implies x = 7.5$

Therefore, $\tan\theta = \dfrac{AD}{DE} = \dfrac{7}{10.5} = \dfrac{14}{21} = \dfrac{2}{3}$.

50. **(D)** $f(x) = \sqrt{x-2} \implies x \ge 2$

Domain of $g(f(x))$ is $x \ge 2$.

$y = g(f) = \left(\sqrt{x-2}\right)^2 + 2 \implies y = x$

Graph (D) is correct.

END

NO MATERIAL ON THIS PAGE

NO MATERIAL ON THIS PAGE

CPSIA information can be obtained
at www.ICGtesting.com
Printed in the USA
LVOW04s1613050118
561974LV00009B/307/P